TORONTO TRAILBLAZERS

Women in Canadian Publishing

TORONTO TRAILBLAZERS

Women in Canadian Publishing

Ruth Panofsky

UNIVERSITY OF TORONTO PRESS
Toronto Buffalo London

© University of Toronto Press 2019
Toronto Buffalo London
utorontopress.com

ISBN 978-1-4875-0557-8 (cloth)   ISBN 978-1-4875-2386-2 (paper)

Studies in Book and Print Culture

Library and Archives Canada Cataloguing in Publication

Title: Toronto trailblazers : women in Canadian publishing / Ruth Panofsky.
Names: Panofsky, Ruth, author.
Series: Studies in book and print culture.
Description: Series statement: Studies in book and print culture | Includes bibliographical references and index.
Identifiers: Canadiana 20190115181 | ISBN 9781487505578 (cloth) | ISBN 9781487523862 (paper)
Subjects: LCSH: Women in the book industries and trade – Ontario – Toronto – Biography. | LCSH: Women publishers – Ontario – Toronto – Biography. | LCSH: Women editors – Ontario – Toronto – Biography. | LCSH: Literary agents – Ontario – Toronto – Biography. | LCSH: Women in the book industries and trade – Canada – History. | LCSH: Publishers and publishing – Canada – History. | LCGFT: Biographies.
Classification: LCC Z488.6.T6 P36 2019 | DDC 070.5092/5209713541—dc23

This book has been published with the assistance of Ryerson University.

University of Toronto Press acknowledges the financial assistance to its publishing program of the Canada Council for the Arts and the Ontario Arts Council, an agency of the Government of Ontario.

 Canada Council for the Arts   Conseil des Arts du Canada

For Gary

Contents

List of Illustrations ix

Acknowledgments xi

Abbreviations xv

Introduction 3

1 "Exceptional in building a Canadian company": Irene Clarke 30

2 A "Principal Architect" of the University of Toronto Press: Eleanor Harman 45

3 The "Editorial Conscience" of the University of Toronto Press: Francess Halpenny 69

4 "She knew the business ... and the Canadian literary market": Sybil Hutchinson 88

5 A "tremendous job of editing": Claire Pratt 113

6 Publishing "Maestro" and Cultural Advocate: Anna Porter 131

7 The "Grande Dame" of Literary Agents: Bella Pomer 152

Conclusion 189

Notes 199

Selected Bibliography 233

Index 251

Illustrations

Irene Clarke, Amen House, in the 1940s. Reprinted with permission of William H. (Bill) Clarke. 32

Eleanor Harman, Frankfurt Book Fair, October 1967. Reprinted from *Press Notes from the University of Toronto Press* 9.11 (November 1967): n. pag. 61

Francess Halpenny in her office, 1972. Photographer: Robert Lansdale. University of Toronto Archives, Toronto, Ontario. 83

Sybil Hutchinson in the 1950s. Reprinted from Sharon Hazen, ed., *Down by the Bay: A History of Long Point and Port Rowan 1799–1999* (Erin, ON: Boston Mills Press, 2000), 239. 98

Claire Pratt, 1950. Box 46, file 8, MCP fonds, Special Collections, E.J. Pratt Library, Victoria University in the University of Toronto, Toronto, Ontario. 114

Anna Porter in the 1970s. Photographer: Diane Pullan. Reprinted from Anna Porter and Marjorie Harris, eds., *Farewell to the 70s: A Canadian Salute to a Confusing Decade*, A Discovery Book (Don Mills, ON: Thomas Nelson, 1979), backflap. 132

Bella Pomer, March 1982. Photographer: Edward Regan. Dated: 26 March 1982. Used: 5 April 1982. *Globe and Mail* fonds, F 4695-2, Archives of Ontario, Toronto, Ontario. See William French, "Writers' Guardian Angels," *Globe and Mail* 5 April 1982: L1. 161

Acknowledgments

The research for this book was undertaken with generous funding from the Social Sciences and Humanities Research Council of Canada, Ryerson University, and the Bibliographical Society of America. The support facilitated my investigation of women who were instrumental in shaping twentieth-century English-language publishing in Canada, and for that I am most thankful.

I welcome this opportunity to acknowledge the archivists, librarians, and staff members who provided vital assistance over the course of this project: senior archivist Erin Strouth of the Archives of Ontario; access specialist Diane Wardle of the British Columbia Archives; Dominique Dery of the David M. Rubenstein Rare Book and Manuscript Library, Duke University; archivists Sarah Hillier and Catherine Hobbs of Library and Archives Canada; Renu Barrett, Beverly Bayzat, and Rick Stapleton of the William Ready Division of Archives and Research Collections, Mills Memorial Library, McMaster University; librarian Val Lem and the interlibrary loan staff of Ryerson University Library and Archives; Chelsea Shriver of Rare Books and Special Collections, University of British Columbia Library; Linda Eddy, Lewis St George Stubbs, and Shelley Sweeney of Archives and Special Collections, Elizabeth Dafoe Library, University of Manitoba; Laureen Wing of Archives and Special Collections, University of Saskatchewan Library; Jessica Barr and Danielle Robichaud of Special Collections, John M. Kelly Library, University of St Michael's College; Barbara Edwards and Marnee Gamble of University of Toronto Archives and Records

Management Services; John Shoesmith and Jennifer Toews of the Thomas Fisher Rare Book Library, University of Toronto; Agatha Barc, Colin Deinhardt, and Roma Kalil of Special Collections, E.J. Pratt Library, Victoria University; Theresa Regnier and Leslie Thomas-Smith of the Archives and Research Collections Centre, Western University; and Michael Moir and Anna St Onge of the Clara Thomas Archives and Special Collections, Scott Library, York University.

A number of individuals granted me interviews and graciously allowed me to draw from our personal and electronic exchanges: William H. (Bill) Clarke, the late Francess G. Halpenny, John W. Irwin, Bella Pomer, Anna Porter, and Susan Wallace.

I have benefited from the expertise of colleagues who assisted me at various stages of this work. Early on, I was guided by Carl Spadoni, former director of McMaster University's William Ready Division of Archives and Research Collections, who offered critical research direction, and Carole Gerson of Simon Fraser University, the leading scholar in the field of Canadian women in print culture.

Along the way I have received help from many others and I am pleased to take this occasion to thank them for their generosity. Nancy Colbert afforded me access to the restricted Colbert Agency fonds housed at Library and Archives Canada; Bella Pomer granted me access and permission to cite from her restricted papers housed at the Thomas Fisher Rare Book Library, University of Toronto; Patricia Lockhart Fleming, Janet Friskney, George Parker, Alison Rukavina, and Rex Williams each suggested avenues of research; Penney Clark supplied details about Copp Clark; David Kent sent me photocopies of his privately held Sybil Hutchinson correspondence; Robert Lecker shared his knowledge of Canada's earliest literary agents; Jane Loughborough forwarded a copy of Francess G. Halpenny's privately published memoir, *A World of Words*; James Stewart Reaney and Susan Wallace lent me their privately held correspondence and personal photographs of Sybil Hutchison; Aritha van Herk offered helpful commentary on the chapter on Anna Porter; and Dianne Woodman made me a compact disk copy of her 1988 audiotaped interview with Gladys Neale of the Macmillan Company of Canada, the original of which is now held in the William Ready Division of Archives and Research Collections, McMaster University.

Student assistants have contributed to every phase of this project. They brought enthusiasm and dedication to their work with archival documents as well as secondary source material in both print and digital formats. I am indebted to them and owe each one special thanks for their collaboration: Evanilde Bekkout, Melissa Carroll, Anne Dmytriw, Tatum Dooley, Holly Edejer, Rosalind Gunn, Rachel Kearney, Mirjana Mandaric, Evan Mauro, Daniela Barrera Murcia, Emma Renda, Maria Rossi, Katarina Ryder-Recas, Rahaf Sheikh-Khalil, Chloe Stelmanis-Cali, the late Christa Zeller Thomas, and Jessica Whitehead.

I extend thanks to University of Toronto Press, in particular to acquisitions editor Mark Thompson, for his invaluable guidance and attention; copy editor Anne Laughlin, for her editorial expertise; and general editor Leslie Howsam of the Studies in Book and Print Culture series, for her encouragement.

An earlier version of chapter 5 on editor Claire Pratt appeared in *Papers of the Bibliographical Society of Canada*. Portions of my work in progress were presented at the After the Digital Revolution workshop; the Canadian Literature Symposium; the Canadian Women Writers Conference: Connecting Texts and Generations; and at conferences of the Association of Canadian College and University Teachers of English; the Bibliographical Society of Canada; and the Society for the History of Authorship, Reading and Publishing. At Ryerson University, my home institution, I presented my research on Sybil Hutchinson at an English Department Colloquium. The probing questions and insightful comments proffered by colleagues at each of these events helped me develop and then focus this book.

Finally, my husband, Gary Gottlieb – always my greatest champion – and our grown children, Bram and Liza, spur me on in all my scholarly ventures. To my family, I am deeply grateful for the love and support that have made this book possible.

Abbreviations

Archival Collections

BP	Bella Pomer papers
CI	Clarke, Irwin and Company Limited fonds
FGH	Francess Georgina Halpenny fonds
HK	Henry Kreisel fonds
JR	James Reaney fonds
M&S	McClelland and Stewart fonds
MCP	Mildred Claire Pratt fonds
MU	McMaster University
UM	University of Manitoba
US	University of Saskatchewan
UT	University of Toronto
UTA	University of Toronto Archives
UTP	University of Toronto Press fonds
VU	Victoria University
WU	Western University

Other Abbreviations

BBC	British Broadcasting Corporation
CBC	Canadian Broadcasting Corporation
DCB/DBC	*Dictionary of Canadian Biography/Dictionnaire biographique du Canada*
NCL	New Canadian Library

NDWT   Ne'er-Do-Well Thespians
RCAF   Royal Canadian Air Force
SHARP   Society for the History of Authorship,
                Reading and Publishing
TPL   Toronto Public Library

TORONTO TRAILBLAZERS

Women in Canadian Publishing

Introduction

The agency for change – in the forms and practices of book culture – lies not with the technology, but rather ... remains in the hands of authors, publishers and readers – and editors and booksellers and librarians ... whose labour, creativity, investment, knowledge, and responses together give shape to a book culture.

– Leslie Howsam
SHARP President, 2009–13[1]

The story of publishing in Canada, once you get past the figureheads, is a story of women.

– William H. (Bill) Clarke
Publisher, Clarke, Irwin[2]

Canada's print and publishing trades have always relied on the labour of women. Soon after 1751, when the country's first printing press arrived in Halifax via Boston, women began to participate in print production. In the eighteenth and nineteenth centuries, daughters, wives, and widows were often employed as compositors, printers, and bookbinders. They worked in family businesses and adopted "patterns of shared labour" already established in England and France, as described by Carole Gerson in volume 1 of *History of the Book in Canada*.[3]

Until his death in 1761, Canada's earliest printer was John Bushell. A "drinker and an uncertain businessman," who nonetheless was appointed King's Printer in 1752,[4] Bushell could not have produced the country's first newspaper, the *Halifax Gazette*, without the assistance of his daughter Elizabeth. Pioneer printer Fleury Mesplet, who launched the short-lived literary weekly *La Gazette du commerce et littéraire, pour la ville et district de Montréal* in 1778, was aided by his first wife, Marie Mirabeau, until her death in 1789. He went on to found the bilingual weekly *Montreal Gazette/La Gazette de Montréal* (now the *Montreal Gazette*) in 1785, which, for a brief time, was run by his second wife, Marie-Anne Tison, following Mesplay's death in 1794. Other publishing women, all widows, included printers Elizabeth Gay, active in Halifax in 1805; Ann Mott, active in Saint John in 1814; Marie-Josephte Voyer, active in Quebec in 1828; and Anne Lovell, active in Toronto in 1868; as well as Sophia Simms Dalton, the first successful woman publisher in Toronto, who issued the semi-weekly newspaper *Patriot* from 1840 to 1848.[5]

By 1871, as Éric Leroux points out, 471 women and 130 girls were employed in the printing trades, "representing 14.3 per cent of the labour force."[6] Half of these women worked in printing offices, while the other half worked in binding shops. In printing offices, women were compositors and, later, typesetters, but most were press feeders. They were held back professionally, not only by their wages, which were less than half those of their male co-workers, but by the unwillingness of printers' unions to allow them entry into apprenticeship. As a result, they found employment in non-unionized offices, where they were exploited as cheap labour. In binding shops, women folded, collated, and sewed sheets, and, given their considerable numbers, were permitted entry to binders' unions. Employers, however, persisted in viewing single women as temporary workers who would leave the labour market upon marriage, and married women as secondary wage earners, attitudes that kept female workers in precarious employment.[7]

In the early part of the twentieth century, a growing number of women entered the labour market. By 1921, they comprised 17 per cent of the total labour force[8] and were employed primarily as domestic workers, clerical staff, library workers, nurses, and teachers. At the same time, many found their way into the English-language publishing houses clustered in Toronto.

I

As more women entered the field of publishing – women's rate of participation rose from 11 per cent of the industry's workforce in 1871 to 20 per cent in 1921– their involvement at all levels of the trade expanded.[9] Firms such as the venerable Ryerson Press (established in 1829 as the Methodist Book and Publishing House) and Copp Clark (established in 1841 under the name of Hugh Scobie, its founder), and the more recently formed University of Toronto Press (established in 1901), Oxford University Press Canada (established in 1904), the Macmillan Company of Canada (established in 1905), and McClelland and Goodchild (established in 1906, now McClelland and Stewart), hired women as clerks and secretaries, manuscript assessors, and proofreaders.

For these women, the majority of whom forfeited their positions upon marriage – as per custom and expectation – a change came in 1930, when Irene Clarke, along with two family members, co-founded Clarke, Irwin. It was a seemingly inauspicious time to launch a publishing company – so soon after the stock market crash of 29 October 1929, and early in the Depression. It was also a daring move for Clarke, who thus became Canada's first female publisher of English-language books. At the helm of Clarke, Irwin from its inception, she assumed even greater responsibility following her husband's death in 1955.

Women who were drawn to publishing recognized Clarke as a trailblazer and over the course of the twentieth century many more entered the field. Increasingly, as Gerson notes, they were involved in "the material production of print, working in printing plants as typesetters and binders, and in publisher's offices" as acquisitions and copy editors, book designers, production staff, and publicists.[10] There are, in fact, two watershed years in the seven decades covered by this study. The first is 1930, for it marks Clarke's breakthrough, which in itself heralded the advent of women editors in trade and scholarly publishing. The second is 1969, the year Anna Porter joined McClelland and Stewart as editorial coordinator. Porter's hiring signalled the undeniable rise of women as career professionals – in-house editors, publishers, and literary agents – in Canadian trade publishing.

With the spread of second-wave feminism and in the wake of the Royal Commission on the Status of Women in Canada, which began in 1967, women made fresh inroads into publishing. As opportunities expanded across the country under new government initiatives to support the production of Canadian literary culture, women became active members of small presses, for instance, Linda Davey and Sarah Sheard of Coach House Press (established in 1965) and Shirley Gibson and Ann Wall of House of Anansi Press (established in 1967). They formed publishing houses especially for children's books, such as May Cutler's Tundra Books (established in 1967), Anne Millyard's Annick Press (established in 1975), and Patsy Aldana's Groundwood Books (established in 1978). Women also set up cooperative-run feminist presses, such as Toronto's Canadian Women's Educational Press (established in 1972, now Women's Press) and Vancouver's Press Gang Publishers (1970–2002), and founded feminist periodicals, including Marion Lynn and Shelagh Wilkinson's *Canadian Woman Studies* (established in 1978, now edited by Luciana Ricciutelli). In partnership with the En'owkin Centre, Jeannette Armstrong created Theytus Books (established in 1980), the first Indigenous-owned publishing house in Canada, while Makeda Silvera and Stephanie Martin co-founded Sister Vision Press (1985–2000), which published works by Black women and women of colour.[11] These examples, and so many other publishing initiatives undertaken by women, though relevant to this study, lie outside its scope and initial aim, which is to lay the foundation for expansive scholarship on the subject of women and Canadian publishing by first considering the significant gains made by key women in mainstream publishing houses.

As the historical locus for most English-language publishing in the country and home to major publishing firms, Toronto is the setting for this book. In 1930, when Clarke, Irwin set up shop in the city, the company joined a number of firms that already were producing books for readers located across Canada. At the time, however, domestic publishing was still in development. Over the course of the century, it would undergo dramatic changes, all of which had inevitable effects on the women who laboured in publishing.

One turn of events was especially hard on educational publishers. Prior to 1968, the majority of Canada's large houses were, first and foremost, educational publishers. Historically, publishers competed – sometimes unscrupulously, as Penney Clark details in her history of Copp Clark[12] – for the opportunity to supply textbooks to the primary and secondary school markets. Those who were successful received lucrative publishing contracts issued by the department or ministry of education of each province. Since these contracts often extended over many years, publishers could rely on stable revenue to sustain their firms and underwrite less profitable trade publishing programs. According to Clark, publisher Jack McClelland viewed educational contracts as the "brightest star on the publishing horizon"; she herself called them "the bread and butter that allowed major firms to also publish in the less financially reliable area of Canadian fiction."[13]

In 1968, Ontario's Ministry of Education cancelled its long-standing program of textbook stimulation grants, which had included designated funding for schoolbook purchases. The province then authorized an expanded list of textbooks and gave its various school boards new budgetary autonomy. Many, as Clark points out, chose "to divert funds to expenses such as teacher salaries and building maintenance rather than to textbooks."[14] Moreover, since teachers now had greater choice in classroom texts, publishers could no longer count on income generated by strong sales of authorized titles.

Ontario's actions had serious consequences and by 1970 publishers' "profits were dropping significantly."[15] One firm deeply affected by the changed circumstances was Clarke, Irwin, which had come to rely heavily on textbook sales. The company lost its financial footing and, like most other educational publishers, never fully recovered from the setback. In fact, the elimination of textbook stimulation grants radically altered the economics underlying publishing in Ontario, so much so that it produced a "before and after" effect that haunts the narrative arc of this book.

While they were producing schoolbooks, all major Canadian houses also acted as exclusive agents for American and British publishers.[16] As George Parker explains, the "agency system" emerged out of historical necessity, since Canada's relatively small population, and thus readership, often could not support print runs sufficient to offset the high costs associated with publishing and distributing books across a vast country. In order to mitigate these difficulties, Canadian publishers formed agency agreements with foreign publishers. Each agreement provided "an annual commission and a share in the profits from individual sales" of titles that originated with international publishers.[17] In return, American and British firms received careful attention from local agents. Clarke, Irwin, for example, gave its agencies white-glove treatment in the form of regular correspondence and occasional visits from the head of the firm herself, Irene Clarke.

As agents, Canadian publishers were at great disadvantage, however. Since Canadian rights were typically ceded as part of "Empire/North American/world rights,"[18] foreign publishers often issued Canadian editions, which meant that domestic agents – who were obliged to sell those same editions – were acting against their own publishing interests. They had to market "books they didn't want" and "had no say in [either] editing or advertising."[19] Moreover, if an agency no longer proved profitable, foreign publishers could cancel their agreements at will. Hence, the agency system made Canadian publishers uncomfortably dependent and highly vulnerable.

As agency sales grew, several American firms established branch plant offices in Toronto and terminated their agreements with Canadian publishers,[20] which brought agency publishing to an eventual close. In 1947, for instance, the cancellation of the Doubleday agency – the company had opened a Canadian subsidiary – was devastating to McClelland and Stewart, which lost, according to James King, "half of its sales and more than half of its income."[21] The experience was "a turning point"[22] for Jack McClelland. As Judy Donnelly recounts, "he realized the precariousness of the firm's reliance on foreign agencies, and began to understand that the company had to become more independent, and even more Canadian in its focus."[23]

McClelland made it his mission to try to free himself from the bondage of agency agreements – by 1963 the firm had "severed distribution ties with foreign publishers whose lines" were unprofitable[24] – and to forge ahead as a domestic trade publisher. That he achieved his goal – if not his financial ambition – is evidenced by his legendary and enduring status as the most nationalist of Canada's publishers, and by the fact that he was largely responsible for the rise of modern Canadian literature. Not only did McClelland launch the New Canadian Library in 1958, a paperback reprint series that continues to feature the work of Canadian writers (now issued by Penguin Random House Canada under the McClelland and Stewart imprint),[25] he published many of Canada's best-known authors of the last century, including several who figure prominently in this volume: prose writers Matt Cohen, Jack Hodgins, Henry Kreisel, Margaret Laurence, Farley Mowat, and Sheila Watson, and poets Earle Birney, Irving Layton, and James Reaney.

As a result of recommendations made by the Royal Commission on National Development in the Arts, Letters and Sciences (better known as the Massey Commission, for its chair Vincent Massey), which issued its report in 1951, the federal government funded the expansion of universities, the establishment of the National Library of Canada (now Library and Archives Canada) in 1953, and the Canada Council for the Arts in 1957. Eli MacLaren explains that "these material developments amplified each other, gradually expanding and deepening the culture of writing, publishing, and reading Canadian books."[26] More improvement followed when Canada signed the *Universal Copyright Convention* in 1962, which further strengthened copyright protection offered by the *Copyright Act of Canada* of 1921 (enforced since 1 January 1924).

Support for domestic publishing and a burgeoning nationalism, which intensified after the Second World War and grew exponentially during the 1960s in anticipation of Canada's centenary in 1967, also accounted for the decline in agency publishing. In addition to McClelland and Stewart, for instance, firms such as Clarke,

Irwin and the Macmillan Company of Canada – though a branch plant operation, Macmillan became a major publisher of Canadian literature[27] – were pursuing local publishing with increased vigour in the 1960s.

In 1970, however, two separate events took place, which have since come to be seen as marking a decisive shift in Canadian publishing. On 24 September 1970, the book trade publication *Quill and Quire* announced the forthcoming sale (on 1 January 1971) of textbook publisher W.J. Gage to the American educational publisher, Scott Foresman, of Chicago. Gage was a long-established Canadian company; it had its beginnings in the 1840s and was incorporated in 1883. Just two months later, on 1 December 1970, Ryerson Press – with its origins in the Methodist Book and Publishing House, it was the country's oldest firm – was sold to yet another American company, New York's McGraw-Hill. If the imminent sale of Gage sounded disaster, the sale of Ryerson was a serious blow. It shocked the public and devastated the publishing community, which went into mourning: it had not only surrendered an eminent publishing house, it had lost a great cultural institution that had championed Canadian writers.[28]

In 1971, in an effort to forestall a similar transaction, the Ontario Development Corporation lent a financially ailing McClelland and Stewart $961,645 to help sustain the firm.[29] In return, as Donnelly records, it was issued "debentures amounting to one-third of the company's assets."[30] Two years later, on the recommendation of the Ontario Royal Commission on Book Publishing, a loan guarantee program for Canadian publishers was put into place. One firm that availed itself of the program was Clarke, Irwin, but in 1983 it was forced into receivership by the same provincial government that had sanctioned the financial support – an example of the painful ironies known well to Canadians publishers. The loan guarantee program survived until 1995, when the Conservative government of Premier Mike Harris slashed its funding[31] – a move reminiscent of the cuts that forced the closure of Clarke, Irwin.

Other types of funding were made available to Canadian-owned publishers through the Canada Council for the Arts, the Ontario Arts Council, as well as the Canadian Book Publishing Development

Program (established in 1979, now the Book Publishing Industry Development Plan), and newer initiatives such as the Canada Book Fund (administered by the Department of Canadian Heritage) and the Ontario Media Development Corporation's Book Fund.

These welcome schemes may have lessened the precarious nature of book publishing, but they did not stabilize an industry that historically has operated as a combined business venture and cultural undertaking – a distinctive blend of economics and art that has appealed largely to intrepid individuals determined to make books and reach readers. Enterprising women like Irene Clarke, and others who toiled alongside male colleagues, have always been among the most purposeful in publishing. By issuing books, editing manuscripts, and supporting authors, they brought ideas to life and helped forge Canada's literary culture. Though their work was essential, it has garnered little recognition and, until recently, was generally carried out behind the scenes.

Although women have continually been part of the print and publishing trades, it was men who dominated both fields. Men, moreover, gave English-language book publishing its historic status as a "gentleman's profession,"[32] associated with well-known figures such as Blackwood, Bentley, and Macmillan in the United Kingdom; Knopf and Simon and Schuster in the United States; and McClelland in Canada.[33] Since publishing practice was shaped by men, it is not surprising that publishing history has focused on the firms that carried their names.

In Canada, memoirs of publishers Bill Clarke, Marsh Jeanneret, Mel Hurtig, and Robert Lecker, editors Kildare Dobbs, John Metcalf, and Douglas Gibson, and book designer Frank Newfeld are complemented by studies of publishers Lorne Pierce, John Morgan Gray, and Jack McClelland, and editor William Toye. Two volumes of Jack McClelland's selected correspondence are available as well.[34]

Women also sustained long and meaningful careers as publishers and editors, but there are few firsthand records of their participation in book publishing. In separate memoirs, for example, scholarly editor Francess Halpenny and book designer Laurie Lewis recollect their respective careers at the University of Toronto Press, while Anna Porter's *In Other Words* recalls her many years in publishing.[35]

More scholarship exists on the subject of women in the print and publishing trades. The bilingual three-volume *History of the Book in Canada/Histoire du livre et de l'imprimé au Canada* is the first source for foundational articles on women in the printing trades (by Claude Galarneau and Gilles Gallichan; by Éric Leroux; and by Christina Burr and Éric Leroux), in the binding trades (by Patricia Lockhart Fleming); and in print culture and publishing (by Carole Gerson). Christina Burr has examined the role of class and gender in the Toronto printing trades between the years 1850 and 1914. Mary Lu MacDonald has studied the *Montreal Museum, or Journal of Literature and the Arts* (1832–4), the country's first periodical "specifically intended for female readers"[36] and edited by Mary Graddon Gosselin. Dean Irvine, who shares MacDonald's interest in literary journals and women editors, focuses on the twentieth century in his monograph *Editing Modernity: Women and Little-Magazine Cultures in Canada, 1916–1956*. In *Literary Culture and Female Authorship in Canada 1760–2000*, Faye Hammill analyses the various ways in which authorship is thematized in the prose works of Frances Brooke, Susanna Moodie, L.M. Montgomery, Margaret Atwood, and Carol Shields.[37]

The digital projects *Canada's Early Women Writers* and *Database of Canada's Early Women Writers*, produced under the direction of Carole Gerson and housed within the Canadian Writing Research Collaboratory, include biographical entries for numerous women who acted as publishers' readers, editors, and literary agents prior to 1950. Lois Pike, Thaba Niedzwiecki, Christine Kim, and Tessa Elizabeth Jordan provide analyses of more recent feminist book and periodical publishing. Especially pertinent to this project are pivotal monographs by Gerson on Canadian women in print culture to 1918 and Lorraine York on the celebrity authorship of Margaret Atwood, Carol Shields, and other writers.[38]

The relative paucity of such foundational work indicates the need for this volume, which presents seven chapter-length studies of career women – publisher Irene Clarke, scholarly editors Eleanor Harman and Francess Halpenny, trade editors Sybil Hutchinson, Claire Pratt, and Anna Porter, and literary agent Bella Pomer – who occupied leading positions in twentieth-century

Canadian publishing. By capturing these women's "contributions to print culture," which have already "fade[d] from view,"[39] and by analysing their lasting influence on publishing practice in Canada, this project seeks to fill an obvious gap in the scholarly and public record.

This investigation of publishing women is situated within the interdisciplinary framework of book history studies and is informed by the approaches and ideas of international publishing historians Robert Darnton and Andrew Nash, as well as sociologist Pierre Bourdieu. Methodologically, it heeds Darnton's injunction to "tap the papers of publishers ... the richest of all sources for the history of books,"[40] to uncover women's diverse roles within the human communications circuit that connects ideas, books, and readers. Conceptually, it is guided by a chief tenet of publishing history, as affirmed by Nash, that all "makers of books are generators of meaning"[41] for the reading public and the culture at large. It is a historic fact that women have participated in the making of books, yet the various ways they have generated meaning through their cultural work have not been properly examined.

Each of the women discussed in the chapters that follow was a central agent in what Bourdieu terms the field of cultural production, which includes publishing and editing. Through their day-to-day efforts and influential decisions – such as selecting publishable manuscripts, conceiving new journals, and determining how best to edit both, or devising ways to advance their companies and promote their authors – they created "cultural capital," the symbolic value a culture assigns to immaterial aspects of cultural production, such as the ideas forged via the publication process.[42]

To the economic, social, and historic conditions attended to by Bourdieu, this study adds the critical category of gender, which bears a significant influence on the cultural work enacted by women who operated within the dominant paradigm of conventional publishing. Leslie Howsam, who regards book history as "a male domain" that has been gendered "masculine,"[43] observes, for example, that "little attention has yet been paid to the woman publisher, or printer, or book trade worker."[44] There is, moreover, a lack of "scholarship on how gender norms ... have shaped editorial practice within book publishing,"[45] as Trysh Travis discovered when researching the Women in Print Movement.[46]

Simone Murray's *Mixed Media: Feminist Presses and Publishing Politics*, an analysis of the feminist press movement and how it altered British publishing, is one such scholarly study. Murray's chapters on Virago Press, Women's Press, Pandora Press, Sheba Feminist Publishers, and several other imprints blend feminist and book history methodologies to show how publishing is a gendered undertaking.[47] Although my own research does not focus on feminist presses, this volume follows Murray in foregrounding gender as a principal factor shaping the career paths of women in publishing. Howsam's call to attend to the historic women whose labour helped turn publishing into a flourishing industry further drives my examination of the major contributions made by seven women to Canada's book trade.

This study is decidedly Canadian in focus. In adopting such a lens, I am encouraged by Carole Gerson's final valuing of the national *History of the Book in Canada/Histoire du livre et de l'imprimé au Canada* project, "however imperfectly it may have been researched and written."[48] More importantly, I am responding to Gerson's recent charge to carve out a "visible Canadian space on the international map of print culture," especially at the present "time when participating in post-national or global intellectual endeavours too often means yielding to foreign cultural hegemonies."[49] My work on publishing women is one such attempt to put Canadian print culture on view.

Gerson's own sustained research program has concentrated on women's historic participation in Canadian print and publishing. As she has shown through "slow and arduous effort,"[50] it is possible to lay bare "the gender politics ruling the largely public sphere of the book trade and the behind-the-scenes role of women,"[51] which reviewer Roxanne Rimstead discerns as the outcome of Gerson's work, and to thereby "reconfigure the literary field so that the areas in which women achieved a presence receive greater acknowledgment."[52]

In fact, Gerson's re-visioning of what Howsam aptly deems a "male domain" underscores the need to regard women "as active agents in the material production of literary culture."[53] Thus, by de-emphasizing their "historical marginalization,"[54] but underlining women's gendered experience in publishing, I mean to demonstrate – to cite Murray – that "invigorating re-examination of received analytical paradigms"[55] can make visible the signal achievements of cultural workers who have been either overlooked or underestimated by publishing scholars.

Irene Clarke, Eleanor Harman, Francess Halpenny, Sybil Hutchinson, Claire Pratt, Anna Porter, and Bella Pomer became pivotal figures in "the literary field"[56] of Canadian publishing, but it would be a mistake to argue they did so by openly identifying as either pro-women or feminist. Although keenly aware of their gendered positions in a field where the majority of their co-workers were male, as were their superiors, they were motivated less by political aim than personal objective and a desire to pursue rewarding work. My research reveals, for instance, that they were central to the idea and practice of editing, as well as the development of authors' rights and professional literary representation in Canada. Nevertheless, in deliberately pursuing careers that aligned with their vocational interests, showcased their respective abilities, and won them promotions and peer recognition, they challenged the prevailing bias against working women and enacted what in essence constituted a feminist practice that further served to encourage other women who saw them as role models and potential mentors.

Clarke, Harman, Halpenny, Hutchinson, and Pratt entered publishing in the 1930s, 1940s, and 1950s, decades when women were under-represented in the workforce, comprising just 18.6 to 22.3 per cent of the total labour market.[57] In a field historically dominated by men, and where they regularly encountered sexist expectations, their drive and career ambition can be read today as signs of an emerging feminism.

Porter and Pomer, on the other hand, began their careers at a time when more jobs were open to women and soon after the commencement, on 16 February 1967, of the Royal Commission on the Status of Women in Canada, whose 1970 report brought new attention to the position of women in Canadian society. Partly as a result of the wide-ranging recommendations made by the commission, Porter and Pomer knew the benefits of autonomy and authority earlier in their publishing careers than the other women featured in this study.

At the same time, all seven women enjoyed several advantages, particularly in terms of race and social class, which afforded them access to unique employment opportunities. They were white, middle-class, educated, and mobile, free to move in search of fulfilling work. Moreover, when they first entered publishing, whether single (Harman, Halpenny, Hutchinson, Pratt, and Porter) or married (Clarke and Pomer, each a mother), all appeared to conform, at least superficially, to contemporary social and sexual norms for women. As a result, they were given entry to Toronto mainstream publishing, a predominantly male realm that held to the status quo. There, though they may not have seen the racial and class privilege that aided their success, they redefined their respective roles and eventually gained valuable influence.

It must be noted, too, that a number of men provided access to professional opportunities and offered personal support to these resourceful women. Clarke partnered with her husband and brother to form her own publishing company. Harman trained under publisher Bill Clarke and was invited to join the University of Toronto Press by editor George Williams Brown. The University of Toronto Press hired Halpenny on the recommendation of her English professors E.K. Brown and A.S.P. Woodhouse. As a creative writer, Hutchinson was encouraged by poet Earle Birney, and as an editor she was championed by publisher John Irwin. Editors Pratt and Porter progressed under publisher Jack McClelland, while Pomer was enlisted to handle subsidiary rights for the Macmillan Company of Canada by president Hugh Kane, and was later prompted by her husband, Harold Pomer, to establish her own literary agency. These women, among the first to occupy senior positions in publishing, would themselves act as advisers to the increasing number of women joining their ranks.

All the same, each of these women confronted gender bias while pursuing professional advancement. Clarke, a formidable publisher, was perceived as aloof for safeguarding her privacy;

Harman was presumed to be inferior to male editors; Halpenny aspired to a career in academe but was advised to pursue high school teaching; Hutchinson was a resolute agent who was judged as too bold; Pratt's editorial compliance was encouraged, then tested; Porter's desire for children was met with resistance from Jack McClelland; and Pomer's role as mediator was challenged by intractable male editors and publishers.

Marital status was yet another aspect that affected these women's working lives. Though we cannot fully know the circumstances of their personal lives, we do know that, by remaining single, editors Harman, Halpenny, Hutchinson, and Pratt never had to make the difficult choice between a career and marriage. The wedded Clarke, on the other hand, retained control over her professional life only because she was head of her own firm. Porter and Pomer were more fortunate, for by the time they entered publishing in 1969 and 1971, respectively, workplace discrimination on the basis of gender and/or marital status, though prevalent, was no longer sanctioned.

Motherhood further influenced the professional lives of Clarke and Porter. Although they were of different times and cultures, both struggled to balance the demands of a career and motherhood and regularly brought work home when their children were young. Pomer, in contrast, did not accept full-time employment until her daughters were teenagers, when she had more time to devote to her career aspirations.

In the face of gender bias, Clarke, Harman, and Halpenny, Hutchinson, Pratt, Porter, and Pomer made the most of their vocational prospects, first by securing their respective positions, and then by refining their professional methods. Individually, each woman asserted her agency as publisher, executive, editor, or literary agent by adapting orthodox ways of acquiring titles, handling manuscripts, and liaising with authors; managing internal operations and advancing the company; initiating new and revitalizing existing editorial projects; and promoting Canadian writers and their books. Collectively, their overarching approach emerged as a feminist practice guided by a resolve to make industry-wide improvements and a matching desire to establish women's place in publishing. Their efforts served to disrupt the dominant masculine paradigm and reinvigorate the culture of publishing and authorship in Canada. Through their cultural work – expressly their vision and method – they became agents of change who helped transform publishing practice in this country.

The world of English-language publishing centred in Toronto was comparatively small, and an individual would likely work for a number of companies over the course of a career. Colleagues often crossed paths, too. This was the case for Harman and Hutchinson. Harman trained at Clarke, Irwin and Oxford University Press Canada – the two firms shared space and staff – under the guidance of Irene Clarke and then Bill Clarke. When Harman left in 1944 to join Copp Clark as editor, Hutchinson was hired by Oxford as her successor.

Two years later, in 1946, Hutchinson became editor-in-chief at McClelland and Stewart, but she exited in 1950 and found a permanent home at the Book Society of Canada, the company founded in 1945 by Irene Clarke's brother, John Irwin, after he left Clarke, Irwin.

Hutchinson's departure from McClelland and Stewart made way for the 1956 hiring of Pratt as senior editor. In turn, when Pratt resigned from her position in 1965, she made room for Porter, who joined McClelland and Stewart's editorial department in 1969.

At the University of Toronto Press, Harman and Halpenny worked together from the 1940s onward, charting the field of scholarly editing in Canada – always more collaborative than the usual editor-author dyad of trade publishing. While she pursued subsidiary rights for Macmillan of Canada in the 1970s, Pomer made lasting connections with international publishers and editors that helped boost her own literary agency, which she started late in the decade.

In 1985, just over a half-century since the launch of Clarke, Irwin and seven years after the creation of the Bella Pomer Literary Agency – the two founding events that bookend this volume – journalist John Lownsbrough proclaimed that women had made significant advances in publishing and had "become a powerful force in this traditionally male field."[58] Two years later, that view was corroborated by the *Toronto Star*'s Ken Adachi:

> There was a time when women were the gofers of the publishing industry. They toiled unseen in the editorial department on meagre

salaries, watched enviously as their male colleagues took bestselling authors to lunch and never reached executive level. Conversely, they were expected to become underpaid publicity girls, of strong liver and femme fatale looks, chatting up recalcitrant book-review editors and gossip columnists or catering to the outsized egos of minor authors on promotion tours.

But this notion now seems clearly out of date.

Adachi went on to cite a recent survey in *Publishers Weekly*, which found that "gender no longer carefully defines – or limits – one's career, and at every level, from secretary to sales rep and upward from there to publisher and to president, men and women are competing for the same position."[59]

If Adachi's positive spin on gender equity in publishing – especially the claim that men and women were competing equally for secretarial positions – seems hyperbolic, it was true that a relatively small number of visible women in publishing bore influence in much the same way that "Canadian women may seem to 'predominate' in literature because writing is one of the few areas in which women have made a consistent public impact,"[60] as Gerson has noticed.

The situation was no different in Britain, where most publishing houses were still dominated by men. In 1987, Liz Calder, founding director of Bloomsbury Press, remarked that "female voices are being heard more and more in senior ... positions," but, she cautioned, "we've only just begun."[61] Calder's comments apply to Canada, as well. In the late 1980s, men remained at the head of most firms. At the same time, female publishers like Anna Porter, who formed Key Porter Books in 1979, and Louise Dennys of Lester and Orpen Dennys – Dennys entered publishing in 1972, starting out as an editorial assistant at Clarke, Irwin – had already become prominent figures who wielded influence in the publishing arena. Despite women's involvement in all aspects of the book business, which flourished in the 1970s and 1980s, formal recognition was lacking. Aside from the occasional magazine or newspaper profile, the public was not informed of women's vital presence in Canadian publishing.

To this day, most discussion of women's participation in publishing still takes place largely in the press, both print and digital.

Outside of *Quill and Quire*, where women are featured regularly, newspapers such as the *Globe and Mail*, the *National Post*, and the *Toronto Star* offer intermittent coverage. Obviously wanting are sustained analyses of women's critical contributions to the book trade – this despite journalist Carol Toller's large claim in 1999, two decades ago, that Canadian publishing was "already dominated by women."[62]

In contrast, international scholarly interest in the subject of women and twentieth-century book trades has heightened. In Europe, *Bibliologia: An International Journal of Bibliography, Library Science, History of Typography and the Book*, edited by Fabrizio Serra and published out of Italy, devoted its ninth volume in 2014 to the theme of women in publishing around the globe. It featured divers articles, including studies of women in Slovenia's book trade and Irish publisher Blanaid Salkeld of the feminist Gayfield Press. Belgian scholar Marianne Van Remoortel's project on European women periodical editors, entitled "Agents of Change: Women Editors and Socio-Cultural Transformation in Europe, 1710–1920," received funding in 2015 from the European Research Council.

In Britain, the subject of women in publishing has received significant scholarly attention. *The Library: Transactions of the Bibliographical Society* (U.K.) has published many articles that deal with women in the book trades.[63] The digitized *Modernist Archives Publishing Project*, an international, collaborative undertaking, has curated a history of the Hogarth Press, which includes references to its several women book travellers, or sales representatives, and managers.[64] An academic conference entitled "Men and Women in the Book Trade: Changing Gender Roles over 500 Years," was held in November 2017 at London's Stationers' Hall.

The influence of Women in Publishing, an organization launched in 1979 by publishers Liz Calder, Carmen Callil, Ursula Owen, and literary agent Anne McDermid "to promote the status of women working in publishing and related trades,"[65] has likely stirred public interest in British women of the press. In June 2010, for example, BBC Television One aired a documentary on the life of celebrated editor Diana Athill of André Deutsch. Part of its Imagine series, the episode was ironically titled "Growing Old Disgracefully." That same summer, Eunice Frost, Penguin Books editor from 1937 to 1960 – the Penguin logo was nicknamed Frostie in her honour – was the subject of a biographical article by Gaby Wood, head of books at the *Telegraph*.[66] In 2013 and 2014, BBC Radio Four also showcased the work of pre-eminent women in publishing. Its program *Woman's Hour* aired on 19 August 2013 an episode entitled "Women in Publishing," which featured interviews with publishers Lennie Goodings of Virago Press and Ursula Mackenzie of Little, Brown. The two-part series Publishing Lives (30 September to 4 October 2013 and 10 to 14 March 2014) included three out of ten episodes on women: editor Kaye Webb of Puffin Books, publisher Norah Smallwood of Chatto and Windus, and publisher Carmen Callil, founder of Virago Press.

The existence of Exceptional Women in Publishing, a non-profit organization founded in 1998 "to educate, empower and support women in publishing,"[67] does not appear, however, to have fostered comparable public curiosity in the United States, where women have also held high-ranking positions in publishing. Scholarly interest in the subject is extensive, however, as evidenced by the number of sources cited in the digital *Women in Book History Bibliography*, prepared by Cait Coker and Kate Ozment out of Texas A&M University.[68] Cited in the *Bibliography* – to name a particularly relevant title – is James P. Danky and Wayne A. Wiegand's edited volume of essays, *Women in Print: Essays on the Print Cultures of American Women from the Nineteenth and Twentieth Centuries*, which examines women authors and readers, editors and journalists, librarians and booksellers.[69] As part of the annual meeting of the Shakespeare Association of America, a number of scholars held a seminar entitled "Women, Gender, and Book History" in Los Angeles on 30 March 2018.

Among the notable American women who enter this study are Virginia Barber, literary agent; Ann Close, senior editor at Alfred A. Knopf; Nan Talese, senior vice-president of Doubleday; and Mindy Werner, one-time editor at Viking Press. Like their British and Canadian counterparts, these women began their careers at a time when American publishing was still the domain of men. Their motivation yielded unprecedented success in a competitive field that required complete commitment and offered them less recognition and remuneration than their male colleagues. For their various accomplishments, they, too, deserve consideration beyond the customary press coverage allotted to women and publishing – a subject, as my research suggests, that is still wide open to scholarly exploration.

II

In their introduction to *Literature in the Marketplace: Nineteenth-Century British Publishing and Reading Practices*, editors John O. Jordan and Robert L. Patten assert that publishing historians must "recognize the impossibility of composing a single metanarrative ... no history is likely to comprehend the whole range of paradoxical and messy consequences of unleashing the power of the press."[70] In place of the "linear paradigms of production that commence with the writer's idea and proceed straightforwardly through composition to publication and reception," they propose "conceptions of the activity of producing and consuming books that decenter the principal elements and make them interactive and interdependent."[71]

The present examination of women involved in English-language publishing in Canada follows Jordan and Patten and is purposely "decentred" in scope. First, though it covers a broad sweep of time – from 1930, when Irene Clarke co-founded Clarke, Irwin, to 2002, when Bella Pomer's literary agency ceased representing novelist Carol Shields – it eschews a thorough overview of more than seventy years of Canadian publishing. Instead, it furnishes historical context as it probes the careers of seven individual women.

Second, chapters are arranged chronologically, not by each woman's year of birth, but by the year she entered publishing: publisher Irene Clarke in 1930; scholarly editors Eleanor Harman in 1930 and Francess Halpenny in 1941; trade editors Sybil Hutchinson in 1942, Claire Pratt in 1956, and Anna Porter in 1969; and literary agent Bella Pomer in 1971. This arrangement is intended to show women's gradual but significant progress as publishers, executives, editors, and literary agents, and their increasingly central role in furthering the development of the publishing industry. Taken together, the chapters form a larger narrative of shared and incremental – not hierarchical and "linear" – achievement and present an "interactive"[72] community of publishing women. At the same time, separate chapters underline the distinctiveness of each woman's accomplishments.

Finally, this monograph is delimited by my focus on women who worked solely in mainstream publishing and whose professional lives were accessible through extant archival records. In addition, the foregrounding of literary production, with an emphasis on trade and scholarly publishing by women who were in the privileged position to facilitate that production, reflects my training and special interests as a literary scholar.

My prior archival research into the role of women employed by the Macmillan Company of Canada – most notably, editor Ellen Elliott and executive Gladys Neale – gave rise to this wider enquiry into women's participation in publishing. In fact, the commanding figures of Elliott and Neale, who are fully present in my study of Macmillan, also hover over the chapters of this book. They, too, must be counted among the women whose dedicated efforts to shape Canada's publishing industry are limned in this volume.

Since the essential details of women's historic contributions to publishing reside largely in archival collections, the availability of archival materials and a further willingness on the part of originators or executors to provide access to particular fonds helped steer the course of this book and determined the subject of each chapter. Happily, several individuals and many more institutions – referenced in the selected bibliography – opened their archival vaults and allowed me to consult a remarkable range of primary materials out of which this book was written.

Regrettably, the inverse situation – inaccessibility or the refusal to grant archival access – has meant that this work elides the contributions of numerous women to twentieth-century Canadian publishing. Since the archives of Oxford University Press Canada, for example, are retained in-house, it was not possible to include an analysis of women's role at that scholarly press, or to achieve a deep understanding of the early training Oxford afforded Irene Clarke, Eleanor Harman, and Sybil Hutchinson.

Similarly, though I had hoped to complement my chapters on Sybil Hutchinson and Bella Pomer with an examination of the careers of literary agents Matie Molinaro – with Hutchinson, Molinaro co-founded Canada's first commercial literary agency in 1950 – and Beverley Slopen – Pomer's colleague and head of the Beverley Slopen Literary Agency – I faced closed access to their respective archives: the Canadian Speakers' and Writers' fonds housed in the Clara Thomas Archives and Special Collections at York University, and the Beverley Slopen papers housed in the Thomas Fisher Rare Book Library at the University of Toronto.

As a scholar who has worked in numerous archival fonds held in North America and the United Kingdom, I am cognizant that all archival collections – those of institutions and individuals alike – are incomplete and reflect principles of selection and arrangement adopted by their originators, often with the intention of shaping their records. As Linda M. Morra observes, the reasons for "absences" in archival fonds range "from the archival practices of institutions, to individual concerns about privacy, to familial interventions made on behalf of authors. Sometimes, these gaps are willfully constructed ... because authors [and other individuals] wish to shape the interpretive lenses that are thereafter applied to their records and that generate narratives about their lives."[73] Further gaps in the archival record result when materials are misplaced, destroyed inadvertently, or discarded deliberately.[74]

Nonetheless, as archivist Catherine Hobbs admits, invoking the insight of Maryanne Dever, "there is a life narrative that suggests itself to readers of archives, particularly caused by reading the documents in sequence and in our interpretation of their omissions."[75] In fact, archival documents revealed the lasting influence of the women covered in this study. They were essential to the writing of this specialized "life narrative"[76] of publishing women, which exists by virtue of access to unique primary resources, however fragmentary or incomplete.

I was especially fortunate in being able to interview three women who are featured in this book. The late Francess Halpenny shared her insights into the rigours of scholarly publishing and her appreciation for the stimulating work she carried out at the University of Toronto Press; Anna Porter recalled the exciting years she spent at McClelland and Stewart and Seal Books; and Bella Pomer recounted the challenges and triumphs she experienced as one of Canada's first literary agents.

Conversations with several others helped contextualize my archival findings. Publisher William H. (Bill) Clarke offered a detailed and fond recollection of his mother and her leading role at Clarke, Irwin. Publisher John W. Irwin, who worked alongside Sybil Hutchinson at the Book Society until her retirement in 1974, remembered "Hutch" as a "gifted career editor of both general and educational books";[77] while Susan Wallace provided an invaluable picture of Hutchinson as the pioneering literary agent who represented her father-in-law, the poet and playwright James Reaney. In writing this book, I have drawn on these interviews for understanding as much as citation.

In the past, my research into publishing has focused on the nineteenth and twentieth centuries and has drawn on the assorted materials typically found in archival collections: personal documents such as notebooks, journals, and diaries; correspondence with family members and friends; and memorabilia; as well as professional documents, which include manuscripts and typescripts; correspondence with writers, editors, publishers, and agents; reader's reports; in-house memoranda; minutes of meetings; galley proofs; production records; catalogues and promotional material; publishing contracts and other legal documents; and ephemera. All of these documents originate in print. I have, in addition, made use of archived audiovisual material, such as radio broadcasts and television programs; audio interviews, film and video recordings; photographs and slides.

This project, however, extends into the twenty-first century, and so for the first time I have had to interpret archival content, specifically email correspondence, that originated in digital format. In fact, my investigation of Bella Pomer's later decades as an agent – Pomer, who is still active, was quick to incorporate email into her professional practice – could not have been written without access to such material.

I have studied hand- and typewritten correspondence retained in archival collections and have found it to be a valuable source of information, both explicit and implicit. To give one example, the letters of Canadian novelists Margaret Laurence and Adele Wiseman – which I know from having co-edited a selected volume of their correspondence[78] – were written over a period of forty years and serve as a record of their long friendship and extraordinary lives. Between 1947 and 1986, Laurence and Wiseman exchanged lengthy, fluent letters about their personal circumstances, various writing projects, and the difficulties of the writing life. The length of the letters, along with the idiosyncrasies of handwritten doodles, asides, and signatures, suggests a shared intimacy, while their depth conveys the profound feelings the women had for one another.

An email exchange differs considerably in both form and content from its paper-based cousin. First, as Lise Jaillant notes in a piece written for the *Times Literary Supplement*, with regard to email correspondence included in the Ian McEwan Papers held at the Harry Ransom Center of the University of Texas at Austin, a "subject line reminds us"[79] that email was modelled after business memoranda. Historically, business correspondence was formal in presentation: courteous, concrete, and concise. Email, however, emerged during the 1990s, when formal address was already less common. It embraced the tone and lexicon of everyday speech and preferred the present tense,[80] while still favouring precision and brevity. Thus, it evolved as an immediate and practical form of exchange, not as a forum for weighty discussion, since "convenience of communication is [generally] antithetical to depth,"[81] as writer Cathal Kelly recently quipped in the *Globe and Mail*.

As Jaillant goes on to explain, since they must comply with privacy security provisions laid out in the U.K.'s *Data Protection Act* (2018), British institutions often prohibit access to email archives.[82] This is normally not the case in North America, where researchers can gain access to restricted archival content. Once I secured her permission, for example, I was given access to the restricted email correspondence included in Bella Pomer's closed archive.

Jaillant points to yet another salient fact: "few institutions have solved all the technical issues specific to digital archives, including an appropriate interface to make these documents available to researchers."[83] In the case of email correspondence, one way of circumventing "the technical issues" has been to print out email threads and include them as part of a print archive. While printing does provide access to email content, it also retains the distractions of subject lines, dates, and times. Moreover, since most email threads are protracted and include superfluous exchange, they can be difficult to follow in print.

Email threads that form part of print archives often contain too much of insignificance. This is certainly true of Pomer's email correspondence with writers Matt Cohen, Jack Hodgins, and Carol Shields – three of her clients foregrounded in this study – which includes a great deal of negligible content that must be combed by a researcher. On the page, these email threads are challenging to navigate. They are also stripped of their original immediacy. Even so, I am fortunate in having been able to study Pomer's email correspondence.

The distinguishing features of email threads confirm that the meaning of all archival materials inheres in their original format. Thus, as a scholar whose research now engages with printed email correspondence, I believe it is necessary to draw attention to the specific qualities of born-digital source material – even in the preliminary way I have done here – and to try to account for the influence of those qualities on one's findings and scholarly analysis.

In researching Pomer's professional representation of Cohen, Hodgins, and Shields, I differentiated between typewritten letters and printed email, knowing that the latter originated in digital format. I also acknowledged that a brief email exchange might mean that a full discussion had taken place separately, most likely over the telephone. Thus, I recognized the importance of telephone calls, which were an absence rather than a presence in the archive. This might seem illogical, but I was always aware that what was addressed in a telephone call could have direct bearing on what was communicated via email. In fact, Pomer's email correspondence, some of which would have either preceded or followed a telephone conversation, often makes reference to comments that remain inaccessible to a researcher.

Hence, in my analysis of printed email threads in Pomer's archive I was careful to interpret what was on record, first in terms of its original digital format, and second in light of what would remain unavailable, such as the content of unrecorded telephone discussions. In fact, since the "absences" and "omissions" Morra and Hobbs identify as characteristic of all archival collections "shape[d] the interpretive lens"[84] I brought to my reading of Pomer's email communication, I found it possible to read across or through – without trying to fill – gaps in the email record.

The wide range of archival sources – in print and born-digital format – that informs this study[85] of publishing women attests to the profound cultural value of such primary material and signals the need to continue preserving literary and publishing archives. As bookseller Ken Lopez wrote, following his recent sale of a literary archive that "was about two-thirds digital" in format, "much digital storage of personal materials is [now] moving from residing on one's own personal computer, iPad, or smartphone and into the so-called 'cloud' ... These digital materials stand at risk of getting lost at this moment in time in a way that they didn't when they had a primarily physical manifestation."[86] I would argue that publishers' archives are threatened in a similar way.

Preservation has always been imperative, but is especially so in the current digital age, when most of the day-to-day work that takes place in publishing is done electronically and may be perceived as lacking historical significance. I hope this monograph, which avails itself of born-digital email correspondence to show the influence of Bella Pomer on publishing practice in Canada, demonstrates that nothing could be further from the truth. For, as Jaillant declares, "the preservation, access and use of born-digital records is central to our [cultural] heritage."[87] Ironically, women's part in producing that shared heritage may now be at even greater risk of erasure than it was in the age of print.

Indeed, access to the full range of archival materials generated across the literary field is essential if we are to expand the global canvas of publishing history, and if women are to be given a place of record alongside the male publishers, editors, and literary agents of the past, present, and future. This book offers one such record.

It develops a narrative of vision, determination, and resilience on the part of seven women who, by helping to shape the publishing industry over the course of the twentieth century, were instrumental in advancing a modern literary culture for Canada. In making "visible"[88] their efforts in publishing – by underscoring their labour and studying their influence as cultural workers – I seek to redress the conspicuous absence of women from our gendered understanding of a publishing culture whose "structuring feature" is "masculinity."[89] Such a counterbalancing representation of female achievement in the public sphere is not only necessary; it is, as Elizabeth Long contends, "an intervention in print culture"[90] where women's history and publishing history merge.

chapter one

"Exceptional in building a Canadian company": Irene Clarke

Irene Clarke (1903–1986) was a trailblazer. In 1930, by co-founding Clarke, Irwin, she became the first woman publisher of English-language books in Canada. At the time, with the world economy in collapse and the country in the grip of the Depression, the decision to launch a publishing company would have seemed imprudent. Under "Irene Clarke's leadership," however, Clarke, Irwin grew to such size and stature that by the late 1940s it was "one of the five largest"[1] educational and trade publishers in Canada, clear evidence of Clarke's business acumen.

Clarke stood in contrast to women of earlier generations "whose intellectual and craft ambitions were frustrated" in a field dominated by men, but "whose domestic and behind-the-scenes labour," as Leslie Howsam notes, nonetheless "made the family business possible, or made it flourish."[2] Clarke was, in fact, an active lifelong partner in the publishing firm that bore both her maiden and married names. Not only did she oversee the Clarke, Irwin enterprise, she was recognized for her pioneering role in Canadian publishing.

Clarke was a complex figure – both traditional and forward-thinking, shy of publicity and publicly engaged – who used her position as publisher to advance women's writing and women's rights. Most notably, she issued the prose of Emily Carr, whose work had been rejected by other publishers. Clarke's choice to back the unconventional Carr and champion the writer's original voice and subject matter was but one example of her early feminism, which also led her to support other women who entered publishing – among them executive Gladys Neale and editors Eleanor Harman and Sybil Hutchinson – and endorse women's causes throughout her life. When, however, the same racial and class privilege that underwrote her defence of women gave rise to overt prejudice, Clarke was blind to her own hypocrisy.

The Public Face of Irene Clarke

Clarke, Irwin and Company was first and foremost a family firm, founded by Irene Clarke (née Irwin), her husband William Henry (Bill) Clarke, and her brother John Coverdale Watson Irwin. Although John Irwin left the partnership in 1944, Clarke, Irwin continued to thrive. From its inception, Irene Clarke, in her dual capacity as vice-president and director, helped manage the company. In 1955, she rose to the position of president and general manager. Thus, throughout its history, Irene Clarke retained a formidable presence at the helm of Clarke, Irwin.[3]

The company was first housed at 86 Richmond Street West in downtown Toronto. In 1936, Clarke, Irwin relocated to the offices of Oxford University Press Canada, where Bill Clarke had become manager. The two publishing houses were financially independent of one another, but were jointly staffed and managed by Clarke. Theirs was an unusual publishing arrangement: Oxford issued the trade edition of a book, while Clarke, Irwin held the exclusive right to issue the educational edition. At Amen House, an elegant Tudor-style property at 480 University Avenue – designed specifically for Oxford by Toronto architects Henry Sproatt and Ernest Rolph, the building opened its doors in 1906 – Irene Clarke had her own office.

In 1949, when Bill Clarke resigned as manager of Oxford University Press Canada, Clarke, Irwin moved to new premises at 103 St Clair Avenue West. The refurbished home in mid-town Toronto was decorated with "cheerful colors ... bright drapes,"[4] and boasted a fireplace in the library; the shipping and warehousing departments were housed in a nearby building. Finally, in 1958 the

Figure 1. Irene Clarke, Amen House, in the 1940s

company purchased Clarwin House, a spacious, two-storey brick building located at 791 St Clair Avenue West. There, Irene Clarke's large office overlooked "an open-air courtyard."[5]

Gladys Neale arrived at Clarke, Irwin in December 1980 to revitalize the company's educational program. Neale, who had been head of the Macmillan Company of Canada's education department from the early 1940s until her recent retirement from the firm, was a longtime colleague of Irene Clarke. She described Clarke's presence: "When Irene Clarke entered a room crowded with publishers, you could almost hear them snap to attention and straighten their ties ... [She was] a genuine pioneer ... a woman who was exceptional in building a Canadian company."[6] Despite her "indomitable"[7] bearing, Clarke "was friendly, approachable, and willing to share her expertise and experiences."[8] She was also a "tough and demanding"[9] business woman who protected Clarke, Irwin's copyright investments and the company's reputation as a publisher of note.

As principal of the firm, Clarke fostered its formal atmosphere, which included a weekly "ritual of afternoon tea," described by Neale as "a ceremony complete with silver tea-service and china cups."[10] Smoking was not permitted and alcohol was prohibited at all company functions, which was atypical for the publishing industry. In the 1940s, Clarke, Irwin and Oxford University Press Canada celebrated Christmas jointly. Publishing historian Roy MacSkimming describes the annual Christmas dinner, sans liquor, held at the King Edward Hotel, which featured an Oxford University Press "author as guest speaker, skits by the staff, and the gift of a silver spoon"[11] in lieu of an employee bonus.

Neale noticed "a large measure of loyalty, respect, and admiration" for Clarke: "She had a maternalistic attitude towards her staff, dealt with them fairly and sympathetically, and at all levels stimulated them in their work."[12] Clarke took an "immense interest"[13] in her employees. They were paid appropriately – Clarke privately hoped each employee could afford to purchase a home – and rewarded with a trip after twenty-five years of service.[14] As her son William Henry (Bill) Clarke remarked in a 2010 interview, "people were drawn to her on a personal level"; many, however, "were a little in fear of her on a business level."[15]

Poet Alden Nowlan, who was based in the Maritimes but maintained a strong connection to his Toronto publisher,[16] characterized Irene Clarke as "sure of her convictions."[17] Clarke was, in fact, an early feminist who sanctioned female ambition. On 18 October 1942, for instance, she reviewed Jennie Lee's autobiography, *This Great Journey*, on the radio for CFRB's Fireside Book Club. Clarke admired Lee, who, at the age of twenty-four, was the youngest woman to be elected to the British House of Commons.

Clarke also condemned discrimination against women. On 10 May 1958, she gave an address to the Victoria College Alumnae Association on the occasion of its diamond jubilee – she was an alumna of the University of Toronto, having earned a BA with first class honours (1924) in classics and English and an MA (1932) in Greek literature and philosophy, and she served on the board of regents of Victoria University from 1946 to 1954 – in which she urged her audience of privileged women to "remember that our duty is not only to ourselves but to the larger community of women the world over. They must look to our full acceptance as responsible persons for their hope of enfranchisement from degrading and inexcusable conditions."[18] The following year, as a newly appointed and the first-ever female member of the University of Toronto's board of governors, she opposed initial plans to restrict Massey College (which opened on campus in 1963) to male graduate students alone.[19]

Clarke's activities in support of women were wide-ranging, even as she was careful of her public persona. In 1940, she was a founding member of the Canadian Women's Voluntary Services. From 1949 to 1952, she chaired the Canadian Federation of University Women's committee on the legal and economic status of women. She represented the International Federation of University Women of Canada at the coronation of Queen Elizabeth on 2 June 1953. From 1954 to 1957, she was an honorary member of the Canadian Council of the Girl Guide Association. Clarke was also a member of the University Women's Club of Toronto and the Zonta Club of Toronto, part of Zonta International, a global organization still working to advance the status of women.

At the same time, Clarke was not alert to her own prejudices. In 1958, for example, she protested her inability to distribute Nora Case's *Ten Little Nigger Boys* (1959) on behalf of its British publisher, Chatto and Windus. "There is very strong opposition in this country now to the term 'nigger,'" which, she attested, "is carrying the whole question of discrimination too far."[20] This comment, which shows a publisher untouched by the suffering of racialized groups, undermined Clarke's claim that she was an advocate for women worldwide. In truth, her class privilege and gendered experience allowed her to see only the difficulties facing white women like herself.

Journalist Robert Fulford once described Irene Clarke – somewhat disparagingly – as "the enigma at the heart of Clarke, Irwin."[21] In reality, Clarke was less enigmatic than private. She generally eschewed publicity and, in later years, wielded power through her son, who functioned as intermediary between his mother and the media. Yet, her professional voice does not dominate the company's archives housed at McMaster University; it is heard best in the agency correspondence included in the Clarke, Irwin fonds. Moreover, with the exception of Emily Carr's publishing record, Clarke left little editorial trace. This lack of detail is deeply frustrating, especially for the scholar who is interested in uncovering all facets of her role as publisher. One thing is certain, however: in life, Clarke loomed large over her firm.

Managing Clarke, Irwin

From the outset, Irene Clarke was involved in all aspects of publishing at Clarke, Irwin. In the early years, she sought out authors; read and reported on countless manuscripts; served as copy editor; and oversaw much of the firm's correspondence. When her children were young, she often brought home stacks of manuscripts, which she read at the kitchen table, as her son Bill recollected vividly.[22] During the six weeks of each year when her husband travelled across the country to sell and promote Clarke, Irwin's books, Clarke took charge of the company.[23]

When her husband died of a heart attack in 1955, Clarke's publishing responsibilities increased. She also became the office manager, one whose decisions held sway. She managed the business, first alongside her son Garrick, who worked for the firm for a brief period before pursuing theological studies, and later her younger son Bill, who joined Clarke, Irwin in 1963 as a director and in 1967 became assistant to the president. Later, when she developed heart problems that kept her from the office – Clarke often worked from her nearby flat on Spadina Road – Bill Clarke's duties expanded and he rose to the position of vice-president and general manager of Clarke, Irwin.[24]

As president, Irene Clarke "maintained a high profile in the company," notes Judy Donnelly.[25] She handled administrative matters, both small and large. Clarke oversaw the upkeep of Clarwin House, designated office space, and dealt with staffing issues. She planned launches and wrote the advertisements for Clarke, Irwin books that appeared regularly in Toronto's *Globe and Mail* and other newspapers. More importantly, she supervised the company's finances and royalty payments.

Clarke's extensive correspondence with publishers was detailed, incisive, and at times, personal; it also showed a conscious commitment to agency publishing, which formed a large part of her business. Among the prestigious houses represented by Clarke, Irwin were American publishers Henry Holt, Noble and Noble, and Rinehart. British publishers included Jonathan Cape, Chatto and Windus, George G. Harrap, Rupert Hart-Davis, and the Hogarth Press. Managing Clarke, Irwin's agency agreements may have been more "time-consuming" and less satisfying than "creative publishing," but it was "profitable."[26] Thus, during her frequent travels Clarke made certain to visit the American and British publishers represented by her firm.

Over the course of her long career Clarke faced critical challenges. In January 1956, for instance, she journeyed to New York to meet with literary agent Willis Kingsley Wing. At the time, Wing represented novelist Robertson Davies, whose first publisher was Clarke, Irwin. Clarke, who sought wide dissemination for Davies's work, was troubled by the "marketing problems confronting a Canadian publisher in the United States"[27] and probed those difficulties with Wing. Until the late 1970s, as Robert Lecker notes, Wing "was easily the most prominent agent for many Canadian writers."[28] In addition to Davies, he represented Ralph Allen, Pierre Berton, Robert Kroetsch, Margaret Laurence, W.O. Mitchell, Brian Moore, Sinclair Ross, Jane Rule, Adele Wiseman, and Scott Young.

Clarke and Wing both aspired to promote Canadian writers. They also shared a desire to build commercial bridges between Canada and the United States, but could not overcome the key obstacle preventing Canadian publishers from penetrating the large American market: the protectionism of American copyright law that prohibited importation of books not manufactured in the United States. In the end, Davies was led away from Clarke, Irwin to the Macmillan Company of Canada – in 1958, the firm published *A Mixture of Frailties*, the final novel in his Salterton trilogy. As the Toronto branch of the renowned London house, Macmillan had the international reach Davies sought for his work.

Normally, Clarke avoided public controversy. When necessary, however, she took action on behalf of Ontario's educational publishers. This was the case in the late 1960s when she requested a meeting with Ontario minister of education Bill Davis, whom she knew through her participation on the board of governors of the University of Toronto. Clarke opposed the elimination in 1968 of textbook stimulation grants by the province's ministry of education, as well as the recent amalgamation of Ontario school boards, which were no longer required to allocate a portion of their funding towards the purchase of textbooks. As a result, school boards were taking far too long to pay their bills, causing severe financial distress for publishers.

In a 1999 interview, Bill Clarke, who was present at the meeting with the minister of education, captured his mother's boldness – "She let him have it right between the eyes!" – and her objection that "the school boards were sitting on the money ... They were taking the money they were supposed to be paying their bills with and putting them into deposits. And getting interest. And so our accounts receivable from school boards were going up [to] ... 90 [days], 120 [days], six months."[29]

Clarke saw the situation worsen when relaxed "rules governing the annual list of approved textbooks"[30] gave individual teachers new flexibility in their choice of classroom texts. Thus, the budgets for textbook expenditures in provincial school boards fell significantly, from "2.5 percent ... in 1967 to 1 percent in 1978."[31]

Ontario's actions and the resulting loss of revenue had a devastating effect on Clarke, Irwin. Educational sales, Donnelly explains, had once "accounted for seventy-five percent of the firm's business."[32] By 1970, however, "print runs for textbooks [had] dropped from 50,000 to 5,000 ... editorial staff numbers had been reduced from forty-two to nine, and the company had only ten educational projects in progress, compared to forty-seven in 1963."[33] Clarke, Irwin, whose reputation was founded on a "meticulous approach to publishing well-crafted textbooks,"[34] struggled to rebound from the financial reversal.

Proceeds from educational publishing had also made it possible to develop an ambitious trade list that illuminated Canada's past. Notable titles in history and architecture, for example, were William Kilbourn's *The Firebrand: William Lyon Mackenzie and the Rebellion in Upper Canada* (1956), Richard Gwyn's *The Shape of Scandal: A Study of a Government in Crisis* (1965), Marion MacRae's *The Ancestral Roof: Domestic Architecture of Upper Canada* (1963), and Marion MacRae and Anthony Adamson's *Hallowed Walls: Church Architecture of Upper Canada* (1975), which won the Governor General's Literary Award in the category of non-fiction.

Clarke, Irwin also published books on Canadian art, including Group of Seven artist A.Y. Jackson's *A Painter's Country: The Autobiography of A.Y. Jackson* (1958), Naomi Jackson Groves's *A.Y.'s Canada: Pencil Drawings by A.Y. Jackson* (1968), and Canadian art historian and critic Paul Duval's *Four Decades: The Canadian Group of Painters and Their Contemporaries, 1930–1970* (1972), which won the Leipzig Award for the world's most beautifully designed book, and *Ken Danby* (1976).

Irene Clarke's own appreciation for the Stratford Shakespearean Festival (founded in 1953, now the Stratford Festival) and its Canadian brand of Shakespearean theatre led to a string of publications: *Renown at Stratford: A Record of the Shakespearean Festival of Canada, 1953* (1953), by Tyrone Guthrie and Robertson Davies; *Twice Have the Trumpets Sounded: A Record of the Stratford Shakespearean Festival in Canada, 1954* (1954), by Tyrone Guthrie and Robertson Davies; and *Thrice the Brinded Cat Hath Mew'd: A Record of the Stratford Shakespearean Festival in Canada, 1955* (1955), by Robertson Davies.

Known for its quality editing and book design, Clarke, Irwin attracted important Canadian writers. In addition to his books on Stratford, Robertson Davies published five prose works with the firm: *Shakespeare for Young Players: A Junior Course* (1942); *The Diary of Samuel Marchbanks* (1947) and *The Table Talk of Samuel Marchbanks* (1949), the first two titles in the Marchbanks trilogy;

and *Tempest-Tost* (1951) and *Leaven of Malice* (1954), the first two novels in his Salterton trilogy;[35] the latter novel received the Stephen Leacock Memorial Medal for Humour.

Clarke, Irwin helped establish Timothy Findley's literary career by publishing *The Wars* (1977), his breakout novel that won the Governor General's Literary Award and was made into the 1983 film starring Brent Carver. The press also issued the first three of Howard Engel's Benny Cooperman detective novels: *The Suicide Murders* (1980), *The Ransom Game* (1981), and *Murder on Location* (1982).

In addition to fiction, Clarke, Irwin published the work of prominent poets: Douglas Le Pan's *The Net and the Sword* (1953), which won the Governor General's Literary Award, and Alden Nowlan's *Bread, Wine and Salt* (1967), another winner of the Governor General's Literary Award (shared with Eli Mandel's *An Idiot Joy*, published out of Edmonton by M.G. Hurtig), *The Mysterious Naked Man* (1969), and *Between Tears and Laughter* (1971).

Two stand-out memoirs were Will R. Bird's *Ghosts Have Warm Hands: A Memoir of the Great War, 1916–1919* (1968) and Adele Wiseman's *Old Woman at Play* (1978). Also significant was the firm's decision to issue the plays of Gratien Gélinas in English translation – *Bousille and the Just* (1961; translated by Kenneth Johnson), *Tit-coq* (1967; translated by Kenneth Johnson), and *Yesterday the Children Were Dancing* (1967; translated by Mavor Moore)[36] – which showed a commitment to fostering dialogue between French- and English-speaking Canadians.

Clarke, Irwin's short-lived Canadian Paperback series, issued between 1963 and 1970, featured the work of Kilbourn, Gwyn, Jackson, Davies, and Gélinas, as well as Emily Carr. The series of thirty-eight titles was an attempt to capitalize on the paperback market and further promote the firm's own publications.[37]

Emily Carr

Irene Clarke, Neale claimed, "learned early the fine art of the care and nurture of authors"[38] and chose to involve herself in key projects, most notably the publications of west coast painter and writer Emily Carr. Ira Dilworth, the British Columbia regional director of CBC Radio who became her adviser, editor, and confidant, brought a selection of Carr's unpublished sketches to the attention of Bill and Irene Clarke. Carr's sketches were based on her experiences among the Indigenous people of British Columbia; she had visited Ucluelet on the west coast of Vancouver Island in 1898, and had travelled to the northern coast and the Queen Charlotte Islands (now Haida Gwaii) in 1912 and 1928. Carr's series of sketches had not yet found a home – they had not found favour with either the Macmillan Company of Canada or Ryerson Press, for example – and Dilworth hoped the Clarkes would agree to issue her work.

After some wooing by Dilworth, Bill and Irene Clarke were charmed by Carr's original voice and unpretentious writing style. The three travelled together to Victoria to meet the author in late March 1941, a publishing contract was signed in May, and the manuscript was submitted by June.[39] Dilworth was delighted – he set "the terms of ... publication, from beginning to page proofs"[40] – while Carr was euphoric. The Clarkes' faith in her work brought "great happiness"[41] to the elderly Carr, who had taken to writing in her late sixties, when she was ill and "invalided in bed"[42] following a heart attack in early January 1937.

Klee Wyck was issued by Oxford University Press Canada in November 1941, just before Carr's seventieth birthday on 13 December.[43] The title, which translates as "laughing one," was the nickname given to Carr by the Indigenous people of Ucluelet. A first printing of 2,500 copies[44] included four colour plates of Carr's paintings and a foreword by Dilworth. In early 1942, a second Canadian printing appeared alongside an American edition issued by Farrar and Rinehart.[45]

Klee Wyck was Carr's first book and – somewhat ironically in light of her current renown as an artist – it brought her more recognition than her paintings had to date. Novelist Robertson Davies, for instance, who reviewed *Klee Wyck* for *Saturday Night*, lauded its "original" style "completely free of fripperies and self-conscious[ness]," with "every thought ... as clear as the note of a bell."[46] The publication of *Klee Wyck* also proved fortuitous for its publisher. When the volume won the Governor General's Literary

Award for non-fiction, Bill Clarke proclaimed *Klee Wyck* "the greatest find in Canadian literature since [Louis Hémon's novel] *Maria Chapdelaine*."[47] Irene Clarke believed its success made Carr "an interesting and magnetic figure to thousands"[48] of readers.

Before Carr's death on 2 March 1945, Oxford University Press Canada issued two further works in rapid succession. *The Book of Small* appeared in late fall 1942. Maria Tippett, Carr's biographer, recounts that 3,000 copies, "a fairly large first printing for wartime ... sold quickly."[49] Reprinted "in December/January," it was praised by "*Saturday Night*, the *Canadian Forum*, the *Winnipeg Tribune*, the *Calgary Herald*, and the *Edmonton Radio Book Review* ... as 'the Canadian Book of the Year.'"[50] *The House of All Sorts* followed in 1944 and was dedicated to Bill and Irene Clarke. Irene Clarke was intensely proud of her discovery of Carr and her decision to publish the work of the writer/painter. She took a deep interest in "everything that concern[ed Carr's] ... life or her work."[51] Clarke also developed a "great affection" for Carr herself, who was easy to talk to and "full of fun."[52]

Irene Clarke handled all matters pertaining to Carr's writing and supervised production of Carr's posthumous publications. In 1966, for example, Clarke, Irwin, which eventually acquired copyright to all of Carr's works, issued *Hundreds and Thousands: The Journals of Emily Carr*. The volume reproduced Carr's journal entries from originals "written in faint pencil,"[53] dating from 1927 to 1941. On 19 October 1966, *Hundreds and Thousands* was launched at a reception for 250 guests at Vancouver's Bayshore Inn. Five days later, on 24 October, a second reception for 400 guests was held in Victoria at the Empress Hotel.[54]

Esteem for Carr drove Clarke's efforts to promote the artist's books. As she admitted to artist Ina Uhthoff, founder and principal of the Victoria School of Art: "[You have] a fellow feeling for our pleasure and sense of responsibility in [having published *Hundreds and Thousands*]."[55] Among Clarke's cherished possessions were 114 Carr letters, as well as original manuscripts and a number of her paintings, all of which she "prize[d] very highly ... for the illumination" they cast on Carr's "personal feelings and the development of her creative energies."[56]

It "was not always easy,"[57] however, to be Emily Carr's publisher. The ailing Carr longed for human interaction, but she was separated from the Clarkes, first by distance and second by the time it took for mail to travel between Ontario and British Columbia. Impatient for letters from Irene and Bill Clarke, Carr often complained bitterly of her publishers' inattentiveness. In correspondence with Ira Dilworth, Carr expressed her deep dismay – verging on insult – at what she perceived as neglect: Irene Clarke is a "'going-to-write' blow-bag"; "Those Clarkes are tombstones!"; "Irene's *long* letter now 4 o[r] 5 months overdue has *not come* yet"; "No word from the Clarke or Clarkess."[58]

That Carr was exuberant, however, when she received the attention she desired signalled the strength of her attachment to Irene and Bill Clarke: her publishers were "so loving & kind. I am lucky"; "Irene says they *both love me*[.] I am so glad"; and "This afternoon came a lovely cyclamen from Irene & Bill's[.] No wonder I'm happy ... I want to hug them both all over again. Aren't there times when you want to hug the whole world?"[59] In the end, Carr's frustration was exceeded by appreciation for her publishers.

If tension ever erupted between author and publisher, it neither dampened Irene Clarke's "special interest in the dissemination of accurate information"[60] about Carr, nor did it pre-empt her lifelong advocacy on behalf of the writer/painter. Clarke considered Carr much more than a "minor factor ... in the Canadian literary scene"[61] and sought to foster appreciation for Carr's writing.

Clarke discussed Carr's books with audiences at Toronto's Granite Club and Heliconian Club, and gave talks on Carr's writing to various women's groups. In January 1943, she reviewed *The Book of Small* on the radio. Later, she took the *Victoria Daily Times* to task for publishing Robin Skelton's scathing review of *Hundreds and Thousands*, in which the critic condemned the book's lack of apparatus. For Clarke, the "insulting" review was an "extraordinary diatribe" that "showed a complete ignorance of [publishers'] production costs."[62]

Clarke also boosted appreciation of Carr's paintings. She expressed hope that the Vancouver Art Gallery would mount an exhibit of Carr's work in 1967 to mark Canada's centenary year, and criticized a 1972 Carr exhibit held at London's Commonwealth Institute for its uninspired presentation and lack of publicity.

Clarke seized an opportunity to publicly promote Carr's art when she opened the Royal Ontario Museum's Emily Carr exhibit of 15 February to 14 March 1972. She "broke a self-imposed rule of no personal publicity"[63] and was interviewed in Toronto on radio (CBC and CFRB) and television (CBC), where she described her experience of publishing Carr's writing and discussed their friendship.

Clarke once claimed to have been mystified by the unfriendly public reaction to Carr "in her own day."[64] She admired Carr's vivid prose, powerful paintings, and fighting spirit. Clarke identified with Carr's strength of character and wilfulness, qualities she knew in herself and relied on to further her own career. Throughout Clarke's life, she "fought for ... [Carr], sympathised with her, and estimated accurately her place in our ... cultural heritage."[65]

As a result of her publisher's appreciation for her authentic voice and distinctive style, Carr's writing endures alongside her painting. Clarke predicted as much in July 1944, when she wrote the following to Carr: "When the rest of us are gone & forgotten except by one or two you will be spoken of by thousands as one of the greatest Canadian women – who in two fields of art & literature made her country's name honored & loved in the world."[66] In 1941, Carr was an undiscovered writer when Oxford University Press Canada undertook to issue her award-winning *Klee Wyck*. Irene Clarke, along with her business partner/husband Bill, embraced Carr's unique work and went on to shape Carr's brief but significant literary career. Her lasting reputation as an author is due, in no small part, to Clarke's dedicated efforts on her behalf.

A close bond formed between Clarke and Carr, two women who broke historic ground, one as a publisher, and the other as a writer and a painter. In fact, the singular relationship between Clarke and Carr showcases the tie that can unite publisher and author. An astute publisher who recognized and embraced Carr's originality, Irene Clarke never wavered in her commitment to Emily Carr as a writer, an artist, and an individual.

In 1980, Clarke's position as "one of the most influential women in Canadian publishing"[67] was celebrated at a grand party honouring Clarke, Irwin's fiftieth anniversary. Irene Clarke delivered a dinner speech with characteristic eloquence, but later that evening suffered a massive stroke that left her bedridden and unable to work. From that point forward, Bill Clarke was fully in charge of the firm and his mother was chair of Clarke, Irwin's board in name alone.

In the 1970s, in an effort to regain ground after the enormous loss of educational publishing revenue, Clarke, Irwin had expanded its trade program and had begun to publish children's books under the editorship of Janet Lunn. The "first children's editor in Canadian publishing," Lunn was with the firm from 1972 to 1975.[68]

Clarke, Irwin also took advantage of the financial assistance made available to publishers following the Ontario Royal Commission on Book Publishing of 1970. Chaired by lawyer and author Richard Rohmer, the commission included Conservative politician Dalton Camp and University of Toronto Press director Marsh Jeanneret. Its final report of 1973, *Canadian Publishers and Canadian Publishing*, recommended loan guarantee and interest subsidy programs for Canadian-owned companies. Such a program of loan guarantees, which narrowly defined a Canadian book by the citizenship of its author, soon was implemented for Ontario book publishers and administered by the Ontario Development Corporation.[69]

Clarke, Irwin, as Donnelly details, "benefited enormously" from the loan guarantee program and by 1980 its bank debt "stood at 1.5 million" dollars.[70] Three years later, "at the bottom of the 1982–1983 recession,"[71] the provincial government determined the firm would "not recover from its economic crisis."[72] The government refused to heed Bill Clarke's "strong objections"[73] or his plea for more time to secure further funding and forced the company into receivership. After fifty-three years, Clarke, Irwin ceased operation. Bill Clarke was shocked, but he chose to shield his mother and bear the anguish alone.

For her leading contribution to Canadian publishing, Irene Clarke was invested as a Member of the Order of Canada in 1976. At the time of her death in 1986 – three years following the closure of her eponymous company – she was publicly lauded as "one of Canada's top business women,"[74] one who shifted Clarke, Irwin's emphasis away from textbooks to "the development of Canadian authors."[75] Bill Clarke's personal remembrance of a "smart and courageous woman"[76] is an equally powerful tribute to Irene Clarke's achievement as a pioneering publisher and the head of Clarke, Irwin.

chapter two

A "Principal Architect" of the University of Toronto Press: Eleanor Harman

Eleanor Harman (1909–1988) entered publishing as an editorial, promotional, and business assistant to Irene Clarke and went on to become a highly skilled editor and executive. Over the course of her career, Harman worked for four publishing houses: Clarke, Irwin and Oxford University Press Canada (from 1930 to 1944), when the two firms shared staff and premises; Copp Clark (from 1944 to 1945); and the University of Toronto Press (from 1946 to 1975), where she made her greatest contribution. Harman joined the University of Toronto Press as associate editor and production manager, was appointed assistant manager in 1952, assistant director in 1953, and rose to the position of associate director in 1970. An accomplished leader, she was "one of the principal architects of its growth during the '50s, '60s, and '70s."[1]

Harman's career was unique.[2] For over forty years, she was involved in "nearly every aspect of publishing: apprenticing as a traveller, or sales representative, developing manuscripts and editing them, designing books, supervising production, writing promotional copy, dealing with the details of administration, training and encouraging staff, and writing books herself."[3] She was also founding editor of both the house newsletter *Press Notes from the University of Toronto Press* and *Scholarly Publishing: A Journal for Authors and Publishers*. Most notably, she and her colleague Francess Halpenny were of the generation of women who limned the parameters of scholarly editing in Canada.

Harman may not have been fully cognizant of the gender bias she experienced and perpetuated at the University of Toronto Press. She faced discrimination as a female editor, but was herself a harsh judge of female employees. Meanwhile, she had to endure director Marsh Jeanneret's occasional reproaches and his regular treatment of her as a secretary rather than a senior officer of the press. In truth, Harman occupied a complex gendered position and never conceded – or chose rather to ignore – the degree of compromise that led to her becoming second-in-command to Jeanneret.

Clarke, Irwin/Oxford University Press Canada

At the age of nineteen, immediately after completing her studies in English – she received a BA (1929) from the University of Saskatchewan and an MA (1930) from the University of Toronto – Eleanor Teskey Harman entered the world of publishing, where she remained for the rest of her working life. Harman's academic training shaped her aesthetic principles. She did not, for example, defer to "the best-seller lists,"[4] for she believed a book that sold "a million [copies] may have less merit than one that sells 10,000."[5] Harman's favouring of serious literature was typical of the literary elitism of the day that defined itself in relation to a mass culture that it generally devalued. Meanwhile, and apparently untroubled by the contradiction, she saw herself as open and democratic, and claimed that snobbery and class-consciousness set her "anticolonial teeth on edge."[6]

A one-time member of the executive of the Toronto branch of the Canadian Authors Association and the Zonta Club of Toronto, Harman joined Clarke, Irwin the year it was founded. At first, she worked under Irene Clarke, who mentored the recent graduate. She also made one trip west to sell Clarke, Irwin books, becoming the first female "traveller" or sales representative in Canada, but Harman preferred editing books to selling them. Eventually, her duties expanded and she was appointed editorial assistant to Bill Clarke in his capacity as manager of Oxford University Press Canada, which he oversaw in tandem with Clarke, Irwin.

Under Bill Clarke's tutelage, Harman "imbibed the [rigorous] editorial values"[7] he had acquired in the 1920s as an editor of educational and medical textbooks at the Macmillan Company of Canada working under the inimitable Hugh Eayrs, a charismatic publisher with a nationalist vision. She reviewed the page proofs of Emily Carr's *Klee Wyck* and managed the design and production of trade books, including Carr's *The Book of Small*, which "involved the use of eight different inks besides the foil used in stamping the [binding] cases."[8] Thus, under one roof, Harman edited, designed, and produced textbooks, handled trade titles, and gained the invaluable experience and knowledge that led her to educational publishing.

Copp Clark

During her years at Clarke, Irwin and Oxford University Press Canada, Harman learned the trade and refined her editorial skills. Her editorial proficiency led to her appointment in 1944 as assistant editor at the Copp Clark Publishing Company, a major educational publisher. Launched in 1841 by the Scottish-born lawyer Hugh Scobie and purchased in 1869 by William Walter Copp, Scobie's former apprentice, and Henry J. Clark, Copp Clark was a venerable establishment by the time Harman joined the firm. Located in the Copp Clark building on Wellington Street in downtown Toronto, the company was a key supplier of textbooks for the elementary and secondary school markets.[9] In keeping with contemporary practice, "which became increasingly common after 1940,"[10] most were American textbooks adapted for the Canadian educational system. As Penney Clark explains, for educational publishers who serviced the Canadian market, it was "cost effective" to replace portions of American text "with Canadian content."[11]

At Copp Clark, Harman seized the opportunity to hone her expertise as a textbook editor. She also became a writer herself and made the professional connections that determined the course of her career. As assistant editor, she worked closely with Marsh Jeanneret. Jeanneret had joined the firm in 1938, soon after graduating from the University of Toronto Law School. His intention had been to pursue graduate studies at Harvard University following a one-year stint at Copp Clark, but Jeanneret abandoned his plan and chose educational publishing over law.[12]

Jeanneret and Harman were among the educated staff hired by Copp Clark to raise its editorial standards. Jeanneret was a self-taught editor who rose to the position of "publisher in all but name,"[13] and Harman absorbed his hard-won knowledge obtained through hands-on experience with educational books. Together, they edited and wrote textbooks for Copp Clark. Their first joint project was *A Story Workbook in Canadian History*, a spiral-bound "paper-covered loose-leaf work combining story-text, illustrations and questions."[14] Published in 1946, over 60,000 copies were sold by 1949.[15]

Next came *The Story of Canada*, a history textbook for students aged nine to fourteen authored by Harman, Jeanneret, and George Williams Brown, a University of Toronto historian. Together, the three collaborators spent countless hours on a project that married "scrupulous research" with "simple narrative."[16] J. Merle Smith provided watercolours that "appeared on every two-page spread of the book, which thus 'could not be opened except at a picture.'"[17] Along with a teacher's manual, *The Story of Canada* was issued in 1949 with an initial print run of 10,000 copies. It sold for three dollars and was adopted in every province, with the exception of Quebec.[18] That same year, 3,000 copies were purchased for the American market.[19] *Notre Histoire*, a French translation by Charles Bilodeau, appeared two years later and was adopted for use in the Maritime provinces, northern Ontario, and Manitoba.[20]

The Story of Canada, presented as "a thrilling adventure from beginning to end,"[21] was a monumental and unprecedented success. It sold well over 1 million copies[22] and earned its authors handsome royalties, which financed the purchase of neighbouring cottages on Lake Muskoka by Harman and Jeanneret. *Quill and Quire* celebrated the book's proud "conception of Canadian citizenship"[23] and William Arthur Deacon, literary editor of the *Globe and Mail*, lauded its "spirited harmony."[24] Deacon could not detect "the slightest clue as to whether any passage was written by Professor

Brown ... or by Miss Harman ... or by Mr. Jeanneret. They seem to have sunk their respective personalities in a common task."[25] When *The Story of Canada* was not short-listed for a Governor General's Literary Award, Deacon lamented its omission as "the most unfortunate choice that judges have made for several years."[26] The 1952 French edition was similarly praised by Maurice Lebel in *Enseignement primaire: Journal d'éducation et d'instruction*: "*Notre Histoire* reads from beginning to end like an adventure novel because its authors knew how to reconcile the exactingness of historical facts with those of the imaginative and plausible narrative."[27]

Throughout her editorial career, Harman drew on the writerly strengths showcased in *The Story of Canada* and hailed by reviewers. She and her co-authors sought to build on their success with a two-volume series also published by Copp Clark: *Canada in North America to 1800* (1960) and *Canada in North America 1800–1901* (1961). A single volume, *Canada in North America since 1800*, was produced by Harman and Jeanneret and appeared in 1967 (Brown had died in 1963).[28] The books drew heavily on material first included in *The Story of Canada*, but they did not have the same impact. The 1960s, a decade of heightened nationalism in anticipation of Canada's centenary, called for an expanded and more culturally nuanced history of the country.[29]

University of Toronto Press

When *The Story of Canada* was published, Harman would have celebrated its appearance from her new office at the University of Toronto Press, located in Baldwin House at the corner of St George and College Streets. George Williams Brown had lured Harman to the press. He was the press's part-time editor-in-chief and editor of its journal *Canadian Historical Review* when he offered Harman the position of associate editor and production manager. Her two years at Copp Clark had made it clear that she was eminently suited to the world of scholarly publishing, so she gladly accepted Brown's invitation and joined the University of Toronto Press in 1946. It was a decision she never regretted.

The University of Toronto Press was "the first scholarly press to be established in Canada and the tenth to be established in North America."[30] Brown's purpose in enticing Harman to leave Copp Clark was clear. He understood that the University of Toronto Press was in dire need of overhaul – according to MacSkimming, its printing plant "had only two typefaces and bound its unjacketed books in one of two colours, dull green or dull red"[31] – but it lacked the capable leadership needed to bring about significant change. Harman, who was known for having "good ideas,"[32] had the necessary administrative and editorial expertise to advance the press's operations and the quality of its publications.

Francess Halpenny, who had recently returned to the editorial department after serving in the women's division of the Royal Canadian Air Force, hailed "the coming of Eleanor Harman ... [whose] role was really to develop ... first of all, the standard of [book] production ... that meant we got some new typefaces, [and] the books suddenly began to look better ... then she worked with Professor Brown in the development of publishing projects."[33]

Harman's appointment received its greatest endorsement, however, from distinguished French professor François Charles Archile Jeanneret, father of Marsh Jeanneret and later chancellor of the University of Toronto (from 1959 to 1965). Having worked personally with Harman on the various textbooks he had published with Clarke, Irwin and Copp Clark, Jeanneret Sr proclaimed: "With Miss Harman around it ought to be possible to turn the place into a Canadian Oxford [University Press]."[34]

From the outset, Harman "had her work cut out for her,"[35] but the chance to focus exclusively on scholarly publishing was vitalizing. At the same time, she had to overcome authorial bias against female editors, even from women themselves. One aspiring writer, for instance, was incensed to learn that her submission had been rejected by E. Harman, who turned out to be a mere "*gir-r-l*."[36] Harman dealt with entrenched negative attitudes towards women editors with resolve, for she did not allow the prejudice to dampen either her taste for scholarly publishing or her ambition.

Simultaneously, however, she endorsed prevailing workplace norms that held female staff members to the strictest standards of professional conduct. Book designer Laurie Lewis remembers Harman's "eagle look" and aversion to "uproarious laughter";[37] she was "reserved but strong-willed,"[38] formidable but "truly exceptional."[39] She was also openly pleased to "never hear a word about"[40] her secretary's three children. In fact, Harman's unexamined belief that married women with children must keep their private and professional lives separate reflected the same gender bias she herself confronted as a single woman in publishing. That she was thus aligned with married female colleagues on the lower rungs of the organizational ladder would have come as a surprise to Harman.

When she joined the press, "the exact scope" of Harman's "duties was not well defined."[41] Soon, her responsibilities grew so that it was near impossible to define her position. In practice, she oversaw the administration of each of the four departments in the press's publishing division: editorial, design and production, sales, and warehousing. In addition, she developed and edited manuscripts and, following his appointment as director in 1953, became assistant to Marsh Jeanneret, with whom she worked collaboratively.

Immediately, as Halpenny described, Harman set herself to improving the design and production of the press's books. Not only did she bring in many new typefaces and bindings, she instituted the use of book jackets, which had been missing from University of Toronto Press books – a glaring omission that highlighted, as Jeanneret himself conceded, "how far removed university publishing was from the market-place,"[42] where attractively produced books were more likely to find ready buyers. In 1954, when Antje Lingner was hired to work under the direction of Barbara Plewman, the press became "the first Canadian publisher to employ a full-time staff designer."[43] Still, Harman continued to oversee the production of numerous titles. She paid equal attention to the financial side of book production and monitored the costs associated with typesetting, printing, and binding. Following publication, she kept abreast of sales figures and the stock of warehoused titles.

The day-to-day administration of the press was Harman's responsibility and it demanded great executive skill. She successfully balanced a range of activities that called for knowledge of scholarly publishing, flexibility, and personal composure. First, she handled correspondence. In fact, she introduced Jeanneret to the workings of the press by giving him the task of sorting the daily mail for one full month. Since many incoming letters registered complaints, it is not surprising that Jeanneret found the work both disagreeable and disheartening. As soon as he could, he relinquished the job to Harman, whose replies to such letters, according to Jeanneret, "were masterpieces of their kind, and achieved the immediate purpose of soothing tempers and maintaining friendships."[44]

Similarly, Harman was required to take the minutes at each meeting of the press's advisory committee. Although he "was technically the committee secretary,"[45] Jeanneret delegated the task to Harman. His excuse – "I must keep my wits about me"[46] at each meeting – belies the fact that he felt entitled to ask Harman, his second-in-command and a senior member of the same advisory committee, to assume a secretarial role when he deemed it necessary. Harman always behaved as part of "a team," however, even on those occasions when Jeanneret chastised her in public.[47]

Laura Macleod offers the following explanation for Harman's compliance: she "was not the sort of woman who pushed to get above what she considered her proper place."[48] Her motive was likely more complicated. In the interest of retaining her position at the press, Harman may have been loath to challenge Jeanneret's assumption that women were better suited to the emotional labour of fielding complaints, as well as the secretarial work of recording the minutes of meetings. Particularly in the case of public rebuke, her silent acquiescence may have been less a personality trait than an adaptive strategy, aimed more at career advancement.

Many other details of lesser or greater significance fell to Harman. She reviewed the annual selection of company Christmas cards, for example, and the in-house practice of docketing hours spent on book production. She supervised all activities pertaining to book promotion: producing catalogues, maintaining mailing lists, distributing review copies, arranging book displays, and filing book reviews. She also wrote jacket blurbs and advertisements.

When the press was designing its own building, to be located at 21 King's College Circle on the St George campus, Harman was deeply involved in the planning process. Throughout 1956, she "spent countless hours conferring" with Harald Bohne, manager of the retail book department, discussing "the layout of the interior of the building."[49] Moreover, when "the blueprints called for space behind every door that was one inch too narrow for a standard filing cabinet,"[50] Jeanneret recalled that it was Harman who caught this serious flaw in the proposed design. When the building opened in 1958, its editorial offices were both functional and comfortable – due, in no small part, to Harman's attention to detail.

Harman was also an adept negotiator who helped secure a Ford Foundation grant in support of scholarly publishing. In October 1956, when she and Jeanneret travelled to New York to meet with director W. McNeil Lowry, "armed with all the Toronto publishing records"[51] they could carry on board their flight, they succeeded in convincing him to include the University of Toronto Press in its program to expand scholarly publishing. In 1957, the press was granted $42,500 over five years, and in 1962 an additional $20,000 over three years[52] – the only Canadian publishing house to benefit from the Ford Foundation's visionary project to help disseminate scholarly work.

Expert Management and "Good Ideas"

Harman's calm demeanour often helped win over authors and smooth the publication process. It was she, along with Jeanneret, who secured Robert MacGregor Dawson's *The Government of Canada* (1947) for the press. Harman acquired the book through a conversational tactic that involved Dawson's distinctive voice booming forth over "royalty percentages or editorial revision or ... sales promotion" during "lunch at a moderately posh downtown restaurant"[53] while she listened attentively, without seeming embarrassment.

Later, over a similar lunch at the Park Plaza Hotel (now the Park Hyatt) in Toronto, and by promising Dawson the editorial support of Francess Halpenny – Halpenny had edited *The Government of Canada* – Harman and Jeanneret obtained his final book for the press. Regrettably, Dawson did not live to see the 1958 publication of his best-selling *William Lyon Mackenzie King: A Political Biography, 1874–1923*; he died of a heart condition on 16 July of that year.

Floyd Chalmers, president of Maclean Hunter, brought the work of renowned photographer Yousuf Karsh to the attention of Jeanneret and, after some serious negotiation, Karsh agreed to publish his first book, *Portraits of Greatness*, with the press. The project, however, did not progress smoothly. It was both costly and delayed, since the Dutch printers Royal Joh. Enschedé chose to use a special black ink to print the portraits.

When she inspected the first volumes to arrive from overseas just prior to the publication date of 21 November 1959, Harman was aghast. As Jeanneret later reported, "seated at her desk" she broke down in tears, "a heap of gravure prints of Karsh's portraits in front of her ... The nature of the tragedy was only too easily discernible. The bound volumes were handsome; their contents were impressive. One little thing, however: ... a good proportion of ... pages fell loose and tumbled forth across the floor, one by one!"[54] A thermoplastic binding had been used instead of stitching to secure the pages, but the black ink of the portraits reacted with the glue and the binding would not hold.

Harman's ingenious response to the mishap – an insertion in each volume stating expressly that the binding allowed for the removal of individual portraits for mounting and framing – hastened a remedy. In the end, a crisis was averted. The binding elicited no negative comment from reviewers and the first printing sold out. Moreover, the new binding of the second printing held fast. *Portraits of Greatness* – which featured images of Winston Churchill, Robert Frost, Martha Graham, Ernest Hemingway, Audrey Hepburn, Carl Jung, Thomas Mann, Georgia O'Keefe, Pope Pius XII, Queen Elizabeth II, Eleanor Roosevelt, George Bernard Shaw, John Steinbeck, Thornton Wilder, Tennessee Williams, and many others – sold over 40,000 copies.

Harman helped save Karsh potential distress over the faulty binding of *Portraits of Greatness* and gained his loyalty. He continued to publish his work with the press, including his 1962 autobiography *In Search of Greatness*, which drew "on more than sixty hours of taped interviews"[55] with Harman and Jeanneret. As MacSkimming notes, Karsh and Jeanneret also "became fast friends";[56] no doubt, Harman's expert handling of an early misadventure in book publishing helped fortify their friendship.

That Harman was both a forward-thinking editor and business-minded executive was evident in her unequivocal endorsement of author Marshall McLuhan. While it took Jeanneret some time to recognize the significance and value of McLuhan's work, Harman was quick to grasp the importance of his groundbreaking ideas – yet to appear as *The Gutenberg Galaxy: The Making of Typographic Man* in 1962 – and even quicker to prevent his defection to another publisher. Following a talk by McLuhan at the University Women's Club of Toronto, where he was approached by an acquisitions editor from Longman Canada, she "set the competitor back by loudly proclaiming, 'Marshall is the *Press*'s author!'"[57] Harman was right to stand her ground, for *The Gutenberg Galaxy* eventually sold over 60,000 copies in hardcover and paperback editions,[58] bringing both its author and publisher much acclaim and remuneration.

In addition to individual titles, Harman was involved with large-scale projects. She was a member of the planning committee for the Collected Works of John Stuart Mill, issued in thirty-three volumes between 1963 and 1991.[59] Her role as administrative overseer of the *Dictionary of Canadian Biography/Dictionnaire biographique du Canada* was more significant, however. In 1963, she submitted an application to Canada's Centennial Commission that resulted in an award of $160,000 to the DCB/DBC. Once the funds were received in 1965, Harman supplied the commission with regular budgetary reports that enumerated all costs – staffing, editorial, design, and production – associated with the *Dictionary*.

Harman approved the lease for the *Dictionary*'s Ottawa office, the hiring of DCB/DBC staff, and their moving and travel expenses. She also assisted during personal crises. When editor Marc La Terreur required a salary advance in 1967 to help support the wife and four children of a brother who had died tragically in a house fire, she came to his aid.

Harman supervised the design and production of the DCB/DBC, paying particular attention to the 1965 Laurentian edition of volume 1, a limited edition of 500 copies with "de luxe"[60] paper stock and a leather spine. That same year, in a promotional effort, she submitted sample mock-ups of the *Dictionary* to the Canadian National Exhibition and the Pacific National Exhibition, where they were displayed prominently. Harman also used the house organ *Press Notes* as a vehicle to regularly showcase the DCB/DBC's progress.

The Practice of Editing

Eleanor Harman and Francess Halpenny, who regularly "put in some friendly time"[61] over lunch at Eaton's department store on College Street, came together through their editorial work. They soon formed an alliance of two women who shared a commitment to refining editorial practice and an interest in editing as a scholarly subject.

At first, MacSkimming explains, Harman and Brown assessed all manuscripts while encouraging "the evolution of ... Halpenny and her colleagues from journal editors into book editors, a task that involved handling more complex texts and approaching specialists in many disciplines to obtain peer evaluation of manuscripts."[62] Harman, who was ten years older, had the benefit of hands-on experience and lent Halpenny her considerable knowledge. She provided the essential training opportunities that led to Halpenny's editorial autonomy and eventual oversight of the editorial department.

Harman was a lifelong learner who read widely in the field of publishing practice. She admitted to perusing "every official publishing history and every unofficial reminiscence with empathy and ... interest."[63] She also read essays on writing, editing, and publishing, most notably by Jacques Barzun. Her purpose in doing so was twofold: she sought to professionalize her own editorial practice and enrich her substantial body of writing on the art of editing.

In 1947, one year after she joined the press, Harman reported on a historic debate – still relevant today – that took place at the annual convention of the Association of American University Presses, which she attended in Princeton, New Jersey. In the pages of the *Globe and Mail*, Harman revealed that scholarly editors often responded to the mediocre writing skills of most academics by extensively revising their manuscripts. The result, she feared, was fraud "in offering the public under the name of the author a work for whose 'finish' ... he is not responsible."[64] Harman understood the academic imperative to publish one's research – it brought career advancement – and recognized the ethical dilemma of revisionary intervention that lay at the heart of much scholarly editing. She faced the problem herself at the press and went on to write about it over the course of her career.

To avoid "the danger of substituting their own ideas and style of writing for those of the author," Harman reminded editors that the "law of diminishing returns begins to apply earlier in manuscript editing than most of us realize."[65] A "notable trap" for seasoned editors was the "thirst for perfection," which they must avoid;[66] instead, editors should always "look for the possibility of simplification."[67] Harman's sense of humour and intuitive grasp of the editor's personality showed in one call for such simplification, which is cited here for its appeal and continued relevance:

> Consider the rule about ellipses in broken quotations ... When one thinks how many authors have been queried about that blessed [fourth] dot, and how many editors have puzzled over it, one feels like weeping at the waste of time and human effort. In my opinion those publishers and journals who ... now invariably use three [instead of four] dots ... must be congratulated on their common sense.[68]

In fact, "common sense" informed Harman's own approach to scholarly editing and her writing on the subject. She applauded the growing professionalization of editing – indeed, her efforts enabled that professionalization – but did not believe in "creating unnecessary functions and developing an artificial mystique of editing."[69]

For Harman, the editor's first responsibility was to ensure clarity of expression and ideas, particularly in the case of mathematic and scientific books and journals, such as the *Canadian Journal of Mathematics* (1949–) and the *Canadian Mathematical Bulletin* (1958–), both published by the University of Toronto Press. In 1954, she sought to streamline the typesetting of scientific texts by urging authors to adopt "standard symbols"[70] instead of inventing their own. Harman always was a progressive and forthright editor, but especially so in the face of rising production costs and increasing demand for scholarly publication.

In a paper presented at the 1975 IEEE (Institute of Electrical and Electronics Engineers) Conference on Scientific Journals, for instance, Harman asked her audience whether a "decision to edit material less closely" might not lead to more publications and "expansion of a field of study," and compel scientific authors "to pay attention to details that up to now ... would be attended to by ... professional editors."[71] A dual commitment to scholarly publishing and editorial standards impelled Harman to openly address the contentious issues facing her profession, in this case the diminishing return on editorial investment in scientific manuscripts. Rather than retreat from such professional challenges, she faced them with characteristic insight and tact.

At the same time, Harman was proud that the press's "publications were edited and produced with a care and expertise not always evident in Canadian publishing."[72] She counted herself among the "good publishers [who] are conscientious in their proofreading, and are genuinely embarrassed by the ultimate discovery of errors they may miss."[73] An expert proofreader, Harman happily read many of the press's publications – books, journals, and in-house material – with an eye for accuracy. She once quipped that each book should be "a masterpiece,"[74] even though "best-sellers and run-away sales"[75] were rare in scholarly publishing.

Press Notes and *Scholarly Publishing*

Harman's landmark contribution to scholarly publishing and editing is most evident in her work on two periodicals issued by the University of Toronto Press: the house organ *Press Notes from the University of Toronto Press* (1959–74) and *Scholarly Publishing: A Journal for Authors and Publishers* (established in 1969, now the *Journal of Scholarly Publishing*). The launching of *Press Notes*,

Jeanneret claimed, proved to be "the most effective step we ever took to inform our constituents about the Press."[76] Its success led to the founding of *Scholarly Publishing*, a quarterly devoted to all facets of university publishing and which flourishes today.

The call for a house organ indicates the degree to which the press had matured into a publishing house of many departments and staff. Intended as a vehicle to foster a sense of community and to highlight the work of individual departments and key publications, *Press Notes* soon expanded its reach to include authors, faculty members, "the board of governors, university and student officials, book publishers in Canada, other university presses ... newspaper editors, [and] selected officers at other universities,"[77] each of whom received a free copy of the periodical. Harman was the editor of *Press Notes*, which appeared approximately every second month as a "pamphlet"[78] of eight to sixteen pages, with photographs. The project became one of her most rewarding "personal responsibilities"[79] at the press.

Harman's early excitement over *Press Notes* was infectious. She envisaged a more modest version of Oxford University Press's own house organ, "dignified"[80] in both content and form, and solicited Halpenny's input. She asked for "excerpts from current and forthcoming books," as well as "good illustrations," sample title pages, or book jackets: "Variety is quite important, so is wit, eloquence, and so on ... All sorts of possibilities."[81]

Harman's devotion to *Press Notes* was apparent to her colleagues, no one more than Jeanneret. In addition to her other duties, as Jeanneret recounted, "she found time to plan and supervise every issue, more often than not at home after hours. Quietly but persistently, she co-ordinated a steady inflow of stimulating articles that kept readers posted on the Press's wide-ranging activities and concerns. To each staff contributor she supplied just the degree of expert editorial assistance which that person wanted."[82] Moreover, when promised articles did not materialize – as was often the case – Harman wrote them herself. In the end, she was the primary contributor to *Press Notes*.

Harman's contributions addressed the press itself, scholarly publishing more generally, and book design and editorial practice.

Several articles showed her engagement with all employees of the press and all levels of its business operations. She wrote profiles of staff members: Basil H. Cosgrave, caretaker (in November 1959); Tom Baker, type-metal librarian (in January 1960); Arthur Verrall, stockroom supervisor (in March 1960); James Taylor, production planner for the printing department (in April 1960); and Harald Bohne, then assistant director of the press (in February 1974). Harman's human touch was felt in each profile, which celebrated the individual's personal achievements as much as his role at the press.

Two pieces described the press's buildings: its expanded shipping and warehousing facilities at 70 Bond Street, leased in May 1961 (in October 1961), and the fall 1966 opening on Huron Street of the University of Toronto textbook store (in March–April 1967). Historic details about the press provided context for the spread of its premises during the 1960s. "Where the Action Is" (in November 1974) was an illuminating introduction to the work performed by staff in the production department, and "A New Way in an Old Age" (in February 1975) offered an overview of the printing department, in particular its innovations in computerized typesetting. Harman's detailed portrayals of the various buildings and departments of the press showed her to be at the very heart of the firm.

Press Notes also gave Harman the opportunity to examine facets of scholarly publishing that highlighted her professional interests and writerly style. In clear, evocative prose, enlivened with humour, she distinguished printing from publishing (in January 1964); differentiated the spring and fall seasons in book publishing (in October 1963); probed the costly practice of distributing free desk copies (in June–July 1963); and derided the annoying popularity of certain words – the press rejected the overuse of "viable" and the misuse of "hopefully" (in October 1973).

Harman also covered developments in the publishing industry, both international and local. The announcement in May 1960 that the Rockefeller Foundation had granted $225,000 over six years to the Association of American University Presses to fund translations of Latin American books "of scholarly or literary importance"[83] made the front page of *Press Notes*. When Jeanneret testified at the federal Royal Commission on Publications, established in September 1960 under chairman Gratton O'Leary solely

Figure 2. Eleanor Harman at the Frankfurt Book Fair, October 1967

"to study the impact of foreign publications in Canada on domestic periodicals,"[84] Harman reported on the proceedings and presented Jeanneret's view that contemporary copyright legislation, which favoured the United States over Canada, hampered the publication of local scholarly journals (in January 1961).[85]

The July–August 1967 issue of *Press Notes* included Harman's overview of the annual meeting of the Association of American University Presses, held in Toronto from 11 to 14 June. She wrote as a proud host of "the largest assemblage of publishers ever brought together in Canada for any purpose."[86] In November 1967, she published a detailed report on the Frankfurt Book Fair, the world's biggest book fair held each October, where competition for the right to issue foreign works was impeded by the "high cost of translation"[87] services in Canada. One result of Harman's attendance at the fair was her increased sense of "isolation ... from world ideas," but it also provided "a liberal education in international publishing as a reward for the many miles trudged around the vast halls of the Buchmesse."[88] An accompanying photograph captured Harman with her colleagues at the fair's Canadian exhibit.

Meeting with colleagues from the United States and Europe broadened Harman's knowledge of publishing. Her perspective on editing, however, was shaped by her experience in Canada, where editorial practice was slow to professionalize. Notwithstanding Lorne Pierce's long and impressive tenure as editor of the Ryerson Press,[89] it was not until the 1950s that editing was regarded seriously in Canada. In fact, Harman and Halpenny were among the first and most accomplished practitioners to provide systematized analysis of the editorial function. At the University of Toronto Press, the testing ground for their ideas, they helped lay the foundation for editorial practice in this country.

For the benefit of editors and authors alike, Harman sought to demystify the process of manuscript editing. To that end, she invited her colleague Patricia Lagacé to take readers through the press's editorial process. Lagacé – who was appointed director of the University of Manitoba Press in 1979 – described the scholarly editor as "a first reader and critic" whose job was "straightforward" and "best when it is least visible." In the interest of producing an ideal book, however, the relationship between editor and author should be collaborative.

First, the editor read through a "manuscript to discover the shape of the work and uncover any major problems ... [while] keeping one eye on the progress of the argument." While doing so, she also attended to faulty diction and sentence structure, inconsistencies in spelling and style, errors in punctuation and documentation, the fair use of copyrighted material, and potentially libellous content. She then moved on to consider the structure of individual chapters and "the logical flow of ideas." To avoid "over-editing" and "rewriting," this second stage required a "lighter hand."

The editor saw a book through the press and served as liaison between the author and production staff, which included the book designer, production manager, and printer. She conferred with the designer on material aspects of a book, read the final corrected draft, and sent it to the author for approval. Before a book went to press, the editor checked galley proofs. Finally, after so much effort, the editor "has become as possessively proud" of a book as the author and as eager "for the first reviews and the sales reports."[90]

Harman's own articles on various aspects of editing dominated the pages of *Press Notes*. She addressed the aesthetics of book design: choice of paper, typeface, and illustrations; book titles and preliminary pages; book jackets and paperback editions. She also covered the practical side of scholarly editing: subsidizing scholarly publications; journal budgeting; the impact of computer typesetting on scholarly editing; publishing conference proceedings; peer review; securing permission to cite material; and hints on proofreading, which demanded a "certain amount of horse-sense."[91] A desire to elucidate and validate the editor's work drove Harman's writing.

In 1961, *Press Notes* gave rise to *The University as Publisher*, a volume planned and edited by Harman to mark the diamond anniversary of the University of Toronto Press. The book reproduced articles from *Press Notes*, alongside an original chapter by Jeanneret, "The University as Publisher," and another by Harman, "Founding a University Press," the first extensively researched history of the University of Toronto Press. The volume was produced to Harman's specifications – "a bang-up job from the standpoint of design ... modern ... but ... [not] too demure"[92] – and her achievement was noticed by at least one American reviewer: this "best short guide to scholarly publishing ... is not parochial, [and] seldom exclusively Canadian. Even the chapter on the history of the Press – ably written by the editor of the volume ... – could be the story of several distinguished presses elsewhere on the continent."[93]

Under Harman's editorship, *Press Notes* reached far beyond its initial goal of uniting the staff and highlighting the work of the University of Toronto Press. It became a vehicle for disseminating valuable information about scholarly publishing, book design, and editing. Jeanneret maintained it "generated tremendous good will" and inspired "more than one other university in Canada to establish its own scholarly-publishing arm."[94]

In 1969, ten years after the first issue of *Press Notes* was published, *Scholarly Publishing* was launched as "a voice for the whole university press movement."[95] Harman relished the opportunity to edit the first "practical journal *about* university publishing"[96] – a forum for discussing "publishing ends as well as means."[97] It was the greatest challenge of her career and Harman gave herself over to the new project. With Ian Montagnes as associate editor, she assembled an international advisory board that included Halpenny, Jeanneret, and directors of university presses at Laval, California, New Mexico, Yale, Melbourne, and Tokyo.

Since editing the journal consumed much of her time and energy, Harman's contributions to *Scholarly Publishing* – on peer review and securing permissions – were based on material first published in *Press Notes*. In addition, she included book reviews and "A Reconsideration of Manuscript Editing," an expanded version of a paper she presented on 20 May 1975 at the annual meeting of the Council of Biology Editors in Gainesville, Florida. She also relied on Halpenny, who contributed several articles on scholarly editing and suggested authors for various topics.

From its inception, *Scholarly Publishing* issued "articles from around the world,"[98] as well as profiles, book reviews, news items, and letters. As MacSkimming reports, the journal quickly "found acceptance internationally as the authoritative source on the subject."[99] Harman, too, gained an international reputation as the journal's accomplished scholarly editor.

Like *Press Notes*, *Scholarly Publishing* produced a collection of essays. *The Thesis and the Book* was edited by Harman and Montagnes and appeared in 1976. Unlike *The University as Publisher*, which featured new material, all of the chapters in *The Thesis and the Book* were drawn from *Press Notes* and *Scholarly Publishing*. Aimed at faculty supervisors and new scholars, the guide – among the first of its kind – offered advice on how to revise dissertations for publication by making "the text more eloquent, more effective, and more easily accessible to the ultimate reader."[100] A chapter by

Francess Halpenny on the differences between a thesis and a book (first published in *Press Notes* in May 1962) lent the book its title and went on to become one of the most consulted pieces in the collection.

Professors welcomed *The Thesis and the Book*; graduate students found it helpful, too. It soon became "required reading for all beginning academic writers"[101] and saved them "considerable"[102] effort. The book's success led to a revised, second edition published in 2003 that continues to offer "useful"[103] advice and "valuable"[104] direction to a specialized audience of emerging scholars.

Jeanneret claimed, without exaggeration, that *Scholarly Publishing* became "the most widely cited reference on its subject ... in the world."[105] The journal's success was largely due to its steward, who edited a total of ten volumes between 1969 and 1979. Just how much Harman truly valued the project was revealed after her death, for she bequeathed "the entire residue of her estate – about $150,000 – ... to be used for the support of *Scholarly Publishing*."[106] Thus, *Scholarly Publishing* was not only founded on Harman's editorial labour, it was sustained by her generosity.

Ontario Royal Commission on Book Publishing

In December 1970, the sales of W.J. Gage and Ryerson Press had a galvanizing effect on publishers, authors, the public, and the media in Canada, all of whom sought an end to further takeovers and called for a full investigation into the state of Canadian publishing. Premier John Robarts responded immediately. That same month, nearly twenty years after the Massey Commission issued its report on the state of arts and culture in Canada, the premier announced an Ontario Royal Commission on Book Publishing.

A timely report to the federal department of industry, trade, and commerce by the accountancy firm of Ernst and Ernst provided much-needed statistical analysis of Canada's book trade. Most tellingly, Ernst and Ernst confirmed that a mere 25 per cent of the $222 million worth of books consumed by Canadians in 1969 had been published in Canada. The report also emphasized the need to rationalize the publishing industry and improve Canadian access to the American market.[107]

Since Ontario's English-language book publishers served the nation, the commission was asked to profile Canada's publishing industry, its contribution to the cultural life and education of Canadians, and the impact of foreign-owned publishers on the book trade. In total, the Royal Commission was presented with 185 briefs and requested 19 background papers that addressed all facets of Canadian publishing.[108]

On 1 June 1971, in a brief to the commission, Harman had the chance to publicize her comprehensive grasp of scholarly publishing. As "second in command" of a press that published approximately 100 books per year and employed "some 450 persons,"[109] she was well positioned to offer an incisive analysis of the challenges facing scholarly publishers in Canada. That she wrote and presented the brief on behalf of the University of Toronto Press showed expertise paired with executive rank.

In a detailed and carefully argued submission, Harman noted that the University of Toronto Press's desire for a strong "university publishing tradition in Canada" was driven by weak "commercial publishing" and a "precipitate trend towards Americanization."[110] To increase domestic publishing and "assist other Canadian institutions to construct active Canadian publishing programs of their own,"[111] Harman proposed something unique: the formation of a central, provincially funded service agency for all university presses in Ontario. She envisaged a centralized distribution centre, provisionally titled the Universities of Ontario Press, to handle warehousing, order fulfilment, and accounting services for all scholarly presses. Such a cooperative service, she argued, would facilitate much-needed expansion of scholarly publishing "without proportionate increase of related overheads."[112] Her aim was to enhance overall efficiency and effectiveness, while reducing the individual operating costs of publishing houses.

Harman's grand vision for systematizing scholarly publishing in Ontario grew out of "two decades"[113] of development by the University of Toronto Press. It also drew on her experience as a consultant (with Jeanneret) to the Université de Montréal, the

University of Alberta, and the University of British Columbia, which established their own scholarly presses in 1962, 1969, and 1972, respectively.

Harman's proposal was the product of her deep knowledge of scholarly publishing in North America, extensive experience as a Canadian publisher, and capacity to form alliances with colleagues in the field. Her suggestions were well received by the commission, but were likely seen as too progressive for a province with just four university presses: the University of Toronto Press (established in 1901), Oxford University Press Canada (established in 1904), the University of Ottawa Press (established in 1936), and McGill-Queen's University Press (established by Montreal's McGill University in 1960, and merged with Kingston's Queen's University in 1968). Had they been adopted, however, Harman's recommendations might have streamlined scholarly publishing and pushed provincial expansion beyond the year 1974, when Wilfrid Laurier University established Ontario's fifth scholarly press.

Harman's brief was an enterprising document, inspired by decades of immersive experience in university publishing. It was also her attempt to leave a lasting mark on future scholarly publishing in Ontario, for the 1970s were Harman's final years in the trade and they were eventful. In 1972, the year following her presentation to the commission, she was elected vice-president of the Association of American University Presses, the first Canadian woman to hold the position. In 1974, she joined the University of California Press's committee on international cooperation and translation. She attended a seminar on scholarly publishing in Kuala Lumpur in 1975. That same year, and just two years before Jeanneret's own departure, she retired as associate director of the University of Toronto Press, although she remained at the helm of *Scholarly Publishing* until 1979. In 1977, Harman was honoured with the Queen Elizabeth II Silver Jubilee Medal.

It took a woman of Harman's formidable ability to lead the University of Toronto Press through twenty-nine years of growth from a modest to a prestige publisher. George Williams Brown must be credited with astute judgment when he persuaded Harman to join the press, for she facilitated its expansion and became one of its greatest champions. With vision, determination, and devotion, she helped shape the culture of the press and the books and journals that bore its imprint.

After a publishing career that spanned five decades, Eleanor Harman died on 29 September 1988. Harman was adept but modest in her calling as publishing executive and scholarly editor. As she conceded in her chapter-length history of the University of Toronto Press: "The words we write now may seem quaint to those who inherit our responsibilities ... But to our successors we would say, even if the words seem quaint: in our time we have tried, we wish you well in yours."[114] Harman did much more than try; with discernment and skill she steered the gradual and steady rise of Canada's premier scholarly publisher.

chapter three

The "Editorial Conscience" of the University of Toronto Press: Francess Halpenny

Editor and scholar Francess Halpenny (1919–2017) was a major force in scholarly publishing in Canada. Halpenny's editorial career spanned five decades. She joined the University of Toronto Press as a junior editor in 1941, was named editor in 1957, rose to the position of managing editor in 1965, and was appointed associate director (academic) in 1978.

Halpenny trained as a journal editor under Eleanor Harman and went on to edit the manuscripts of influential scholars, such as political scientist Robert MacGregor Dawson and art historian J. Russell Harper. Her greatest contribution to the University of Toronto Press was as general editor of the monumental *Dictionary of Canadian Biography/Dictionnaire biographique du Canada*, a position she held from 1969 to 1988.

After completing her master's degree, Halpenny was dissuaded from pursuing a doctorate in English. Though she regretted the sexism that limited educational and occupational opportunities for women, she did not curb her ambition. Instead, she turned to scholarly publishing as a viable alternative to an academic career and set out to acquire the editorial mastery and professional knowledge required to forge the distinctive publishing aesthetic of the University of Toronto Press. As a hands-on editor of scholarly works and an incisive analyst of editorial practice, she was vital to the press's development as a leading scholarly publisher.

University of Toronto Press

The origins of Francess Georgina Halpenny's editorial career can be traced to her undergraduate study of literature and her love of theatre. As a student of English at the University of Toronto, Halpenny studied with Canadianist E.K. Brown and Miltonist A.S.P. Woodhouse – powerful academic impresarios both. In 1935, Woodhouse spearheaded the creation of the annual review "Letters in Canada," the *University of Toronto Quarterly*'s bicultural survey of Canadian literature. Under Brown and Woodhouse, Halpenny received "excellent training in languages" and in "way[s] of analysing the structure of literature"[1] – solid preparation for a future editor.

Writer, producer, and actor Mavor Moore was a classmate of Halpenny's. When he failed second year – theatre claimed too much of his time – Halpenny's borrowed course notes helped him regain his academic footing. Many years later, Moore recovered Halpenny's notes and returned them, with a message. "How good these are!" he declared. "The clarity of mind (and of writing), the careful analysis based on careful note-taking, and the synoptic way in which you've put it all together – all these presage the marvellous person you have become."[2] As Moore acknowledged in 1987, Halpenny's nascent capacity for first-rate intellectual and editorial work dated back to 1936, the first year of her undergraduate studies.

Halpenny completed a BA (1940) and then an MA (1941), all the while pursuing a growing interest in theatre. She acted in countless plays and adapted and directed several performances for the University Alumnae Dramatic Club (now the Alumnae Theatre Company, which was founded by female graduates of the University of Toronto), and went on to become a lifetime member and one-time president of the club. One critic described her as "indefatigable and unfailingly optimistic"[3] as an actor. Her subsequent approach to editorial work reflected these same qualities.

Halpenny had scholarly aspirations and had hoped to earn a doctoral degree in English, but was deterred from doing so. In the early 1940s, young women like her were not encouraged in their ambition: "Women were few in numbers as students and certainly few in numbers in academic appointments," she later reflected, "and I was bluntly told by a senior academic person in University College that the place for a woman graduate was a high school."[4] Halpenny was not surprised at the advice, but she was disappointed. As she later admitted, "Had that been a different world I would have gone on to graduate work."[5] Luckily, an opportunity at the University of Toronto Press prevented early disappointment from turning to rancour.

In fact, Halpenny's vocational dilemma was resolved through a theatrical connection. Since 1932, Alison Ewart (later Hewitt), a friend of Halpenny's through the University Alumnae Dramatic Club, had been general editor at the University of Toronto Press, where she had established its editorial department. While Halpenny "was casting about"[6] after completing her master's degree, Ewart informed her of a vacancy in the department. When Halpenny told professors Brown (now at Cornell University) and Woodhouse about the post, they immediately "took up my cause"[7] – both were impressed by her thoughtful diligence – and facilitated her appointment as junior editor. Her job, as Marsh Jeanneret recalled, was to handle "manuscript-editing and confidential correspondence about readers' reports."[8]

Halpenny joined the University of Toronto Press in the fall of 1941 and was "pleased ... to stay near and connected with a campus and its intellectual and cultural pursuits while ... abandoning a decision about a career in teaching."[9] Publicly, she regularly acknowledged the early support of Brown and Woodhouse, support which gave her entry to the world of scholarly publishing, an environment suited to her career ambitions. Privately, she repaid Brown's generosity by editing his book *Rhythm in the Novel*, issued by the University of Toronto Press in 1950, one year before his death from cancer.

By the time Halpenny assumed her new position, the University of Toronto Press had grown considerably but was still a relatively modest operation. The small editorial department was "housed in a tiny office in Baldwin House," where, as Halpenny recounted, strict gender norms prevailed. That is to say, the house was also "occupied by the Department of History, with whom we always had tea at four o'clock in the afternoon – and for whom, in those days, of course, the ladies always made the tea. So we in the editorial department were swung into duty to make the tea."[10]

That she made light of the ritual – "*of course*, the ladies ... in the editorial department" would swing "into duty" (emphasis added)[11] – suggests that Halpenny saw through the gendered and classed expectation that female editors should defer to male historians by preparing afternoon tea. Rather than defy convention, however, it would seem that she – much like Harman – purposefully adapted her behaviour to secure an intellectually stimulating position and to advance her career at the press.

Jeanneret's "early but inaccurate impression" of Halpenny "was that she had a retiring personality, no doubt because she kept her own counsel and operated unobtrusively over at Baldwin House"[12] – a deliberate strategy meant to quietly disarm opposition to intellectual women operating in a man's world. In fact, Halpenny was anything but retiring and her aspirations reached beyond her editorial office.

After one year as a junior editor, Halpenny joined the women's division of the Royal Canadian Air Force and took a leave of absence from the press. She trained as a meteorologist and from 19 October 1942 to 2 November 1945 was stationed first in Torbay, Newfoundland, where she supported an anti-submarine patrol by tracking weather patterns in the North Atlantic Ocean, and later in Summerside, Prince Edward Island. When she enlisted, Halpenny knew little of Canada; she had not even visited Montreal. She came to value the knowledge of Newfoundland and Prince Edward Island gained through military service; it fed her growing nationalism and later proved advantageous when she became general editor of the *Dictionary of Canadian Biography/Dictionnaire biographique du Canada*.

Before Halpenny returned to Toronto in 1945, Alison Hewitt, having married and adopted a child, had left the University of Toronto Press. Social norms of the day dictated that women leave the workforce upon marriage. Consequently, Halpenny was needed at the press. In fact, her colleagues at the press, anxious for her discharge, had petitioned for her early release from the RCAF, but their efforts were unsuccessful. Thus, upon her return she received an especially warm welcome, and her editorial responsibilities gradually increased.

In the immediate postwar years, the editorial department of the University of Toronto Press was concerned primarily with journals: for example, the *Canadian Historical Review* (1920–), the *Canadian Journal of Economics and Political Science* (1934–67), and the *University of Toronto Law Journal* (1935–). Halpenny was assigned to the *University of Toronto Quarterly* (1931–), where she learned copy-editing skills and prepared the bibliography for "Letters in Canada."[13]

Halpenny once disclosed that the "editorial role is unhappy in many ways because most of the training is done on the job and that can be ... frustrating."[14] She strongly believed "the editorial contribution could be enhanced by some kind of formal preparation"[15] and always promoted "the continued development ... of editorial skills to be put at the service of Canadian subjects and authors."[16]

Halpenny's own on-the-job training – which entailed learning "the complexities of type and book production, the [firm's] back list [and] ... its ways of promoting books, in addition to the procedures of ... [her] own department with bibliographies, tables, and footnotes, capitalization and quotations, illustrations and their captions, preliminary pages and indexes, page proofs and author's alterations, reprints and revisions"[17] – was carried out in Baldwin House, conveniently located next door to the press's printing plant, which housed a composing room, a press room, and a bindery. Halpenny was a constant visitor to the plant, where she saw workers setting type, running presses, and assembling and binding printed sheets.

Working alongside production staff and book designers, as she did, Halpenny soon developed a thorough understanding of books as artefacts and a keen appreciation for the precision craft of book manufacture: "Scholarship is not purer scholarship because it comes forth in drab apparel; an attractive but dignified format will do much to attract readers to it."[18]

At the same time, she apprenticed with the editors assigned to the press's journals and convened with the historians of Baldwin House who shared details of their own scholarly projects. As Halpenny's experience and knowledge grew, she came to see the scholarly editor, who had particular responsibility in preparing manuscripts for publication, as essential to the book-making process.

Halpenny may have been prevented from pursuing a doctorate, but she nonetheless remained drawn to the scholarly life and a reverence for scholarship bore directly on her assessment of the editorial role. For Halpenny, scholarly editors "act as scholars of form. What recommends them as editors, and gains them respect, is their own passion for scholarship."[19] She viewed the editor as a scholar in her own right and believed in editing as a form of scholarship. This credo informed Halpenny's own editorial practice; it also drove her scholarly investigations into editing.

Scholarly Editing – Theory

Halpenny's scholarship concentrated on four key areas: scholarly editing and the role of the university press;[20] bibliography; libraries and librarianship; and the importance of the humanities. Given my emphasis on publishing, I focus here on her analysis of the editorial function within a scholarly context.

In the 1960s, Halpenny began to publish actively. She wrote to plumb the skills and knowledge born of daily practice as a scholarly editor. In truth, for Halpenny writing and editing were scholarly endeavours of equal importance. Writing, however, served an essential expressive purpose: it was the appropriate means to elucidate the importance of editing to the scholarly enterprise and to advance the professionalization of editing.

Halpenny held the common view that publishing combined business, craft, and art. She often explained that scholarly publication was "extremely expensive ... requiring extensive subsidization to ensure that ... the publisher does not actually lose money on his investment ... Subsidy funds from all sources are getting harder ... to obtain, and the amount required increases year by year. Under those circumstances no editor wants to recommend for publication a manuscript which has not received unequivocal endorsement by its readers."[21]

Editing, explained Halpenny, is "an integral part, of the exercise of scholarship,"[22] while dissemination – "to make available the results of scholarly research which might not otherwise be adequately published"[23] – is the primary purpose of any university press. It is this service to university presses that holds scholarly editors to the highest standards. In turn, the character of a publishing house comes largely from "the editors who have built its lists."[24]

According to Halpenny, "constant curiosity and inexhaustible hope"[25] are characteristics of the best editors, those who are engaged by ideas, past and present, and excited by the promise that lay in each new submission. Hence, scholarly editors require "a university background ... and must be alert to what is happening in a general way in academic circles."[26] They are sophisticated readers who consistently draw on their breadth of knowledge. Despite her background in English literature, for example, Halpenny dealt "with manuscripts on microbiology and Sanskrit literature and almost anything else that you would care to mention."[27]

As the first and last person to handle a manuscript, the editor is the pivotal figure in the publication process, as well as the intermediary between author and publishing house. Though Halpenny stressed the advantage of congenial working relationships with authors, she also believed that editors must "remember, with judicious detachment, that they serve an imprint, and that the imprint gains its significance from the level of scholarship it supports."[28] Thus, for Halpenny the editor's responsibility to a scholarly press trumped concern for an author, one indication of the intense pride she felt in her own affiliation with the University of Toronto Press.

Halpenny's theorizing was driven as much by didactic purpose as scholarly interest. Experience had taught her the difference between a manuscript and a book – a manuscript was only potentially a book – and she resolved to share her hard-won knowledge with aspiring editors. In so doing, she facilitated editorial training while elaborating the complexities of editorial practice.

Halpenny always knew what Darcy Cullen, acquisitions editor with UBC Press, acknowledged in 2012, that the scholarly editor is "an active participant in the making and disseminating of texts."[29] She also knew that the work of an editor, though "vital and significant,"[30] is difficult to learn and "most successful when least observed."[31]

In many of her writings Halpenny described and defined the role of the scholarly editor, and her statements still apply today. The editor's first job, she believed, is to assess the merit and fit of a manuscript with the standards and direction of the scholarly publisher. To do so, she must engage specialist peer reviewers who are best positioned to evaluate and comment on the quality of a manuscript. Thus, she has to acquire knowledge of experts in a wide range of scholarly disciplines, which entails campus visits and regular attendance at scholarly conferences at home and abroad. The editor must then, if necessary, send a manuscript to various granting agencies in an effort to secure subsidies to underwrite publication. Once funding is assured, she must present a manuscript for approval to the advisory board of a publishing house.

When all approvals are in place, editors work directly with authors as they revise their manuscripts for publication. Unlike anonymous peer reviewers, editors are known and thereby free to offer "sympathetic, imaginative, firm, and clear guidance to authors, who are likely to be nervous and sensitive."[32] Like Jane Isay, one-time executive editor of Yale University Press, Halpenny perceived the "built-in inequality between the authority who is writing the book and the editor who is trying ... to help bring forth the very best work of which the scholar is capable."[33] Therefore, the editor's attitude "should be one of informed respect and interest for the author's subject"[34] and she advised editors to use "tact and judgment"[35] when "presenting queries to authors in order to make clear the reason for them."[36]

Halpenny considered the copy-editing of a final manuscript to be a "delicate art,"[37] born of training and experience, which requires technical mastery and careful attention to the minutiae of grammar, style, and scholarly apparatus. In her view, the aim of copy-editing is a publishable manuscript that is clear, accurate, and efficiently organized: "a set of ... pages in good trim which does justice to the ... effort the author may have given to his subject."[38]

Scholarly Editing – Practice

The first beneficiaries of Halpenny's editorial skill and insight were the University of Toronto Press and its authors. In her memoir, published in 2002 in the *Papers of the Bibliographical Society of Canada*, Halpenny recalled some of the more remarkable books she edited. One of the earliest she was assigned after returning to the press from military service in 1945 was Robert MacGregor Dawson's landmark text, *The Government of Canada*, which is still in print today. In the heat of late August 1947, Halpenny toiled on the final manuscript of Dawson's "stirring and sterling text."[39] She even "chugged away through it over the weekend," as she did not "want to get behind."[40] Her efforts were amply rewarded when later that year *The Government of Canada* won the Governor General's Literary Award for non-fiction.

Subsequently, and at his request, she worked with the political scientist on his biography of William Lyon Mackenzie King. Then, when Dawson died in July 1958, aged 63, Halpenny sorted out the final editorial details of the work and brought the project to completion. At Eleanor Harman's cottage on Lake Muskoka, she prepared the index to the volume, a task so absorbing that she did not notice the burning and sinking of "a large motor-launch ... its occupants being rescued from the water, some fifty yards"[41] away.

When Dawson's widow, Sarah, received her copy of the biography, she wrote to convey her profound appreciation for Halpenny's "personal contribution" to the book: "[My husband] told me so often last winter that he could never have done it but for your help. You were so patient and understanding with him."[42] Few editors, it is clear, were so attuned to the needs of scholarly writers.

Halpenny felt the "great loss" of Dawson personally as well as professionally: "No one who heard his booming voice, intense with the energy of his living and thinking, has ever forgotten the sound."[43] In life, Dawson had returned her regard. He once "boomed" his acute awareness of Halpenny's editorial ability down the hall of Baldwin House to historian and editor George Williams Brown: "this young lady's got me down, and now she's going over me with a harrow."[44]

Another recipient of Halpenny's expertise and friendship was the pioneering art historian J. Russell Harper. When she was managing editor, Halpenny "had the privilege of working with Harper as he reflected [on] and wrote"[45] *Painting in Canada: A History*. Published in 1966 in time for Canada's centenary, Harper's "historical and critical study [of Canadian art] ... left largely anecdotal attempts behind."[46] In the 1970s, she worked on three other Harper books: *Paul Kane's Frontier* (1971), *A People's Art: Primitive, Naïve, Provincial, and Folk Painting in Canada* (1974), and *Kreighoff* (1979).

Halpenny acknowledged Harper's energy and scholarly vision. She valued their "close and long working relationship during which I never ceased to respect and admire his dedication and sensitivity about his subjects, and to be grateful as my own eyes were trained to see the special qualities of Canadian art as they had developed over the centuries."[47] Halpenny delivered a eulogy at Harper's funeral (he died on 17 November 1983 in Cornwall, Ontario) and published a memorial tribute in *Quill and Quire* in February 1984, in which she publicly affirmed her warm feelings for her fellow innovator.[48]

In addition to encouraging authors and improving their manuscripts, Halpenny offered genial mentorship and a "training ground"[49] to scholarly editors. In the 1950s and 1960s, scholarly editing in Canada was dominated by a "cohesive and interesting group"[50] of women, several of whom were employed by the University of Toronto Press. Halpenny – who also recommended promotions and oversaw salaries at the press – shared the benefits of hands-on instruction with her colleagues and passed on her knowledge to the female associates who joined her staff. This burgeoning in-house network included Jean Houston and Jean Jamieson, for example, who themselves became respected editors. Houston rose to the position of executive editor, while Jamieson succeeded Halpenny as humanities editor. Rosemary Shipton, who joined the press in 1968 and also trained under Halpenny, went on to co-found Ryerson University's Publishing Program in 1990.[51]

As well as an adviser and collaborator, Halpenny was an educator. Throughout the 1960s, *Press Notes* carried her instructive pieces on editorial practice.[52] She led training courses for junior editors through the Association of American University Presses. On 25 January 1965, she gave a presentation entitled "The Business of Editing" to the editorial staff of the Toronto publishing firm W.J. Gage. From 1967 to 1984, she offered a well-received graduate course on contemporary publishing to students in the Faculty of Library Science (now the Faculty of Information). Moreover, Halpenny's editorial reach broadened when she edited and introduced two volumes of essays that emerged from the University of Toronto's annual conference on editorial problems, *Editing Twentieth-Century Texts* (1972) and *Editing Canadian Texts* (1975).[53] In producing these collections, which explored contemporary approaches to editing and the challenges facing editors, Halpenny's three editorial interests – the practical, the pedagogical, and the scholarly – meshed seamlessly.

Dictionary of Canadian Biography/Dictionnaire biographique du Canada

On 1 July 1969, after three years as managing editor of the press, Halpenny was appointed general editor of the *Dictionary of Canadian Biography/Dictionnaire biographique du Canada*, a groundbreaking bilingual series that spans the nation's history and vast geography. One of the press's most ambitious publications, this monumental project drew on the full range and depth of her editorial skill and administrative ability, knowledge of Canadian literature and history, and wide scholarly network.

Halpenny took over from David Hayne, who held the position of general editor from 1965 to 1969. Though she claimed never to have faced gender-based discrimination at the press[54] – the assertion may have been self-protective – she was openly "pleased that a woman was [now] given the job"[55] of general editor, an acknowledgment of how far she had come since entering publishing. In 1969, however, she could not have foreseen the indelible mark she would leave on the *Dictionary*, or that she would come to be even more widely known because of her award-winning work on the DCB/DBC.

The *Dictionary of Canadian Biography* was made possible by the generous bequest of James Nicholson, a Toronto businessman and co-founder of Nicholson and Brock, who made his fortune selling Brock's Bird Seed. In 1952, Nicholson gifted 2.5 million dollars to the University of Toronto to produce a Canadian biographical dictionary to be modelled after Britain's magisterial *Dictionary of National Biography* (now the *Oxford Dictionary of National Biography*) and the *Dictionary of American Biography*. The Canadian initiative was formalized on 1 July 1959. On 9 March 1961, with the additional support of a translation grant of $17,000 from the Canada Council for the Arts,[56] it "became a fully collaborative [bilingual and bicultural] effort"[57] – the first of its kind in Canada – under the guidance of historians George Williams Brown as general editor and Marcel Trudel as directeur adjoint.[58] The University of Toronto Press was designated to publish the English-language volumes, with simultaneous publication in French by Les Presses de l'Université Laval.

At the outset, it was decided to organize the complete series chronologically by death date, but alphabetically within each volume. This original format, which departed from the strictly alphabetical structure adopted by the British and American dictionaries, aimed to provide a history of Canada "told through biography, through the lives of the people who were actors in the story."[59] By the time of Halpenny's appointment, volume 1 (which covered the period 1000 to 1700) had been published in 1966; volume 2 (which spanned 1701 to 1740) would appear in the fall of 1969, and several additional volumes were under way.

According to Jeanneret, Halpenny was an outstanding editor and "the logical person ... to head the dictionary."[60] It was he who recommended that she be appointed general editor of the DCB/DBC and he later praised her "unqualified success."[61] Halpenny gave herself over to the project. In a position that called for collaboration as much as editorial competence, she oversaw a combined total of thirty-four staff at the University of Toronto Press and Les Presses de l'Université Laval and worked with hundreds of contributing authors. She provided advice at all levels and, for many years, commuted weekly to Quebec City, where she maintained her own apartment.[62] She became, to quote Jeanneret, the "editorial conscience" of the *Dictionary* and the press.[63]

Since the DCB/DBC was originally housed in the editorial department, Halpenny had "had something to do" with the project "from the day it began."[64] Her editorial involvement had increased rapidly and she had served often as Hayne's "deputy"[65] when he was absent from the office. In 1969, when the DCB/DBC was designated a separate department of the press, Halpenny launched an immediate and incisive review of its editorial procedures. As its newly appointed general editor, she sought to expedite production of individual volumes.

In March 1969, four months prior to her promotion, Halpenny showed that she already had a strong grasp of the DBC/DBC. In a piece written for *Press Notes*, which described the role of DCB/DBC editors in shaping volume 2, her sense of the large-scale editorial project and her capacity to decide its future were evident. Editors, Halpenny explained, were responsible for ensuring the accuracy of incidents recounted in biographies and for giving "suitable play"[66] to the participants in each incident. She believed cross-references were essential to the overall narrative fabric of the volume and were an important means of building continuity across the series. The "major responsibility"[67] of preparing the index to volume 2 also fell to the editors. A massive undertaking, the index listed the names of all individuals, significant and otherwise, mentioned in the biographies. The bibliographies, too, were cumulated and verified by DCB/DBC editors. Finally, editors undertook "a continuous reading straight through of the English text and the French text, complete, pursued as a simultaneous exercise for two people coming to the manuscript as a whole for the first time."[68] Halpenny also reminded readers that translations were "cross-checked meticulously."[69]

Halpenny fearlessly acknowledged the *Dictionary*'s relative weaknesses. Though she believed in literary biography as "an art ... of understanding and interpretation," the "narrow frame of space the DCB/DBC must respect in its volumes" did not always allow for "graceful, accurate, sensitive essays on individual writers."[70] The earliest volumes, she also conceded, emphasized politicians and businessmen over Indigenous peoples and women. The discrepancy in extant copies of authors' works created further difficulty, since the "rarity of copies of some works" and the "often fortuitous plenty of a limited number of others" could easily distort "interpretation and assessment"[71] of a writer's literary achievement. Her contribution to the 1990 collection, *Re(dis)covering Our Foremothers: Nineteenth-Century Canadian Women Writers*, edited by Lorraine McMullen, is an illuminating example of the scholarly editor grappling with the very problem of elusive research subjects. She wrote specifically of women writers "who came to North America from an experience of literature and of literary creativity elsewhere"; native-born Canadians who published poetry and fiction; and "less well-known women writers, some of them also editors."[72]

Halpenny, who prioritized primary sources, was troubled, too, by the dearth of documentation for minor figures, especially women who had died between 1800 and 1900. She sought a wide representation of individuals in the pages of the DCB/DBC and encouraged "earnest striving on the part of the project's staff and its consultants" to uncover "the undeniably important roles women played in the century's society."[73] Her dedication to tracing resources and recovering the narratives of such women yielded important editorial and scholarly results. Whenever possible, for instance, biographies of women – however brief – were included in the DBC/DBC. Moreover, Halpenny's published scholarship on the "problems and solutions"[74] presented by these biographies brought much-needed attention to the efforts driving the *Dictionary*.

In 1965, Canada's Centennial Commission granted the DCB/DBC $160,000 in support of biographical research, specifically for the years 1850 to 1900.[75] Hence, from 1969 onward, volumes covering the eighteenth and nineteenth centuries were published in alternate sequence. In total, Halpenny oversaw the publication of ten volumes of the *Dictionary* – together, they covered the years 1741 to 1900 – as well as an index for 1000 to 1900. The volumes and index were published between 1972 and 1991 – a great feat of general editorship.[76] That three of the ten volumes were issued during the period 1972 to 1978, when Halpenny also served as dean of the Faculty of Library Science, signalled her capacity for leadership and ability to manage varied functions.

Figure 3. Francess Halpenny in her office, 1972

Work on the DCB/DBC was gratifying and Halpenny – in her understated but eloquent manner – promoted the series via print, radio, and television. Ever the educator, she extolled the instructional potential of the series where "teachers will find ready assistance in presenting developments or themes of Canadian history and students will discover means of working out exercises on a region or an event that interests them."[77]

Halpenny also celebrated the narrative aspect of the DCB/DBC, and rightly so. She was especially proud of "the shorter biographies [of individuals] who have never been researched before ... It's the crowd of them that's important. You get a picture of an age, of its people and events."[78] As a cultural historian who was trained in literary analysis, Halpenny hoped the biographical entries would fill the canvas and tell the story of this country, from the broadest stroke to the smallest detail.

Getting to know the people and places of Canada through her work on the *Dictionary* was one of Halpenny's greatest pleasures. Her nationalist vision also embraced the community of scholars who contributed to the DCB/DBC. With each volume she envisaged "canoe brigades of contributors" dispatched "over Canada's stretches of time and space, to seek their riches in archives and libraries,"[79] an especially apt metaphor for the DCB/DBC enterprise.

Her indebtedness to the staff, contributors, and supporters of the DCB/DBC was profound, but Halpenny was the expert inspirational heart of the project. Reviewers invariably lauded her editorial finesse: "the uniform excellence of the series owes much to the skill of the editors of the DCB/DBC,"[80] noted historian Paul Rutherford. Some, like Christopher Moore, remarked gratifyingly on pet facets of the *Dictionary*: "Every volume ... is a window on its times ... To its great credit, the DCB has always tried to find room for more than merely the famous and powerful ... [It] remains the central work in Canadian historical writing."[81]

Under her solid leadership – Halpenny was its longest-serving general editor – the DCB/DBC enjoyed great stability. Inspired by an early reviewer who declared triumphantly of volume 1, "at last we have ancestors,"[82] she always remained true to the founding nationalist spirit of the DCB/DBC.

Posterity would corroborate Jeanneret's assessment of Halpenny as ideally suited to lead the DCB/DBC. In 1983, her contribution to this country's cultural history was recognized by the Canada Council for the Arts, which awarded Halpenny the prestigious Molson Prize for outstanding achievement in the arts, humanities, or social sciences. "Within the Canadian scholarly community," the citation announced, "the editorial procedures of the *Dictionary* have become a model of excellence."[83] Two years later, she received the UBC Medal for Canadian Biography. In honouring a series rather than the usual individual volume, the award lauded the DCB/DBC as "a splendid resource for historians both professional and amateur, with interests in public culture and the daily concerns of ordinary lives."[84] How fitting a tribute to Halpenny's rare combination of editorial and scholarly vision that shaped so many volumes of the *Dictionary of Canadian Biography*.

Halpenny, who was prevented by gender bias from pursuing a more straightforward vocational path, once described her "eccentric career, which took me from years as an editor in scholarly publishing at the University of Toronto Press to an academic role in a library school and joined both with historical and literary interests in the general editorship of the *Dictionary of Canadian Biography*."[85] Though she may have seemed an unlikely decanal candidate, it was precisely her experience at the University of Toronto Press – the unique combination of editorial, scholarly, and administrative responsibilities – that led to Halpenny's appointment in 1972 as dean of the Faculty of Library Science. In 1977, towards the end of her tenure, Halpenny revealed, "I always will be particularly interested in scholarship as such – how it changes and develops, how people are engaged in it, and I feel that essential to its development is the health of the library profession and the service it provides to scholars in all fields."[86]

In 1979, after completing her term as dean, Halpenny returned to the University of Toronto Press, where she continued her work on the DCB/DBC. Although she retired from the press in 1984, she was associated with the *Dictionary* until 1991. In honour of her achievements, Halpenny was invested first as an Officer (in 1979) and then a Companion of the Order of Canada (in 1984).

In retirement, Halpenny took on many new projects. In 1983–4, on behalf of the Book and Periodical Development Council, she directed a study of selection policies for English-language Canadian print materials in public libraries across the country. A fellow of the Royal Society of Canada since 1977, she served as its president from 1984 to 1986; in fact, her presidential address of 3 June 1986 offered a historical overview of the *Dictionary of Canadian Biography*.[87] From 1988 to 1993, she served on the Royal Society's Committee for the Advancement of Women in Scholarship and inaugurated and coordinated a Visiting Women Scholars lecture series. In 1993, she attended the first meeting (held in New York) of SHARP, the international Society for the History of Authorship, Reading and Publishing.

Halpenny also became an outspoken advocate for the humanities – her first and last choice of subject, which came under heavy siege during the 1980s. In the pages of journals and newspapers, she petitioned readers: "Perhaps no area of scholarly activity more needs the belief and sustenance of all of us, whatever our field of study and work, than the humanities."[88] She argued that government policies, "centred upon problems of the immediate and pragmatic, and so focused on technological solutions,"[89] left no place for reflection on the past and future afforded by the humanities.

In her 1995 retrospective article, "The Humanities in Canada: A Study in Structure," Halpenny insisted that the

> Humanities need to reinforce the conviction of their own worth and of their persuasive powers where it matters to ensure that worth can be exercised. They need to be highly "skilful" in considering adaptations of what they do to new realities. "Skilful" means demonstrating tact and sensitivity amid what can be high emotion. "Skilful" requires holding to the policies and processes that ensure disinterested scholarship whatever its areas: that is the significant gift the Humanities can offer to public debate.[90]

As a "highly 'skilful'" editor who once issued the work of countless humanities scholars under the imprint of the University of Toronto Press, Halpenny was ideally situated to rally support for the humanities. Moreover, as a reputable scholar herself, she could elucidate the value of a discipline centred on human experience and understanding.

Halpenny's work in the field of editing brought her awards and honorary degrees, as well as special forms of recognition. Her image, for example, appeared on a street banner outside the Faculty of Information on St George Street as part of Boundless, the University of Toronto's latest fundraising campaign. Her legacy is also reflected in a joint initiative of St Michael's College and the University of Toronto Press. The Francess Halpenny Internship Program in Publishing, established in 2007, offers an undergraduate student enrolled in the Book and Media Studies Program the chance to work closely with a scholarly editor at the press, and to feel what Halpenny described as the heady "excitement of identifying and helping to make accessible in their best dress the results of worthy scholarship, of sensing the movements of disciplines"; she also learned that "publishing gets into the bloodstream; [and that] the editorial instinct is life-lasting."[91]

Halpenny always counted herself fortunate in having been a scholarly editor. In looking back over the first one hundred years of the University of Toronto Press, she celebrated

> those who design, produce, promote, plan what will finally appear in the catalogue and in a finished book. Key to this process of publication are the editors, who sit at the receiving gate, watching the horizon for new projects, seeing them through into the house, concerned about their welfare until they leave it again for the public. They must be constant observers of how the work of scholarship proceeds. UTP has been fortunate in the editors who have built its lists.[92]

Foremost among those editors was Francess Halpenny. She did not make that claim for herself, but Halpenny's record of editorial and scholarly achievement stands as evidence of her profound influence on the culture of the University of Toronto Press, its authors, and its legacy of scholarly publications. Heralded as "an undisputed star of the editing world"[93] following her death on Christmas Day 2017 at the age of 98 – her final four years were spent in the veteran's wing of Toronto's Sunnybrook Health Sciences Centre – Halpenny is remembered not only for her wide-reaching contributions to publishing and scholarship but also for her legendary wisdom, advocacy, and mentorship.

chapter four

"She knew the business ... and the Canadian literary market": Sybil Hutchinson

Canada's first female editor-in-chief was Sybil Hutchinson (1902–1992). Over the course of her long career, Hutchinson worked for three publishing houses: Oxford University Press Canada (from 1942 to 1945), McClelland and Stewart (from 1946 to 1950), and the Book Society of Canada (from 1950 to 1974).

Hutchinson edited poetry and educational series. She also worked closely with novelists Henry Kreisel and Sheila Watson and poet/playwright James Reaney. Especially attentive to the needs of authors and their manuscripts, Hutchinson earned a reputation as a highly skilled editor of both trade and educational titles.

In addition, Hutchinson was a pioneering literary agent. In 1950, she partnered with Matie Molinaro to establish Canadian Writers' Service, Canada's first successful commercial literary agency. When the partnership dissolved in 1959, Hutchinson continued as an independent agent until her death in 1992. She was highly effective in this role, despite open resistance to her determination to represent her clients' interests and her resolve to secure remuneration as an agent. In fact, by breaking ground as a literary agent and forging new avenues of work for women – several followed her lead and set up Toronto agencies in the 1970s – Hutchinson had a profound influence on Canada's book trade.

Teacher/Student/Writer

Sybil Alexandra Hutchinson entered the workforce as a teacher and for many years taught both elementary and secondary school. In 1936, at the age of thirty-five, Hutchinson decided to change course. She enrolled at the University of Toronto, where she studied English and completed a BA (1939) and then an MA (1941) under the supervision of poet Earle Birney. To Birney, Hutchinson was "a real discovery" and he lauded her scholarly work: she "wrote the best Master's thesis I've ever had, on [short story writer] Katherine Mansfield."[1]

Similarly impressed with Hutchinson's own short stories, Birney urged her to refine her craft and publish her creative work. A first story, "Kettleful of Sunshine," appeared in 1942 in *First Statement*, the little magazine edited and published by John Sutherland out of Montreal. Soon afterward, Birney's personal endorsement convinced editor Ralph Gustafson to include Hutchinson's "Second Sight" in *Canadian Accent: A Collection of Stories and Poems by Contemporary Writers from Canada*, issued by Penguin Books in 1944.[2] Several years later, Hutchinson was able to repay Birney's generosity when she brought him to McClelland and Stewart and helped edit his picaresque novel *Turvey*, which was published by the firm in 1949.

Hutchinson's deft use of local dialect was a distinguishing feature of "Second Sight." As she revealed in 1978, "I did quite a bit of research at one time in linguistics, analyzing speech patterns (from written texts and tapes of spoken English) as a technique for delineating character in fiction. Results were rewarding. I don't think we pay nearly enough attention to this in our writing. Excluding obvious differences in dialect, we seem to be content to cut our conversational texts out of one piece of cloth."[3]

Birney admired Hutchinson's stories as "able and vivid recreations of rural characters and doings in the Point Pelée district of Ontario" – his "protegée"[4] was born and raised in Port Rowan, Ontario, which she described in 1942 as a "mere speck of a fishing village on Long Point Bay."[5] Birney was disappointed when Hutchinson did not pursue her interest in writing. "If there had been a Canada Council at that time," he wrote in 1980, "she would undoubtedly have received the financial aid she needed to continue, and might be ranked ... among our leading novelists."[6]

In 1973, Hutchinson offered this terse comment on her writerly ambitions: "[I] wish I had kept on writing. [But there were] Not many markets in those days."[7] She may not have become a writer, but she did immerse herself in the writing life. Moreover, Hutchinson's professional correspondence was distinguished by the easy style and unmistakable voice of a writer – frank, spirited, and enthusiastic – and an abiding interest in the art of writing made her "a highly competent editor."[8]

Oxford University Press Canada

Hutchinson began her editorial training in 1942, when she accepted a position at Oxford University Press Canada. Eleanor Harman had left Clarke, Irwin/Oxford that same year and Hutchinson was hired as her successor. In the 1940s, the Canadian branch of Oxford University Press saw significant growth under the management of Bill Clarke. During Hutchinson's three-year apprenticeship at Oxford, the company's publishing program expanded and its reputation as a publisher of important books was enhanced. In 1943, for example, from plates shipped overseas from England, Oxford issued the King James Bible, "the first time the Bible had been produced in the Dominion."[9] Though printed by Ryerson Press, the Bible was published by Oxford.

Oxford's list also reflected an emerging taste for books about Canada's culture, national identity, and role in world events. No doubt, Hutchinson's own interest in literature and history was boosted by Oxford's publication of Emily Carr's *Klee Wyck* (1941), *The Book of Small* (1942), *The House of All Sorts* (1944), and *Emily Carr: Her Paintings and Sketches* (1945), as well as B.K. Sandwell's *The Canadian Peoples* (1941) and Eugene Forsey's *The Royal Power of Dissolution of Parliament in the British Commonwealth* (1943). In addition, she would have shared in the general excitement when three Oxford titles garnered Governor General's Literary Awards within three years: Carr's *Klee Wyck* (for non-fiction in 1941), Alan Sullivan's *Three Came to Ville Marie* (for fiction in 1941), and Edgar McInnis's *The War: Fourth Year* (for non-fiction in 1944).

As a member of Oxford's editorial staff, Hutchinson formed close working relationships with the management team under Bill Clarke and John Irwin. In a 2013 interview, Irwin's son, who worked with Hutchinson at the Book Society, acknowledged her natural intelligence and capacity for sustained effort. He knew both her "soft heart and sharp tongue; she did not suffer fools gladly."[10] Hutchinson soon acquired the skills necessary to usher a manuscript through the publication process. So in 1946, when McClelland and Stewart offered her the position of literary adviser and editor-in-chief to follow Donald French, who had died the previous year, she was amply prepared for the new challenge.

McClelland and Stewart

When Hutchinson joined McClelland and Stewart, its offices were located at 215–219 Victoria Street; one year later the company moved to 228 Bloor Street West. At McClelland and Stewart, Hutchinson worked cooperatively with Hugh Kane. Kane had joined the firm in 1937 and eventually rose through the ranks to become executive vice-president in 1955, working alongside principal Jack McClelland to transform the one-time agency operation – established early in the century by John McClelland, Jack's father, in partnership with Frederick G. Goodchild – into one of Canada's premier independent trade publishers.

As editor-in-chief, Hutchinson was responsible for editing manuscripts, choosing illustrations, assisting with book design, soliciting jacket copy, and overseeing book production. She also made at least one trip west to visit creative writing professors – Earle Birney at the University of British Columbia, where he was a member of the Department of English since 1946 and would establish Canada's first creative writing program in 1965, and Fred Salter at the University of Alberta – in search of publishable manuscripts.

One of Hutchinson's first initiatives for McClelland and Stewart was the Indian File books, a poetry series published between 1948 and 1958. She may have conceived the Indian File series in response to the Ryerson Poetry Chapbooks, a series issued by Ryerson Press that "had been in production since 1925"[11] and would endure until 1962. As Randall Speller explains in his study of the Indian File books' design, Hutchinson sought to revitalize McClelland and Stewart's lagging "reputation as a publisher of attractive books and [to] reflect the growing post-war interest in Canadian books and original publishing."[12]

Poet Robert Finch supplied the series' name and Paul Arthur, son of Toronto architect Eric Arthur, was responsible for its striking design. Arthur adopted Indigenous motifs from the Northwest Coast and Plains Indians, with patterned paperboards and matching dust jackets. The use of quality paper, Bodoni and Perpetua typefaces, and fine binding consolidated the "distinctive Canadian ... appearance of the books."[13] Like the Ryerson Poetry Chapbooks, the Indian File books made explicit the association between rising Canadian nationalism and book-making, evidence of "nationalist themes spread[ing] beyond the words of texts and into the production of the physical texts themselves."[14]

Nine volumes of poetry comprised the Indian File series: Roy Daniells, *Deeper into the Forest* (1948); Robert Finch, *The Strength of the Hills* (1948); James Reaney, *The Red Heart* (1949); James Wreford Watson, *Of Time and the Lover* (1950); Alfred Goldsworthy Bailey, *Border River* (1952); Patrick Anderson, *The Colour as Naked* (1953); P.K. Page, *The Metal and the Flower* (1956); Phyllis Webb, *Even Your Right Eye* (1956); and John Glassco, *The Deficit Made Flesh* (1958). In both design and purpose, the series was, as Speller affirms, "a remarkable achievement."[15]

Hutchinson was a hands-on series editor. Reaney's *The Red Heart*, for example, was assembled and prepared jointly by Hutchinson and marketing assistant Colleen Thibaudeau (who became Reaney's wife in 1951). The book was published in the fall of 1949, reviewed on the radio by Birney on 14 December 1949, and all 500 copies were sold by January 1950. Although she did not participate in the production of later titles – Hutchinson's departure from

McClelland and Stewart came two years after the launch of the Indian File books – she must be credited with launching the influential series, which also won Governor General's Literary Awards for Reaney, Watson, and Page.

Hutchinson's work with individual authors distinguished her years at McClelland and Stewart. Her connection with novelist Henry Kreisel, for example, brought editor and author enduring satisfaction. Born in Vienna, Kreisel fled to England in 1938 during the Nazi annexation of Austria. Two years later, he was among the many Jews, alleged to be enemy aliens, who were sent by Britain to Canadian internment camps. Kreisel spent his first eighteen months in Canada in Internment Camp B70, near Ripples, New Brunswick, an isolated community located thirty kilometres east of Fredericton. Hutchinson learned of the aspiring writer through Norman J. Endicott, a professor of English at the University of Toronto, where Kreisel eventually enrolled as an undergraduate student. In 1946, when he submitted the manuscript of his first novel to McClelland and Stewart, Kreisel found a champion in Hutchinson: "I can honestly say that I didn't put your manuscript down until I finished it."[16]

In an effort to secure an American publisher for Kreisel's novel, the manuscript was sent first to Little, Brown and subsequently to Random House for consideration. Publication in the United States, with its large market potential, lessened the financial risk. John Morgan Gray, president of the rival Macmillan Company of Canada, once described the practice of sending a "manuscript to a publisher in the [United] States or Britain, or ... the book to a literary agent who will act for the author. This kind of helpful activity has often been ... interpreted as meaning that the Canadian publisher 'won't take a chance' unless somebody makes up his mind for him; but with many books it is the way he can serve the author best."[17] The simultaneous publication of American and Canadian editions of the same work was general practice at mid-century.

Although editors admired Kreisel's work for its atmosphere and poignancy, his manuscript did not win American approval. Hutchinson, however, was not deterred by rejection. Instead, she proffered encouragement and cogent advice that soon became the hallmark of her letters to Kreisel: "Don't be discouraged ... That is easier to say than to do. But it takes determination to be a writer. Make up your mind you're *going* to be one."[18] To further bolster the young writer, Hutchinson offered editorial suggestions. Could he introduce the heroine earlier in the novel? Might he end subtly on a hopeful note? In 1947, however, Kreisel was a newly appointed assistant professor of English at the University of Alberta and was adapting to the demands of his teaching position.

The following year, when McClelland and Stewart's fall list had an opening, Hutchinson seized the opportunity and wrote instantly to Kreisel, coaxing him to revise his novel:

> You ask in your last letter if I have any ideas about your writing. Well, you know, I have. But I don't know how you will react to this suggestion. Quite frankly, we are desperate for a novel this fall ...
>
> I am wondering what you would think of turning back to The Angels Weep [*The Rich Man*'s working title]. You are a little older now, and have put the novel out of your mind for a while. Have you any ideas for working it up a little? Could you make the setting for the tailor [i.e., presser], Toronto? Work in a little Toronto background. Perhaps heighten the European part ... I really think you could do a rework of this in two months ... turn this over in your mind seriously. That is a good piece of work. When you appeared with it you were a poor little lad and it was difficult to get an organization to think you had it in you. You don't understand how difficult that is ... It is quite unfair, but *standing* counts. I am speaking quite frankly. Let me know what you think about this.[19]

Kreisel did give serious thought to Hutchinson's suggestions. He returned to his novel with renewed enthusiasm, inspired by Hutchinson's insightful comments towards revision and her unwavering belief in his writerly ability.

It took Kreisel four months of intense work, "without interruption, with the barest minimum of sleep,"[20] to complete the necessary revisions by Hutchinson's deadline of 1 August 1948. Throughout the process he was buoyed by his editor's regular letters, written "to cheer you on in this work."[21] Finally, *The Rich Man* was accepted by McClelland and Stewart for publication that fall and Hutchinson's excitement was contagious: "if it makes you work with more assurance to know that your book is really sold – go right ahead."[22] She envisaged the day when, having published one novel, Kreisel would be eligible to apply for a Guggenheim Fellowship – "I think you're the very person who should have it" – although "I should not be putting ideas into your head."[23]

Hutchinson counselled Kreisel on the advantages of signing on with New York literary agent Maximilian Becker of the AFG (American-French-German) Agency. Becker was interested in new Canadian writers. He also represented Sinclair Ross, whose 1941 novel *As For Me and My House* Becker had placed with Reynal and Hitchcock in New York. Writing "as a friend, not as a publisher,"[24] Hutchinson advised Kreisel that Becker was more experienced than she to draft an optimal publishing contract. When Becker recommended that Kreisel receive a payment of $250 advance on royalties, she admitted that the idea originated with the agent and apologized, with her usual candour, for not procuring the advance herself. She was the ideal editor, always attentive to the writer's professional interests, especially in the case of first-time authors.

When Kreisel submitted his revised manuscript, Hutchinson's response was unequivocal: "If this isn't one of the best books of the Can. fall book trade."[25] Fall publication meant production was hurried, but she worked to ensure the felicity of Kreisel's text. Hutchinson sought to protect the author from censure by book reviewers and critics. She knew, for example, that the CBC's Lister Sinclair could "be entertainingly scathing"[26] and wanted to save Kreisel from potential embarrassment. Hutchinson also oversaw the typesetting and proofreading of galleys. Rather than send all the page proofs to Kreisel in Edmonton, she saved time by reading some of the proofs herself.

Hutchinson solicited cover copy and worked closely with book designer Paul Arthur to confirm he apprehended the Jewish focus of Kreisel's novel. She served as liaison between Kreisel and salesman Jack Scott, who marketed McClelland and Stewart titles in the Western provinces. She promoted *The Rich Man* among colleagues in the book trade and the scholarly community, distributed review copies, and sent out author's copies. Hutchinson admitted, "We never did a book this fast before,"[27] but she relished the thrill of seeing the novel through the press. *The Rich Man* was published on 12 November 1948; by 7 January 1949 Hutchinson could report that sales had already met production costs. She was jubilant: "I can't tell you how triumphant I feel about Rich Man. Just the feeling that it is possible to put something first rate over here in Canada ... we did it, and that's satisfying."[28]

The opportunity for immigrant writers like Kreisel to find an audience in Canada elicited strong nationalist feelings in Hutchinson. The same nationalist impulse drove her efforts to improve conditions for writers. In the late 1940s, for example, along with writers Pierre Berton and Joyce Marshall and radio broadcaster Lister Sinclair, she proposed the formation of a Canadian Writers' Guild to rival the Canadian Authors Association, which she did not view as "any sort of good organization,"[29] especially for younger writers. Later, through her own agency, she campaigned on behalf of individual authors.

Hutchinson's letters to Kreisel did not lapse in the wake of publication. She kept him abreast of sales and reviews of *The Rich Man*. Since she understood that it took time to establish a reputation, she also prompted the new author to maintain the momentum of writing and prodded him to begin work on his next novel. Hutchinson was convinced that Kreisel would have no trouble securing an American publisher for a second book and, as early as 8 February 1949, asked, "have you had any time at all to work on this?"[30] Later that month, she pressed him to "get started on Novel [number] 2 ... while your name is still in the public notice."[31] Hutchinson admired Kreisel's talent and believed in his capacity to form and retain a loyal audience.

When Kreisel was slow to produce a second work of fiction, Hutchinson's faith in the author did not waver. In August 1960, following a brief meeting in Toronto, she again broached the subject with Kreisel, by then a highly respected senior professor at the University of Alberta: "I feel that it is important for you to do another novel ... to spur you on, Henry, I really think you write well. Just don't let yourself get diverted."[32] In response, Kreisel sent

Hutchinson partial drafts of his second novel, *The Betrayal*, which was published in 1964 under McClelland and Stewart's imprint. By then she was an editor at the Book Society, but Hutchinson – who was both steadfast and patient – celebrated Kreisel's success.

In fact, if not for Hutchinson's foresight and coaxing, Kreisel might have accepted early rejection and *The Rich Man* would have languished unpublished. Instead, he was roused to rewrite his fiction to satisfy his "literary mentor['s]"[33] urging and "sound critical judgment. She saved me [he claimed] from making embarrassing gaffes ... reined in my tendencies to embroider a text with fanciful metaphors and taught me less is more."[34]

Kreisel was deeply appreciative of his first editor and in 1990, one year before his death, proclaimed his indebtedness to Hutchinson. In a retrospective piece entitled "Reflections on Being 'Archived,'" published in the quarterly *Canadian Literature*, Kreisel affirmed Hutchinson's cultural significance. Her letters, he declared, conveyed an

> urgency, the ... feeling that the person is there in the room with you, talking to you ... I am glad that we were thousands of miles apart and she had to write to me, so that her letters are preserved and may perhaps serve as a model of the creative role a fine editor can play in helping to develop manuscripts. We have never in Canada valued editors in the way in which they have been valued in other countries. It pleases me to know that a student or a researcher ... will come across these letters and learn that Sybil Hutchinson mattered in the development of a Canadian literature.[35]

We must all be grateful to Kreisel for preserving a correspondence that shows Hutchinson as a discerning editor who attended equally to the broad strokes and essential details of his literary canvas. Hutchinson was both astute and alert in her approach to the aspiring writer who, at her insistence, produced the fine novel that launched his literary career. Kreisel claimed, "No other editor had the same influence on me as Sybil [Hutchinson]. She was an intensely alive woman ... [who] exude[d] ... vitality and ... enthusiasm."[36]

Figure 4. Sybil Hutchinson in the 1950s

Hutchinson was deeply invested in bringing forth a writer's best work and understood the value of protracted gestation. In addition to Kreisel, she encouraged novelist Sheila Watson in her early efforts on *Deep Hollow Creek*. In 1949, when Hutchinson first read Watson's manuscript, she had difficulty following its plot but was impressed by the text's originality: "It reads very authentically and the idiom is excellent."[37] Always open and curious, she was not at all put off by Watson's experimental style. Rather, she tried to generate interest in Watson's manuscript by sharing it with Robert

Weaver. Weaver had joined the CBC as program organizer in 1948 and immediately had begun to solicit work by Canadians, which aired regularly on programs such as *Canadian Short Stories* (1946–54), *CBC Wednesday Night* (1947–63), *Critically Speaking* (1948–67), and later *Anthology* (1954–85) and *Stories with John Drainie* (1959–65).

Hutchinson also sent Watson's manuscript to noted British editor J.E. (Jack Eric) Morpurgo of Falcon and Grey Walls Press (previously of Penguin Books). She hoped to capitalize on Morpurgo's recent expression of interest in Canadian manuscripts that were "not too long."[38] Ironically, Morpurgo's curiosity may have stemmed from his brief stint at the University of New Brunswick in the mid-1930s, which he denounced as "Hell without possible hope of redemption."[39]

Failed attempts to interest Weaver and Morpurgo in *Deep Hollow Creek* disappointed Watson, but did not deter Hutchinson. Optimistic that each year also brought an "average number of lucky breaks,"[40] she counselled Watson to expand her manuscript and "simplify its style."[41] Hutchinson's express belief in Watson – "Your writing is really excellent, you know. I don't like sending it back to you"[42] – had the desired effect. The young author heeded Hutchinson's editorial suggestions and went on to revise her novel in the early 1950s. Moreover, as archivist Anna St Onge affirms, Hutchinson's early encouragement and criticism led to the belated publication in 1992 of *Deep Hollow Creek* by McClelland and Stewart (under Ellen Seligman's editorship) and its nomination for a Governor General's Literary Award.[43]

The support she gave Watson was among Hutchinson's final acts as editor-in-chief at McClelland and Stewart. Hutchinson and Jack McClelland had both joined his father's firm in 1946, but they had not developed a rapport. To the charismatic McClelland, Hutchinson seemed "remote, almost always looking in the other direction when anyone spoke to her."[44] More significant was McClelland's growing interest in editorial matters – he had quickly assumed a leadership role in the company – which may have felt threatening to Hutchinson. She believed McClelland lacked the requisite knowledge of either literature or publishing and "interfered too much"[45] in her work.

Their general incompatibility and McClelland's sense of being "squeezed"[46] by Hutchinson came to a head in 1950 and, on the morning of 14 April, McClelland dismissed his rival editor. In the heat of her firing, Hutchinson wrote to Kreisel, one of the first people she told she was "leaving McClelland & Stewart, very shortly. I should like to say, quite frankly, that I am leaving on request of Jack McClelland ... As I was not well paid ... I am not too grieved ... it was getting more and more difficult here, with Jack McC[lelland] asserting his bad taste in all matters."[47] With characteristic fortitude, she hoped to secure "a new and different (and I hope, more remunerative) job."[48]

Five days later, after some reflection, Hutchinson's anger at being discharged had intensified. On 20 April 1950, she wrote to Watson to say that she was leaving her position at McClelland and Stewart "as quickly as I can arrange to" and conceded that she was doing so

> with a certain regret, because I felt that while we might have done much more, each year we were able to do even a few worthwhile books. But now young Jack McClelland wishes to be the editor. (Jack graduated with some difficulty in pass arts and wrote supp[lemental exam]s in English). I don't know what his editorial policy will be, but the disturbing thing about him, to date, is that his policy fluctuates from minute to minute.
>
> What I shall be doing I don't know at all. But if Jack is doing the sort of publishing I think he will be, I know I don't want to work at that sort of crap.[49]

In the face of perceived injustice, Hutchinson wrote privately but disparagingly of McClelland. At times, such frankness nettled her colleagues in the book trade. Over the course of her career, however, expertise trumped boldness and Hutchinson was universally regarded as a practised editor.

Professional setback was followed by personal misfortune. In May 1950, Hutchinson was hospitalized and required surgery for cancer that later proved to be benign. As she recuperated at home, Hutchinson had time to consider her situation. To Kreisel she wrote that "M&S is a memory with me now," but admitted, "I just don't like to think about them."[50] Prior to her operation, she had approached John Morgan Gray of the Macmillan Company of Canada about a possible position with his firm and was feeling increasingly hopeful about work and life: "I am very philosophic. I think (not an easy optimism, I hope) that things rather work out for the best, and it's very nice to have so much bad luck, if you call it that, at one fell swoop. I felt so sure that I had cancer, that I feel now what a privilege it is to be able to walk around in the world and feel fine again."[51] Hutchinson was right to be optimistic, for she had her health and would soon find new employment.

Book Society of Canada

In 1950, Hutchinson joined the Book Society of Canada. Publisher John Irwin hired Hutchinson. He knew of her excellent editorial skills – they had worked together in the 1940s at Oxford University Press Canada – and he welcomed her as a new member of the firm.

Unlike McClelland and Stewart, the Book Society was primarily a publisher of textbooks for the educational market. Given her own literary aspirations earlier in her career and her recent work as editor-in-chief at McClelland and Stewart, Hutchinson may have regretted the lack of opportunity to build a distinguished list of trade titles at the Book Society. She did not express dissatisfaction, however. Instead, she brought her usual zeal to her editorial work and remained a dedicated employee until her retirement in 1974.

In fact, Hutchinson's expertise resulted in an expanded list of literary titles for the Book Society. Her ideas were well received by Irwin, who enabled Hutchinson to handle literary acquisitions. She brought playwrights Len Peterson, Edwin Procunier, and Lister Sinclair to the firm. In addition, she corresponded with authors, applied for American copyright, oversaw book promotion, distributed review copies, and sent out author's copies.

Although she was not involved directly with book design, Hutchinson attended to the costs associated with production. Permissions, in particular, could be expensive and she always tried to minimize that expenditure. In her work as a publicist, she urged authors whenever possible to promote the Book Society as their publisher. She herself was invited to represent the company at a preview televised screening of Peterson's play *Almighty Voice* (1974), held at CBC's television studios in downtown Toronto on 11 November 1975.

With educational texts, Hutchinson followed Harman's standard practice and tried "to avoid complicating the [editorial] process."[52] She always "look[ed] for the possibility of simplification" and eschewed "unnecessary refinement."[53] At times, Hutchinson also contributed content to the works she edited. When Canadian material was needed for *Introduction to Better Reading* (1959) by Joseph C. Gainsburg and Lillian G. Gordon, a text that originated in the United States, she unearthed the requisite selections: "until you begin to hunt for these things, you have no idea how difficult it is to locate paragraphs that will have the exact construction you need."[54]

In connection with the Book Society's Searchlight series – inexpensive anthologies prepared for use in high school English courses across Canada – Hutchinson's knowledge and skill as a series editor were on show. Frequently, she was more collaborator than editor. In 1969, for example, she assisted Len Peterson who edited a Searchlight book on Morten Parker's 1965 film *The Red Kite*, produced by the National Film Board of Canada and based on Hugh Hood's short story "Flying a Red Kite." Hutchinson wrote the biographical and textual notes and compiled the list of further reading, distinctive features of each title in the Searchlight series.

Hutchinson embraced the publishing industry's growing "emphasis ... on material with Canadian setting, written by Canadians,"[55] and her editorial suggestions often reflected her sensitivity to nationalist issues. She knew well the geography of Ontario, for instance, and directed editors to evoke location: "Just stating a setting as northern Ontario, does not give a story a Canadian identity."[56] For a project on Indigenous art, Hutchinson advised editor Edwin Procunier to include paintings by Emily Carr and contemporary verse by First Nations and Inuit writers as "the really vital thing."[57]

Hutchinson was an editor who held writers in high esteem and would not alter their work without approval. As someone who once had aspired to authorship, she respected those who wrested meaning from words. There were other times, however, when she ignored professional etiquette and behaved wilfully. Surreptitiously, she read correspondence that lay open on Irwin's desk. When he found that she would enter his office in his absence, Irwin was forced to lock his door. Once, when his patience finally wore thin at her public display of rudeness, Irwin wrote a letter of reprimand: "Miss Hutchinson, what you said to me in public in the office was unacceptable. Let it be understood between us that if this recurs you will leave."[58]

For the most part, Irwin overlooked Hutchinson's indiscretions, for she was a valued editor and loyal employee whose contributions to the Book Society extended beyond her work with authors and their manuscripts. Every spring, for instance, she happily planted the company garden with annuals. Irwin showed his appreciation for Hutchinson's contributions in various ways, once by covering the cost of airfare and ground transportation to the Grand Canyon and California, where she holidayed in 1962, but he rued his inability to increase her salary and often expressed that regret to his son, who became president of the firm in 1971. When she retired in 1974 after a long career in publishing, most of it spent as editor with the Book Society, John W. Irwin took the opportunity to present Hutchinson with a generous cheque on behalf of his late father, who had died on 8 December 1971. The gesture nearly brought her to tears.[59]

Pioneering Literary Agent

The same year she joined the Book Society, Hutchinson partnered with Matie Molinaro to establish Canadian Writers' Service, later known as Canadian Speakers' and Writers' Service. As Robert Lecker points out, Hutchinson and Molinaro were not the first to set up a literary agency in Canada – although they were, I contend, the first to succeed commercially. In 1946, Montreal saw the launch of Hedges, Southam and de Merian, which had links to three major international agencies: D.C. Benson and Campbell Thompson

Limited in London, and W.A. Bradley in Paris. Although Doris Hedges had a reputation as a writer and promoter of Canadian literature, her efforts could not sustain a literary agency and, Lecker explains, "Hedges, Southam & de Merian did not remain a presence in the decade after its founding."[60]

Hutchinson, unlike Doris Hedges, did maintain a literary agency for many years. She did so on a part-time basis while employed as an editor at the Book Society of Canada, where she earned her primary income. After she left Canadian Speakers' and Writers' Service in 1959, Hutchinson operated independently and acted for select writers such as poet Robert Finch and playwright James Reaney, while Molinaro developed a successful career as a full-time commercial agent and gained prominence by representing luminary figures such as media theorist Marshall McLuhan and cartoonist Ben Wicks. Soon, Molinaro's renown eclipsed Hutchinson's, and the latter's achievements as a literary agent were all but erased from view – an oversight this examination of her career seeks to rectify.

Hutchinson's professional role as literary agent, which brought her supplementary income at the standard commission fee of 10 per cent, was formalized in 1950 and sanctioned by John Irwin. In practice, however, the mentorship and career advice she offered Henry Kreisel and Sheila Watson during her years at McClelland and Stewart were signs of her propensity for agency work. Hutchinson's governing belief that a key "function of an agent is to keep authors writing. It is very easy to lapse. That, and to keep ... work circulating in the places best calculated to buy it,"[61] can be traced to her encouragement of Kreisel and Watson.

Home was the base for Hutchinson's agency work: first, a second floor apartment at 40 Avenue Road and later, a fourth floor apartment at 50 Hillsboro Avenue, both in mid-town Toronto. Hutchinson lived on Avenue Road for twenty years, but the building's decline during the 1960s led to her move on 1 November 1971 to an apartment on Hillsboro Avenue that offered "more room, and ... is well kept up. [with a] Resident sup't. – who can take in parcels (like manuscripts)."[62] The building's proximity to public transportation was also important to Hutchinson, who had a driver's licence but chose never to drive.

Hutchinson never intended "to build up a large 'stable' of writers"; instead, she sought to represent authors whose "worthwhile and interesting" work had "a market."[63] In 1953, Alice Cameron Brown was already a published poet when she submitted short stories and a novel for Hutchinson's consideration. Hutchinson sent Brown's stories to Robert Weaver of the CBC. At the same time, she offered her own cogent advice towards revision. She felt one scene in "Ghosts," for example, was too contrived and urged Brown to "work on this – the first of it is good – and the situation in general very humorous ... In the meantime, don't be discouraged – you have talent."[64]

Brown's historical novel set in the West also received careful analysis. Hutchinson believed it lacked development and a consistent point of view and invited the author to "think this over carefully, and don't be offended at my honest opinion. I am only trying to think how we can make this better. So much of it is very very good."[65]

Though she was professional and candid in her assessment of Brown's work, Hutchinson also attended to the author's feelings. When, for example, she succeeded in placing Brown's poem "November Garden" with *Saturday Night* magazine, she sent the writer a cheque for $9.00 accompanied by a conciliatory comment: "I know they should pay more, but verse is hard to market."[66]

Poet Robert Finch, who twice won the Governor General's Literary Award for *Poems* (1946) and *Acis in Oxford* (1961), was another of Hutchinson's clients. The connection between poet and agent actually dated back to 1948 with the publication of *The Strength of the Hills* in McClelland and Stewart's Indian File series.

When Finch's literary career was revived in the 1980s, it was due, in no small part, to Hutchinson's intervention. On 8 December 1979, at the University Women's Club on St George Street, Hutchinson brought together Robert Finch and publisher Tim Inkster of the small prestige imprint Porcupine's Quill – Inkster later claimed he was "*instructed* to attend a lunch, to be hosted by Ms Hutchinson"[67] (emphasis added) – with the impressive result that Porcupine's Quill went on to issue no less than seven elegantly designed volumes of Finch's poetry: *Variations and Theme* (1980), *Has and Is* (1981), *Twelve for Christmas* (1982), *The Grand Duke of Moscow's Favourite Solo* (1983),

Double Tuning (1984) – which was dedicated to Finch's trusted agent and won an Alcuin Society Award for Excellence in Book Design in Canada – *For the Back of a Likeness* (1986), and *Sail-boat and Lake* (1988).

As Inkster recalled in 2010, Hutchinson was "forthright," "formidable," and "intimidating," and she "drove a hard bargain."[68] At the close of 1979, he did not believe his press "the most suitable of candidates" to issue Finch's work, but Hutchinson "was not to be dissuaded,"[69] and so he relented. Although the relationship between publisher and poet "was never easy,"[70] Inkster finally conceded that the Porcupine's Quill benefited from Finch's association with the University of Toronto's Massey College, which provided an ideal setting for many of Finch's book launches.

Hutchinson was a staunch promoter, so much so that even her very own Book Society was charged $25.00 for the right to feature the Robert Finch poem "December 25" on its 1980 Christmas card.

James Reaney

In fact, Robert Finch was brought to the Porcupine's Quill via negotiations over a James Reaney title. As the latter's agent, Hutchinson granted Inkster the right to republish *The Boy with an R in His Hand*, Reaney's children's book (first issued in 1965 by the Macmillan Company of Canada) about the 1826 Types Riot at William Lyon Mackenzie's Toronto printing offices. In return, Inkster had to agree to publish Finch's *Variations and Theme*, which he launched alongside the Reaney volume in 1980.

Hutchinson first met Reaney, like Finch, when she was an editor at McClelland and Stewart. As Reaney's editor, Hutchinson lauded the "originality, wit and freshness"[71] of his 1949 volume, *The Red Heart*, third in the Indian File series. As his agent, she went on to steer the course of Reaney's literary career. From the 1950s until her death, Hutchinson looked out for Reaney's interests and protected his authorial rights. She handled all permission requests; negotiated with radio stations, theatre companies, and publishers; set up speaking engagements; vetted publishing contracts; managed all earnings from his writing; and even assisted with his income tax returns. She was trustworthy and loyal and always closed her letters to Reaney with "love."

For a time, Hutchinson also represented Reaney's wife, Colleen Thibaudeau. She had little success in placing Thibaudeau's poetry and short fiction, but that did not prevent her from forming a close relationship with Reaney's family, especially his daughter-in-law Susan Wallace.[72]

Hutchinson's primary responsibility, which she took most seriously, was to ensure that Reaney, a tenured professor of English at the University of Western Ontario (now Western University), could devote as much time as possible to his writing. As Lorraine York affirms, "One of the most important ways in which the agent provides protection is by shielding the writer ... [who] is deeply engaged in a project, from the very exigencies of the marketplace."[73] Hence, Hutchinson handled correspondence pertaining to Reaney's literary undertakings. She insisted that correspondents "send all letters dealing with the use of Reaney's work to me directly. He otherwise has to redirect requests, or ... there is a danger of their going unanswered. He is a very busy person."[74] For the most part, she navigated all facets of agency correspondence – both the straightforward and more complex issues – with calm and precision.

Hutchinson strategically fielded permission requests. In February 1969, she negotiated with Keith Gill of CBC Toronto for permission to cite twenty lines from Reaney's poem "The Beauty of Miss Beatty" on the CBC radio program *Ideas*. For a fee of $10.00, Hutchinson granted the CBC one-time broadcasting rights. For a fee of 4.5 guineas, the BBC similarly was allowed to cite twenty lines from Reaney's poem "Traffic" on the radio program *The Motor Car in Britain*, which aired on 19 March 1969. Publishers, such as the Macmillan Company of Canada and Ryerson Press, directed customary permission requests to Hutchinson.

Theatre groups contacted Hutchinson for the right to mount Reaney's many plays. Over the years, she corresponded with the National Arts Centre, the Stratford Festival, the Manitoba Theatre Centre, Theatre Calgary, Vancouver's Playhouse Theatre

Company, and countless other professional and amateur theatre companies across North America and the United Kingdom.

When appropriate, she asserted her position as agent and wrote to admonish those who did not follow protocol. In 1967, for example, when he mounted Reaney's play *Listen to the Wind* as part of Saskatchewan's Regional Dominion Drama Festival, Robert N. Hinitt was taken to task for not securing advance permission. Hutchinson did

> not wish to be carping or disagreeable, but you should have been in communication with me *before*. Your programmes should have carried a notice: "Listen to the Wind is copyright. Permission to produce by courtesy of Sybil Hutchinson, Agent for James Reaney".
>
> If you are doing any of Reaney's plays again, please tell me about it in advance.[75]

Such minor transgressions were frequent and Hutchinson managed them with efficiency.

As an awarding-winning poet and playwright, Reaney often was asked to speak at public events. In such cases, Hutchinson oversaw all necessary arrangements, including travel, accommodation, and remuneration. In October 1969, for instance, Reaney's invitation to lead an evening class on poetry and drama as part of a language arts course mounted by Hamilton's Board of Education was dispatched to Hutchinson. She reassured Reaney that he "would be in complete charge of the evening" – "free ... to do anything" he wished – and advised him to charge a fee of "$300.00? (Why not?)."[76] Hutchinson's profound respect for Reaney as a vital and truly innovative writer increased over time and she demanded compensation that reflected his level of achievement.

Hutchinson also wrote query letters on behalf of Reaney. In 1969, when he was working on his trilogy of plays about the legendary Donnelly family of Lucan, Ontario – *Sticks and Stones* (1975), *The St Nicholas Hotel* (1976), and *Handcuffs* (1977) – Reaney learned that H.N. Bawden of Gormley, Ontario, was in possession of diaries kept by William Porte. James Donnelly was said to have murdered

Patrick Farrell on 25 June 1857 and Porte had served on the jury at the inquest into Farrell's death. For the purposes of research, Reaney wished to consult Porte's diaries and asked Hutchinson to contact Bawden on his behalf.

Hutchinson wrote to Bawden several times, explaining her mission and attempting to coax him to allow her to photocopy the diaries:

> I can understand your anxiety about sending them ... But I wonder if you would consider letting me look at them. Dr. Reaney really would like to have a xerox copy of them. This I could do – and he would be quite glad to shoulder the expense of it. We have a xerox machine at the Book Society, and I could do the work myself. You could be here and watch me do it – and see that no harm came to the pages, if you wished. But I can assure you that I am a reliable person, who appreciates the value of this material.[77]

Hutchinson sweetened her request by suggesting that Reaney edit the diaries for publication. She also offered to circulate the edited diaries among Toronto publishing companies that might be interested in such historical material.

Unfortunately, no amount of cajoling or reassurance worked to soften Bawden; he refused to share the diaries with Reaney via his agent. While Reaney acknowledged her attempts to gain access to Porte's diaries, Hutchinson was not accustomed to defeat and did not take the sting of such disappointment lightly.

Hutchinson monitored publishers' handling of Reaney's plays. By August 1971, for example, it was clear that the Macmillan Company of Canada was not doing enough to market *The Killdeer and Other Plays*, which it had published in 1962 to great acclaim – the volume had won the Governor General's Literary Award for drama. Moreover, Macmillan was not prepared to issue more of Reaney's plays, several of which had been staged and were awaiting publication. Vancouver's Talonbooks, on the other hand, which had co-published Reaney's *Colours in the Dark* with Macmillan in 1969, had approached Hutchinson with a proposal to become the primary publisher of Reaney's drama.

Hutchinson understood the importance of "an appreciative publisher, certainly. But a writer doesn't thrive on appreciation, alone. He needs a public ... My concern is to advance Reaney's writing as well as I possibly can. I do not think he should be made a publisher's pawn."[78] Hutchinson thought it was time for Reaney "to go where they want you – & believe your work has a sales, not just a prestige, value."[79] She counselled the playwright to leave Macmillan and urged him to accept the offer from Talonbooks.

Hutchinson felt "a bit sorry for [Donald] Sutherland [Director of Macmillan's Trade Division] – but perhaps not very sorry."[80] In fact, Reaney had twice visited Sutherland at Macmillan's offices at 70 Bond Street to express his keen desire to have all his "completed but unpublished plays printed."[81] When, after having been allowed ample time for consideration, Sutherland finally denied Reaney's request, Hutchinson deemed it necessary to sever ties with Macmillan. She regretted "that this break is happening,"[82] but was moved less by emotion than business sense and determination, precisely what Reaney needed to guide his career.

To the satisfaction of playwright and agent, Talonbooks (and later Press Porcépic) went on to issue Reaney's plays. All too soon, however, David Robinson of Talonbooks would learn that Reaney's agent had low tolerance for unprofessional conduct. When, after some time, she had received neither a publishing contract for a revised edition of *Colours in the Dark* nor replies to several letters, an exasperated Hutchinson was driven to rebuke on 8 February 1972: "I do object to working with publishers who don't send out contracts ... and who don't answer letters. It is preposterous that Colours [in the Dark] (Revised) has been out for some months; that you were to bring the contract with you when you came to Toronto by plane – yet you did not do so, nor have sent it since that time."[83] In view of such failings, Hutchinson was right in her unyielding approach; it served Reaney's interests and facilitated his rise to literary prominence.

Problems associated with remuneration would elicit an even stronger response, for Hutchinson was a careful manager of her client's finances. In December 1977, Reaney received a cheque in the amount of $117.94 from Press Porcépic, publisher of his *Selected Shorter Poems* (1975), *Selected Longer Poems* (1976), as well as the

Donnelly trilogy. Since the payment ought to have been directed to Hutchinson, she wrote to the press, proclaiming herself

> James Reaney's agent, and all payments due to him should be sent to me – cheque made out in my favour as his agent. Instead, this cheque was made to Reaney directly.
>
> Dr. Reaney said in his covering letter to me: "The Godfreys [publishers Dave and Ellen Godfrey of Press Porcépic] have sent this cheque, enclosed herewith, plus a record of sales, etc. In any case, I've lost the sales record, but fortunately not the cheque. Shouldn't this all have been sent to you?"
>
> Of course it should have. And, because of your error, both Reaney and I have been inconvenienced. Please do not let this occur again.
>
> And you will now have to send me a copy of the record of sales that was with the cheque. Otherwise my accountant will not know how to credit the cheque.
>
> I wish to emphasize the fact that we do not appreciate these slipshod, careless ways of dealing with authors.
>
> Please make a note, and remember, that all business dealing with James Reaney should be directed to me.[84]

That Hutchinson managed all of Reaney's literary earnings and was intolerant of lapses in proper remittance is revealed in this emphatic letter to Press Porcépic. In upholding herself as an intermediary figure between author and publisher, the letter further conveys her determination to safeguard her own financial interests as a professional agent.

Hutchinson had to act when the production company Nielsen-Ferns took more than one year to pay Reaney $4,500 for a commissioned screenplay entitled "Brocksden." Hutchinson's initial invoice was submitted to the company in January 1977, but the fact that it had gone astray did not surface until March 1978. At that point, she issued a second invoice, accompanied by a letter emphasizing that "Dr. Reaney is much disturbed at the delay with payment. He worked hard on the script, and in good faith."[85] When the fee finally arrived – the project was never realized – it was due only to Hutchinson's persistence.

Hutchinson's readiness to assist Reaney was made especially clear in early 1977, when she put her feelings aside and solicited a $100 donation in support of the Ne'er-Do-Well Thespians from her one-time adversary, Jack McClelland. A Toronto-based theatre company, NDWT (1975–82) performed out of the Bathurst Street Theatre (now the Randolph Theatre). It was co-founded by Reaney and director Keith Turnbull and was best known for its productions of Reaney's inventive plays.

McClelland was so moved by Hutchinson's letter of appeal – written at Reaney's request – that he pledged his support for the theatre company: "You were always able to write a very persuasive letter and clearly nothing has changed and so you have sold me."[86] A gifted letter writer himself, McClelland could not help but appreciate Hutchinson's inimitable style.

Hutchinson formed a close bond with Reaney and was deeply distressed when he suffered a psychological breakdown in 1987. She prayed "the doctors will be able to bring him back to earth & soon. I am so relieved to know he is *in* hospital & getting proper medication & care."[87] As Reaney regained strength, Hutchinson felt even greater relief.

To Reaney, as well as his family, Hutchinson was a devoted ally whom they admired and valued. As Susan Reaney recalled in February 2014, "Dad had the good luck to come to Sybil's attention early in his career when he really needed a publication ... She knew the business ... and the Canadian literary market, and it was helpful for Dad to have someone represent him who lived in Toronto ... They had a good relationship built on trust and mutual sensibility."[88]

Hutchinson died on 30 September 1992 at the age of 90 and bequeathed her personal library to James Reaney and Colleen Thibaudeau. It was her way of signalling abiding affection for Reaney and their shared enterprise of disseminating his work and protecting his literary interests.

After her death, Reaney struggled to find a new agent, but felt none was as principled as Hutchinson. As he, along with her colleagues in the book trade, had always known, Sybil Hutchinson – who once stated that "in publishing, as in life ... what one loses on the swings, one gains on the roundabouts"[89] – truly was an original.

chapter five

A "tremendous job of editing": Claire Pratt

Editor Claire Pratt (1921–1995) was at the vanguard of mid-twentieth century Canadian publishing. From 1956 to 1965, Pratt was senior editor at McClelland and Stewart, where her focus on Canadian writing enhanced the firm's publishing program. She was also a series editor involved with the New Canadian Library and Design for Poetry series.

When Pratt joined McClelland and Stewart, new writers were gaining ground and the company was enjoying a period of intense growth. She worked closely and effectively with individual authors, among them journalist Peter C. Newman, novelist Margaret Laurence, and poet Irving Layton. By helping authors produce their best work and by bringing books to life – series reprints, prose, and poetry – Pratt advanced the professionalization of editing and made a lasting contribution to literary culture and publishing in Canada.

McClelland and Stewart

After completing a BA (1944) in English and philosophy at the University of Toronto – and winning a gold medal in philosophy – Mildred Claire Pratt went on to pursue graduate work in international studies at Columbia University. She then returned to Toronto and entered the book trade as an entrepreneur. In 1945, she and business partner Olive Smith established the Claire Pratt Book Service,

Figure 5. Claire Pratt, 1950

"a specialized book shipping and addressing service."[1] Pratt closed the purchasing agency in 1949 and undertook freelance editorial work for the Macmillan Company of Canada, Ryerson Press, and the University of Toronto Press. In 1952, she became an editor with Harvard University Press, but illness and the need for further surgery – throughout her life Pratt suffered complications resulting from childhood polio – forced her to leave the position in 1954.[2]

Two years later Pratt joined McClelland and Stewart, where her intelligence, professionalism, and appealing personality were on view. In light of the physical disability and discomfort she had to endure, Pratt was remarkable for her wide-ranging abilities and the degree of her ambition and accomplishment. She took on major responsibilities, which coincided with an era of publishing activity at McClelland and Stewart new to the annals of Canadian firms. She evaluated countless submissions, edited manuscripts, prepared indexes, proofread galleys, ushered books through the publication process, and met and corresponded regularly with authors. In addition, she participated in editorial meetings, attended press conferences, and negotiated with other publishing companies, including Clarke, Irwin and Oxford University Press Canada.

Jack McClelland, who was a shrewd judge of editorial competence, soon came to rely on Pratt for her expertise and dedication. Although McClelland's demands frequently threw Pratt's "day into confusion" and led to general "uproar,"[3] publisher and editor formed a cordial connection. Pratt withstood McClelland's "rampage[s],"[4] attended meetings or met with authors in his stead, and often took over his various projects.

For Pratt, editorial work was a hectic round of activity, akin to "laboring in a whirlwind."[5] Periodically, she travelled out of town to meet with authors who did not reside in Toronto; regularly, she devoted evenings and weekends to editorial projects; and often, she "worked like a devil"[6] to meet publishing deadlines.

Pratt was inundated with work, at times feeling so much tension at the office that she wondered whether she and her colleagues would get through the day without suffering "a nervous breakdown."[7] In April 1958, for example, as she was preparing for a much-needed vacation, McClelland warned her – only half in jest – that her "desk would be piled high with work on my return so that any good my holiday would do me would be undone."[8]

That Pratt would not succumb easily to anxiety is evident in her rejection of an offer from author Farley Mowat who visited his publisher's East York office in 1961 – the firm had moved to

25 Hollinger Road in 1952 – "with a bottle of rum, foisting a glass to me most of which I poured out the window, not wanting to lose my job."[9] Clearly, Pratt thrived in the stimulating, somewhat chaotic atmosphere of Hollinger House and was satisfied in her position. It was "hard work" but "happy times."[10]

Series Editor

A source of particular pleasure was Pratt's work on the New Canadian Library, McClelland and Stewart's landmark reprint series and the first series in Canada to mark the arrival of the 1950s postwar paperback revolution. Launched on 17 January 1958, the success of the NCL has been profound – it continues today as the premier paperback reprint series devoted to Canadian authors.

Pratt was designated in-house editor for the NCL and she welcomed the opportunity to help create a series of books tied closely to her knowledge of and affinity for Canadian literature. A collaborator by nature and editorial calling, she worked alongside Jack McClelland and the series' general editor, Malcolm Ross, an esteemed literary scholar who was then head of the Department of English at Queen's University. Pratt was involved in developing and expanding the paperback series: she communicated with editors and authors, secured publishing rights, and shepherded titles through the press. As NCL historian Janet Friskney affirms, "in-house editors such as Claire Pratt ... demand much more recognition for their editorial influence in the production of certain pre-1900 titles."[11]

Since the nature of Pratt's work on key NCL volumes is described in full in Friskney's 2007 study of the New Canadian Library,[12] I offer here a summary of her editorial mediacy. While Ross assumed the task of securing a critical introduction to each NCL title, Pratt oversaw most in-house matters pertaining to the series. At times, her view of a potential title was solicited. In 1962, for example, she enthusiastically endorsed inclusion of James De Mille's *A Strange Manuscript Found in a Copper Cylinder* (first published in 1888), although it was another seven years before the NCL edition appeared. More often she was asked to "select and proofread the source texts on which NCL reprints were based,"[13] a choice that required thorough knowledge of a work's bibliographical provenance and publication history.

Pratt worked with Robert McDougall on his 1958 NCL edition of Thomas Chandler Haliburton's *The Clockmaker or, The Sayings and Doings of Samuel Slick, of Slickville (First Series)* (first serialized in 1835–6) to ensure stylistic consistency in a text that adopted a Yankee idiom. She also performed a near feat of magic when she managed to expand W.H. Drummond's *Habitant Poems* to 110 pages. When editor Arthur J. Phelps stubbornly refused to include more than twenty-two judiciously selected poems, Pratt devised to spread out the verse and pad the slender 1960 NCL edition with indexes. The next year, she and Carl Klinck established a clear editorial policy in an attempt to align their joint efforts to produce an edition of Frances Brooke's *The History of Emily Montague* that would retain the flavour of the original 1769 publication. The copyright page of the 1961 NCL edition of Brooke's work noted the editorial changes made to the copy-text. Pratt took similar care with Klinck's 1962 NCL edition of Susanna Moodie's *Roughing It in the Bush* (first serialized in 1847), the first abridged title to appear in the series.

Pratt was responsible for bringing Thomas McCulloch's *Letters of Mephibosheth Stepsure* (first serialized in 1821–2) to the New Canadian Library. She served as liaison between Malcolm Ross and literary critic Northrop Frye, philosopher John Irving, and librarian Douglas Lochhead, the three scholars associated with the project. First, she went to great lengths to secure a reading copy of the rare book. She approached Lochhead, librarian of Dalhousie University, who encouraged her interest in McCulloch's work and willingly lent her his library's only copy of the *Letters*. Second, to increase the book's market potential, she endorsed the use of *The Stepsure Letters* as an abbreviated title. Third, when Lochhead's research uncovered six previously uncollected letters, she was called upon to make a selection of new material for inclusion in the 1961 NCL edition.

Further editorial intervention was necessary at the proof stage. Another editor had mistakenly modernized McCulloch's spelling, and Pratt, who was detailed and exacting – she sought "to perpetuate rare and worthwhile Canadian works"[14] and believed it was "important to adhere to the source"[15] of the core title – delayed publication and corrected the proofs to accord with the copy-text of McCulloch's *Letters*.

Pratt deserves recognition for her editorial labour on a number of post-1900 NCL titles, as well. She brought her keen editorial eye to Sinclair Ross's *As For Me and My House* (first published in 1941). As Friskney details, Pratt's few suggestions towards minor revision were made in the interest of clarity – changes to prepositions and conjunctions, for example – and were accepted by Ross for the 1958 NCL edition of his novel. Pratt also assisted Edward Meade, who was grateful for the chance to undertake extensive revision to *Remember Me* (first published in 1946) in preparation for its 1965 publication in the New Canadian Library.

An especially attentive editor, Pratt regularly took the time to convey her appreciation for an author's work. Novelists A.M. Klein and Brian Moore were thanked personally by Pratt for the opportunity to issue *The Second Scroll* (first published in 1951) – an "exceptionally fine book with its fine nobility of language"[16] – and *Judith Hearne* (first published in 1955 as *The Lonely Passion of Judith Hearne*) – in the New Canadian Library in 1961 and 1964, respectively.

That same regard led Pratt to exclude extraneous material that could detract from a text. Hence, she omitted the original introduction to Hugh MacLennan's novel *Each Man's Son* (first published in 1951; NCL in 1962) and the original illustrations in Paul Hiebert's novel *Sarah Binks* (first published in 1947; NCL in 1965).

Pratt's principal, Jack McClelland, did not have the editorial inclination, financial resources, or sufficient personnel to underwrite scholarly editions of early Canadian works – twelve such editions were produced between 1985 and 2012 by Carleton University's Centre for Editing Early Canadian Texts.[17] Nonetheless, through the New Canadian Library, McClelland reintroduced a number of overlooked but critical pre-1900 texts – as well as many more recent titles – to a contemporary audience. And despite early mixed reviews and inadequate profits, he never gave up on the NCL, the one project that best reflected his nationalist impulse.

Today, the reprint series is still used widely in university classrooms, where it continues to reach new generations of readers.

In addition to the New Canadian Library, Pratt was charged with overseeing McClelland and Stewart's short-lived Design for Poetry series. In particular, she served as go-between for book designer Frank Newfeld and the five poets whose verse was featured in the series: Ralph Gustafson (*Rivers Among Rocks* 1960), Leonard Cohen (*The Spice-Box of Earth* 1961), Earle Birney (*Ice Cod Bell or Stone: A Collection of New Poems* 1962), Roy Daniells (*The Chequered Shade* 1963), and Phyllis Gotlieb (*Within the Zodiac* 1964).

Pratt – a woodcut artist herself – was a great admirer of Newfeld, who is now considered "the first notable postwar book designer in Toronto."[18] She regarded him as a collaborator and lauded his achievement in the series' first colophon: Gustafson's *Rivers Among Rocks* "was planned and illustrated by Frank Newfeld, a brilliant young Canadian designer, typographer and art director, whose work has earned him an imposing series of awards in various fields of design."[19] Although she complained about "doing business with Earle [Birney]"[20] – McClelland also found Birney especially abrasive – Pratt handled the series' poets and their volumes with her usual dedication and expertise.

Trade Book Editor

In addition to being a proficient series editor, Pratt was a talented trade editor; she worked tirelessly with noted cultural figures, among them parliamentarian and member of the Co-operative Commonwealth Federation (precursor to the New Democratic Party) Stanley Knowles. When Jack McClelland invited Knowles to write a book on the emerging New Democratic Party, he did not foresee the arrival of a weighty manuscript in need of serious editorial intervention – a task he entrusted to Pratt in January 1961.

McClelland believed Knowles's effort could "become a fairly good book,"[21] but only after extensive editing. He urged Pratt "to be quite ruthless about the revision. The repetition is overbearing particularly in the middle chapters! I think it must be eliminated and you will have to do so with extreme care."[22] McClelland often tested Pratt in this way, since he knew that she could be "ruthless" in her editing without sacrificing the goodwill of an author, a delicate balancing act that would elude a less skilful and humane editor.

Pratt's literary upbringing and love for her poet father – she was the only child of leading poet E.J. (Edwin John) Pratt and magazine editor Viola Whitney Pratt[23] – gave her particular insight into the writerly personality and the profound connection between a writer and his work. She was not a commanding editor; rather, she respected the individual's claim to his or her creation and sought to ensure the publication of a writer's best effort.

After she had worked painstakingly on his manuscript, Pratt wrote to Knowles affirming that she had "never seen such a beautifully prepared script"; she also hoped that he would not be offended by her "recommendations for cutting."[24] Moreover, if he felt "that any vital points have been omitted or your meaning distorted in any way,"[25] Pratt deferred to the author's expertise. In fact, Knowles rejected many of Pratt's suggestions and she was required to undertake further and intensive line editing prior to publication; she also prepared the index. Knowles's *The New Party* was successfully published that same year. That Knowles acknowledged her "tremendous job of editing"[26] – McClelland also reported that "Knowles seemed pleased with your work. Good show"[27] – attests to Pratt's editorial finesse and her ability to work with an author who was precise and detailed.

Pratt's capacity to forge productive relationships with authors was also evident in the case of Peter C. Newman. Pratt worked closely and expeditiously with Newman on *Renegade in Power: The Diefenbaker Years* (1963), a study of Prime Minister John Diefenbaker's government. Undaunted by Newman's reputation – he was known as a formidable and uncompromising journalist – Pratt brought clarity and calm to their editorial exchanges. Although she felt pressed for time and worked diligently to meet the publication deadline of October 1963, she retained her equilibrium throughout the editorial process.

To ensure timely publication, Pratt was required to focus all her attention on Newman's manuscript. She praised Newman's text as "a remarkable accomplishment. It has been great fun to work through,"[28] and sent him a list of editorial changes she had made to his manuscript. Newman also was told he would be free to make alterations at the galley stage.

When she received Newman's emended galleys, Pratt remained diplomatic: "What a lot of corrections there are ... This is going to involve a great deal of re-setting but better now than in pages."[29] While she incorporated the majority of Newman's changes, she also sought to minimize the cost of re-typesetting by ignoring several of his corrections. Newman lauded Pratt's "excellent editing";[30] he was disappointed, however, "that some of the changes I made on the galleys have not been made on the page proofs."[31] In the end, Newman insisted "that [all] the changes that I've marked are made" and offered final revisions that "require[d] the least amount of resetting and NO changes in pages."[32]

Given the pressure she had endured to meet the publication deadline, Pratt worried that mistakes may have crept into the finished work: "I shouldn't be surprised if there were the odd one, considering the speed with which the book was rushed through."[33] Her careful treatment of Newman's "lively and informative"[34] volume won her the gratitude of the author, however. Newman appreciated the "skill with which my manuscript was handled" – so much so, that he even promised to send Pratt a list of further corrections, just "in case there is a second edition."[35]

Despite her affable nature, Pratt no doubt felt great relief following the publication of *Renegade in Power*, which sold phenomenally well and set a new precedent for the critical examination of Canada's political leaders. Happily, she sent Newman his author's copies, returned his "seventeen-pound manuscript,"[36] and turned her attention to other editorial projects.

With renowned historian W.L. Morton, Pratt was equally solicitous. Morton was executive editor of the Canadian Centenary series (1963–86), a nineteen-volume history of Canada and one of McClelland and Stewart's first attempts to issue prestige academic publications. In November 1963, Morton was struggling to pare down *The Critical Years: The Union of British North America, 1857–1873* (1964), number twelve in the series though one of the first titles to be published. Pratt, who had asked for revisions, apologized for having "distressed you so much over the word cutting"[37] and eased the author's anxiety by granting him more time to work on his manuscript.

Morton valued Pratt's understanding and forgave her delayed response to his revised submission when she explained that she had "been slower than I anticipated ... owing to a number of factors, both personal and editorial. You, on the other hand, have attended to the manuscript with great dispatch, and this I appreciate."[38] Ever gracious and obliging, Pratt won the respect and cooperation of authors who shared her genuine enthusiasm for the literary enterprise.

Pratt took great pleasure in her work with fiction writers. Like Hutchinson before her, she advised Henry Kreisel, whose second novel, *The Betrayal* (1964), was issued under her watch. When Pratt asked Kreisel to revise the novel's ending, his changes met with her approval. She found the use of two postscripts appropriate and meaningful, and was gratified to have such "a deeply moving book, with great significance"[39] on McClelland and Stewart's fall list. Kreisel was buoyed by Pratt's words and thankful for her editorial suggestions.

One of Pratt's most important relationships was with prose writer Margaret Laurence. Pratt cherished her association with Laurence – they shared a compassionate nature – and recalled the momentous "day the manuscript for *This Side Jordan* arrived on my desk. Shortly afterwards I had lunch with Margaret Laurence and was enchanted with the warmth of her personality. She was on the eve of leaving for England and was kind enough to invite my mother and me to visit her. This we were fortunate enough to do twice, in 1964 and 1967, at Elm Cottage,"[40] Laurence's beloved home in the village of Penn in Buckinghamshire, England, from 1962 to 1973.

While Pratt was grateful for the opportunity to work with an author whose prose she so admired, Laurence was moved by the editor's favourable response to her writing. In fact, the publication of *This Side Jordan* in 1960 – written and set in Ghana, it was Laurence's first novel – initiated an abiding connection between editor and author, and established McClelland and Stewart as Laurence's Canadian publisher.

The Tomorrow-Tamer (1963), Laurence's collection of African short stories, followed *This Side Jordan*. Pratt's assessment of the volume, incisive and effusive in its praise, bears reproduction here:

> [The stories] are superbly done ... beautifully written, in a style that captures the feeling of Africa in all its turmoil, conflict, and naked pathos. The fragmentary and futile attempts at understanding between black heart and white are described with compassion and insight. Also the rift within Africa itself hopelessly touched with the white man's civilization.
>
> Characterizations are excellent. "The Merchant of Heaven" is a typically unimaginative type characteristic of evangelistic zeal caught up in the mysteries of Revelation. In "The Perfume Sea" two people, lost souls finding romance in a harmless deception concerning the emptiness of their past. "The Rain Child" – African brought up in England (country of rain) unable to adjust to Africa, her supposed home.
>
> These stories are powerful, unique, exquisite. I recommend them unreservedly for publication by us. And my guess is that they would sell.[41]

Pratt intuited Laurence's early lack of confidence and was willing to share this positive view of her stories. In her characteristically open way, she was pleased to offer a glowing report and wrote immediately to Laurence: "One of the best things that has happened to me in a long time is your manuscript of short stories. I wish there were some way in which I could put across to you how really enthusiastic I feel about them, Margaret. Depth of compassion and insight, combined with stylistic beauty and the use of the word or phrase that is exactly right, make of each of them a pure gem, a true union of the artist and the craftsman. In short they are marvellous."[42]

Boosted by such unqualified praise, Laurence sent Pratt the manuscript of a novel she had been working on for some time, her first to adopt a Canadian setting. "Hagar," as *The Stone Angel* was provisionally titled, elicited a more measured response from Pratt, but one that recognized the novel's probing power: "The book is beautifully written, with sensitivity and compassion. In spite of the drabness, the hopelessness of the theme, it is not depressing, at least I do not find it so. In its spotlighting of a condition endemic in our way of life, the book does not present anything new in our literature but does, however, present it in a flawless way. I find it difficult to know how well it would sell here."[43]

Pratt's assessment of Laurence's artistry was accurate. What she did not anticipate was the triumph of the novel and its lasting impact on Laurence's career. The publication in 1964 of *The Stone Angel*, the first in what became a series of works set in the fictional town of Manawaka (modelled after the author's native Neepawa, Manitoba), heralded a new phase in Laurence's productivity and announced the emergence of a new Canadian writer, one with a distinctive voice and an unmistakable appreciation for her country and its people.[44] Pratt was, however, the first Canadian editor to discern the nuances of Laurence's writerly voice and vision and she remained a touchstone figure in the author's life.

Irving Layton

More than any other writer, the spirited poet Irving Layton brought out Pratt's vivaciousness. Layton always sought Pratt's opinion of his poetry. He tested her patience by continually revising a manuscript until the moment it was forwarded to the printers. He negotiated constantly: if he were to remove one poem from a collection, might he replace it with another? He also enriched Pratt's professional life and offered some of the most heartfelt expressions of gratitude she received over the course of her career at McClelland and Stewart.

For her part, Pratt developed a keen understanding of Layton's complex and provocative personality, his profound belief in poetry as salve for the soul, and his glorification of love. She penetrated his grand public persona – Layton was famous for his bravado – and apprehended his innermost need for approval and human connection.

Poet and editor first worked together on *A Red Carpet for the Sun* (1959). They communicated via correspondence, Layton from his home in Montreal and Pratt from her office in Toronto. Layton, who liked to discuss the relative merits of his verse, sent Pratt a copy of "New Tables" for inclusion in the book; he did not think it "a bad poem. How do you feel about it?"[45] Pratt's response – "It is a splendid poem and I am delighted that we shall have the chance to include it in the collection"[46] – assuaged Layton's concern – "I'm pleased, very much so, that the poem ... finds favour with you."[47] In fact, Layton regularly asked for such reassurance and, when appropriate, Pratt bolstered the poet's flagging confidence.

Layton's openness matched Pratt's warm personality and he developed a sense of kinship for his editor. He also admired Pratt and relied on her editorial judgment. Although he offered a rough chronological arrangement for the poems in *A Red Carpet for the Sun*, Layton deferred to Pratt and invited her to "play around with variations, if you feel that a better pattern would be the result."[48] He was "jubilant"[49] when Pratt corrected a serious error in page proofs: the misformatting of many lines of verse. "Bless your dear heart," Layton declared, "I call that splendid, and my spirits are once again skyrocketing."[50]

Early in 1959, poet and editor met in person for the first time and Layton claimed the encounter would have been pleasurable "even under the most distressing of circumstances."[51] When *A Red Carpet for the Sun* was launched later that year – a staggering 5,000 copies sold in three months[52] – Layton and Pratt had a chance to reconnect in Toronto. Layton enjoyed being feted, but regretted that he had not had time for a long discussion with his prized editor.

Cause for shared celebration came when *A Red Carpet for the Sun* received the Governor General's Literary Award for poetry, which confirmed that Layton and Pratt were, indeed, a strong team. The foundation for a mutually satisfying relationship – characterized by respect, trust, and genial humour – and the pattern of exchange between poet and editor were laid through their joint effort to produce this landmark selection of Layton's verse written between 1942 and 1958.

The tie between Pratt and Layton strengthened with each successive project and their correspondence records an increasing frankness, free of rancour. Layton used Pratt as a sounding board for his thoughts on the purpose of poetry. He intended his next work, *The Swinging Flesh* (1961), a collection of stories and poems, "to have the tonic effect of a brisk thunder-shower. I want it to rip through the heavy smog of fellowly liberalism, togetherness, etc. Nowadays if a book of short stories and poems doesn't make some people mad and others glad, it might just as well be left to moulder in manuscript form."[53]

Pratt accepted Layton's desire to "open the door for real living poetry"[54] with poems that were vulgar, sexual, and satirical of the bourgeoisie, but she baulked at his use of "rod-assed" and his reference to the reader as a *dummkopf* in his draft foreword to *The Swinging Flesh*. Pratt knew that Layton's foreword was deliberately inflammatory. Nonetheless, she urged him to consider alternative phrasing and her affectionate closing, "Yours in Dumkopfheit [sic],"[55] signalled her certainty that Layton would not be irked by her editorial suggestion. In this instance, the poet relented and omitted both terms from the published foreword.

Layton's persistent practice of dispatching new and replacement poems – each a self-declared "damn fine lyric"[56] – for inclusion in his forthcoming book may have tried Pratt's patience, but poet and editor only came to an impasse over a single poem, "Why I Don't Make Love to the First Lady," which proclaims in reference to Jacqueline Kennedy, "Of course I could have her! / In a flash, with a snap of my fingers. / An arrogant magician, / I'd put words under her perfect feet / and make her fly to me."[57] After repeated discussions with Layton, Pratt wrote him a measured letter outlining why the poem ought to be excluded from *The Swinging Flesh*. She believed the poem was too topical and lacked taste and humour; she wondered "do you really think it's all that good?"[58]

Evidently, Layton believed strongly in the poem, for no amount of cajoling from his otherwise accommodating editor – "all your requests have been taken care of ... thus far with gladness and delight"[59] – would dissuade him from including the piece in his collection: "this poem makes the kind of statement I feel ought to be made by poets who are lucky enough to live in countries where the censor doesn't decide what's printable or not. I intend to write many more such poems, only sharper and more bitter."[60] Layton was "firm and pleasant"[61] and to object further would prove futile, so Pratt conceded defeat. In fact, as Nick Mount recounts, Layton went so far as to mail a copy of "Why I Don't Make Love to the First

Lady," along with a copy of *A Red Carpet for the Sun*, to the President and Jacqueline Kennedy; he also read the poem aloud at the inaugural Canadian Conference of the Arts held in May 1961 at Toronto's O'Keefe Centre for the Performing Arts (now Meridian Hall).[62]

Layton admired Newfeld's cover design for *The Swinging Flesh* and expressed muted complaint when he was obliged to await arrival of his author's copies. In truth, he was a privileged author, one whose book of stories and poems appeared in 1961 without the formality of a signed contract, evidence of the bond of trust that had been forged between the poet and his publisher.

The personal tie between Layton and Pratt, and his indebtedness to her deft handling of his work, deepened over the production of *Balls for a One-Armed Juggler* (1963), which was issued with alacrity and minimal fuss. In September 1962, Jack McClelland forwarded Layton's manuscript to Pratt with the injunction that she was to meet an impending publication deadline of January 1963. Quickly, Pratt determined that the manuscript needed little editorial intervention. In her view, Layton had "arrived at a certain height from which your message is more thoroughly communicated than at any time previously ... You can accept this from one who ... [has] never pretended to like anything of yours or anyone else's that I didn't like."[63] Not surprisingly, Layton was buoyed by Pratt's "perceptivity and honesty": "If you were here beside me I'd hug you, I am so elated."[64]

As she awaited the arrival of Layton's trademark incendiary foreword, Pratt prepared *Balls for a One-Armed Juggler* for publication. By 28 January 1963, Layton had received his author's copies and, once again, he lauded Frank Newfeld's triumphant design: the front cover adapted a photograph of a bearded and mustachioed Irving Layton. Praise for Pratt came from Layton and McClelland alike, who saluted her expeditious handling of the book. By 1963, she was not only a practised editor with great executive ability; she was also an effective communicator, especially with insistent poets and publishers.

The Laughing Rooster (1964) was the last of Layton's volumes to be seen through the press by Pratt. Its production, unlike that of *Balls for a One-Armed Juggler*, was more typical of Layton and involved the ongoing submission of poems, delayed delivery of a foreword, and heated debate over the inclusion of contentious material.

Upon submission of each manuscript, Layton anxiously awaited Pratt's response to his work and *The Laughing Rooster* was no exception. He felt he had "written most of the poems with my own blood" and claimed – in his usual way – to have assembled a "rich, complex, and many-textured"[65] book. When Pratt endorsed his most recent verse, Layton was "overjoyed"[66] and looked forward once again to working closely with his trusted editor.

Before receiving Pratt's positive assessment, Layton had already begun to send her additional poems for inclusion in the manuscript. He continued to offer replacement poems and, at the final hour, tried to sneak in several poems through Ruth Taylor, Jack McClelland's executive assistant. Pratt's rebuke belied her affection for a poet who nonetheless tried her patience: "You promised me you would not send any more poems so now I have proof that you are not a man of honour. No wonder you slunk the poems in behind Ruth! Irving, there is no room in the book for any more poems."[67]

Layton mustered his playful side to subdue Pratt: "Honestly I didn't mean to go behind your back. I was having some correspondence with Mrs. Taylor and I thought I'd include the poems in one letter I'd written her. Of course I knew she'd show them to you. Knowing the faint-hearted person you are I might have hoped that in showing them to you Ruth would add her plea to mine."[68] In fact, what drew Pratt to Layton was his mischievous nature. She forgave all his foibles, but stood her professional ground and refused to insert the late poems.

In fact, Pratt was far from being "faint-hearted." In January 1964, while she waited for Layton to deliver the foreword to *The Laughing Rooster*, she sought the intervention of Jack McClelland on a separate matter. Pratt was troubled by Layton's poem "In Praise of Eros," which invoked the conflict between John F. Kennedy and Nikita Khrushchev during the Cuban Missile Crisis of October 1962. She believed many readers would find the poem offensive – the November 1963 assassination of Kennedy was still a fresh memory – and hoped to exclude it from the collection. In light of her failed attempt to convince Layton to remove "Why

I Don't Make Love to the First Lady" from *The Swinging Flesh*, Pratt asked McClelland to take on this new battle. He warned her that "the last time I had a confrontation [with Layton], I lost, too,"[69] but he hoped to succeed in this instance.

Pratt was correct to enlist McClelland, for he managed to convince Layton of the risk associated with publishing "In Praise of Eros": "there is no one at this end that feels that this will give us anything but serious trouble. Again let me emphasize that this has nothing to do with the poem. It's clever and witty, but migod, please!"[70] McClelland's argument held sway. For all his zeal, Layton sought to avoid "serious trouble" in the form of legal censure and agreed to the removal of the poem.

Layton solicited Pratt's editorial help with the foreword and the arrangement of poems in *The Laughing Rooster*. Her guiding, conciliatory way suited the poet, who was not naturally compliant. As we have seen, however, Pratt was neither selfless nor humourless in her devotion to Layton and his verse. As she prepared to send Layton his proofs of the volume – Newfeld's elegant and innovative design for the book incorporated woodcuts of a rooster – she asked, "Now that I have, at great pains, done everything you asked, where is my ode?"[71] Layton's own comic reply could not conceal his gratitude: "Claire, my love ... Because you were so patient with my repeated requests, I've put you into my special roster as Saint Claire and I pray to you each night before going to bed. I shall write a poem this summer and title it SAINT CLAIRE."[72]

Regrettably, neither Layton's ode nor his response to the news that chronic ill health finally forced Pratt's resignation in April 1965 is available, but there can be no doubt that her departure left a major gap in McClelland and Stewart's editorial department and a profound mark on the poet who felt allied to his gifted editor. Throughout their association – at once richly productive, deeply satisfying, and frequently trying – Layton expressed his care and admiration for Pratt, a faithful editor who appreciated his best work and always warmed to the life force behind his bold and blustery exterior.

Though Pratt could not physically sustain the unforgiving rigour of the publishing life, she retained her interest in books and writers and continued her editorial work on a freelance basis. She assisted author Norah Story and William Toye on *The Oxford Companion to Canadian History and Literature*, issued by Oxford University Press Canada in 1967. In 1968, she began work on a Canadian style manual for McClelland and Stewart. Press Porcépic was one of her other clients.

She also pursued her own writing projects and was awarded a Canada Council grant in support of a genealogical study of her father's ancestry. In 1970, Jack McClelland was not surprised to receive a polished, elegantly written manuscript from his former colleague and the "best book editor in the country."[73] The following year he published *The Silent Ancestors: The Forebears of E.J. Pratt*, in large part to honour Pratt's "great contribution to McClelland and Stewart."[74]

One of a line of influential editors in a field that was gaining ground in Canada in the 1950s, Pratt's success was the result of a combination of intelligence, resolve, and good humour that set the standard for McClelland and Stewart editors, female and male alike, who would follow her lead. In 1969, Linda McKnight and Anna Porter joined the firm's editorial force. Lily Poritz Miller was hired in 1972, Denise Bukowski in 1973, and Ellen Seligman in 1977. In 1986, Douglas Gibson arrived – via Doubleday Canada and the Macmillan Company of Canada – to launch his own prestige imprint, Douglas Gibson Books.

Having entered publishing at an auspicious time for Canadian writing and writers, Claire Pratt helped foster the literary momentum that drove McClelland and Stewart. In turn, Jack McClelland gave her the opportunity to professionalize the role of editor, which she did with grace and aplomb, proudly proclaiming "I am being taught by my own work."[75] McClelland was right to rely on Pratt's capacity to meet the challenges of working with books and authors, for she became an accomplished literary editor and a central figure in Canadian publishing.

chapter six

Publishing "Maestro" and Cultural Advocate: Anna Porter

In 1969, four years after Claire Pratt's resignation, Anna Porter (1943–) was hired into the position of editorial coordinator at McClelland and Stewart. Porter, like Pratt, joined the firm with some previous experience of editing and seized every opportunity to develop her publishing expertise. She oversaw production schedules, handled submissions, and worked closely with poet Earle Birney and prose writer Farley Mowat. In 1975, after a series of rapid promotions, Porter was named the firm's editor-in-chief.

Four years later, Porter moved into the role of president and editor-in-chief of Seal Books, a paperback publishing company co-owned by McClelland and Stewart and Bantam Books of New York, a position she held until 1982.

Over the years, while struggling to balance the conflicting demands of a career and motherhood, Porter also used her standing as an editor, publisher, and award-winning author[1] to further her guiding interests and promote democratic principles. Today, she is best understood as a proponent of Canadian literature and its writers; a campaigner for the right of individuals to live free of discrimination; and a defender of freedom of speech. Taken together, Porter's editing and publishing, writing and advocacy, show her to be a socially and politically engaged citizen who has persistently carved out a public role for herself in Canada's cultural sphere.

Figure 6. Anna Porter in the 1970s

McClelland and Stewart

After graduating with a BA (1966) and MA (1967) in English from the University of Canterbury in Christchurch, New Zealand, Anna Porter (née Szigethy) worked as a proofreader at Cassell in London and a sales representative for Collier Macmillan, first in London and then New York. In late 1968, when she arrived in Toronto via New York, she joined Collier Macmillan as a copy editor, tasked with adapting American textbooks for the Canadian market, but resigned after six months with the firm.

When a friend told her of an opening at McClelland and Stewart, Porter applied for the vacancy and soon was interviewed by creative director Frank Newfeld. Their informal meeting was less about Porter's publishing experience than her knowledge of French and German, languages she had in common with the Czech-born Newfeld. Newfeld recommended Porter as overseer of editorial and production schedules, but their casual exchange served only as prelude to a subsequent meeting with publisher Jack McClelland, whose hiring decisions held sway in the company.

McClelland and Porter met in early summer 1969 over lunch and vodka martinis at Toronto's Westbury Hotel at the corner of Yonge and Carlton Streets. No more formal an interviewer than Newfeld, McClelland quizzed Porter on her knowledge of Canadian writers. She could name just four – Morley Callaghan, Norman Levine, Margaret Laurence, and Leonard Cohen – but McClelland apprehended the enthusiasm, talent, and drive that would distinguish her rise at McClelland and Stewart. After lunch, he drove her to Queen's Quay to appraise a boat he was thinking of purchasing. As they stood together admiring "a single-masted wooden yawl, gleaming white in the sunshine" and "bobbing gracefully in the water,"[2] McClelland confirmed that Porter could begin work the following week.

Porter was obliged to "learn about Canada by reading Canadian writers."[3] She remembers McClelland pointing out that "his company was called 'The Canadian Publishers,' and how the hell would I manage in the editorial department if I knew nothing about the country? 'It's the price of admission,' he claimed."[4] Porter was required to read all the titles issued to date in the New Canadian Library. Happy to comply, she launched her immersion in Canadian prose with the fiction of Gabrielle Roy, albeit in English translation. She went on to read the work of Stephen Leacock, Thomas H. Raddall, and Brian Moore, but abandoned the struggle with Frederick Philip Grove. She also encountered the fiction of Lucy Maud Montgomery, the verse of Earle Birney and Irving Layton, and the non-fiction of Pierre Berton, Farley Mowat, and Peter C. Newman. "Has anyone ever had such an education in becoming a citizen,"⁵ Porter wondered. She was grateful for the chance to discover Canada through the eyes of its writers.

Porter was involved with the day-to-day operations of McClelland and Stewart and soon felt at home in what she described as its "grungy offices"⁶ on Hollinger Road. Drawing on past experience, she performed various editorial and supervisory tasks. She oversaw the production of book jacket and catalogue copy; fielded permission requests; coordinated editorial and production schedules; assisted with book promotion; participated in editorial and design meetings; advanced book projects; assessed countless manuscripts, both fiction and non-fiction; and most of all, liaised with authors.

Porter centralized the gathering and organizing of editors' notes used to produce copy for book jackets and seasonal catalogues. She directed copyright questions to McClelland and Stewart's permissions department. When reviews of manuscripts were delayed, Porter reminded tardy editor Don Roper of the need for prompt action. She advised Peter Taylor in his role as director of advertising, promotion, and publicity. She also became a "maestro," as journalist Robert Fulford dubbed her in 1985,⁷ of the annual Frankfurt Book Fair, where she boosted McClelland and Stewart's books and made lasting connections with international publishers, editors, and literary agents.

Her recollection of a rather desultory rise from "some sort of junior editorial busybody,"⁸ who "started doing editing ... because of staff changes, people coming and going ... [and] kind of drifted into acquisitions,"⁹ belies Porter's rapid development as a competent editor. Like Pratt, she worked with Malcolm Ross on the New Canadian Library. She also handled the Canadian Centenary series and any number of manuscripts.

Porter participated in editorial discussions, even when the subject of a work lay outside her area of expertise. She met with co-authors Doug Michel and Bob Mellor, for instance, and recommended publication of their draft manuscript *Left Wing and a Prayer: Birth Pains of a World Hockey Franchise*, but only after it had received her husband's enthusiastic endorsement, "because I wouldn't read a book like this myself."¹⁰ In cases where she lacked necessary knowledge, Porter's editorial decisions were informed by the resources at hand – in this instance her spouse, Julian Porter.

Drawing on her own interests and convictions as an environmentalist, Porter proposed a sequence of books on Canada's national parks conceived by Gavin Henderson and James Gordon Nelson, experts associated with the National and Provincial Parks Association of Canada. She envisaged original titles that would "include a lot of informative material, rather than the usual pretty books that tourists might take home from national parks."[11] Although the project did not materialize, McClelland noted Porter's initiative. It confirmed that she had adopted the nationalist ideology that drove his firm's publishing program.

McClelland and Stewart's informal atmosphere suited Porter's own professional style. Her in-house correspondence, for example, was peppered with colloquialisms – "helluva" was a favourite adjective, especially for potentially "hot" books. At the same time, it showed an incisive intelligence, an appreciation for the scope of each issue under consideration, and an ability to penetrate to the core of pressing editorial concerns.

Whenever she came across an extraordinary manuscript, Porter was intoxicated: it was "why those of us who care about this strange business stay with it in spite of all the disappointments, petty day-to-day problems and everything that keeps going wrong."[12] She could discern a work's targeted audience and whether it warranted production as a hardcover book or mass-market paperback. She also intuited a manuscript's timeliness, market potential, and fit with McClelland and Stewart's Canadian focus, vital factors that informed her analysis of all submissions.

McClelland trusted Porter's evaluative insight. When she judged a collection of short stories by David Lewis to be "repetitious" with "no unifying theme,"[13] McClelland accepted Porter's opinion: "I think you should tell him quite frankly that he could hurt his market for the future by coming out with a book of miscellany. I don't think you have to criticize the material directly but just say it doesn't hang together."[14]

Porter's hesitant response to a collection of stories by Leon Rooke was coloured by her earlier rejection of Clark Blaise's

A North American Education, which was published by Doubleday Canada in 1973 and had gone on to win critical praise. She believed Rooke's volume lacked coherence and "didn't have a great deal to say."[15] "No longer certain,"[16] however, of her ability to gauge the merits of a short story collection, she solicited McClelland's response to the manuscript. The seasoned McClelland sought to reassure Porter and had "no great difficulty making a decision ... The answer is that we should reject," especially since Rooke was "American and ... the stories are basically American-orientated ... He is a good writer but not someone we have to publish. I think you are just feeling badly about Clarke [sic] Blaise ... [whose] book has had some good reviews but there is no real reason to believe that it has sold."[17] Later, Porter came to admire Blaise for his unique perspective as a dual American-Canadian writer and regret her decision to reject his work.[18]

Dennis Lee's critical study *Savage Fields: An Essay in Literature and Cosmology* posed a different problem. Unconvinced by the book's claim of significance for novels published by House of Anansi Press, the publishing company that Lee and Dave Godfrey co-founded in 1967, Porter nonetheless felt obligated to give serious consideration to *Savage Fields* out of respect for the intellectual energy of its author. Despite three positive readers' reports, McClelland corroborated Porter's sense of Lee's project "as a blatant exercise in self-justification"[19] for his own publishing efforts. In the end, they decided against publishing a work directed at a small audience, and Anansi brought out Lee's book in 1977.[20]

In 1974, Porter was perturbed when Rudy Wiebe pressed for a paperback edition of *The Temptations of Big Bear* – the novel had appeared in hardcover the previous year – but McClelland was composed: "I don't really think the whole thing is a big deal ... [W]e have treated ... [Wiebe] very well and very fairly and I think we should just cool this situation for the moment."[21] Porter followed McClelland's advice and, three years later, when Wiebe's novel was issued as volume 122 in the New Canadian Library, the author was appeased.

When she worried about rejecting the flawed work of an author who had been encouraged to write a book about widowhood in favour of Betty Jane Wylie's stronger manuscript on the same subject, Porter sought McClelland's counsel on how to handle the problem. She expressed a hope that he had "some wonderful solution" up his sleeve that she hadn't "thought of yet."[22] Once again, McClelland was unequivocal, prepared to decline a work of non-fiction that was "loosely written, not well organized," and made for "unpleasant reading."[23] "I don't think you have to sweat this one all that much," he added, "and if we didn't get either of the books, I wouldn't lose all that much sleep anyway."[24] Porter's confidence in Wylie's work proved sound. *Beginnings: A Book for Widows* appeared in 1977 under McClelland and Stewart's imprint and was successful enough to warrant several reissues.

As writer Sylvia Fraser once commented, McClelland had "the forgiveness of the old sinner."[25] He was also "complex and contradictory"[26] – as Pratt would attest – and could be as demanding as he was supportive. As a result, the day-to-day relationship between McClelland and Porter was tumultuously productive. They were a creative team: allies who disagreed regularly and vociferously. Both had personal convictions and were unafraid to proffer criticism of the other. When, for example, Porter sought to curb McClelland's impulsive and extravagant nature and advised against rash decisions, he baulked at her attempts to control his behaviour. At times, the publisher lost patience with his protégée, who was a quick learner but whose occasional lapses were irksome. Nonetheless, McClelland came to rely heavily on Porter's diligence and obvious strengths, in particular her organizational and interpersonal skills.

In March 1971, to boost Porter's further development, McClelland recommended a salary increase to at least $15,000. Porter, who quickly learned that the publishing industry was – and remains – notorious for underpaying its employees, later quipped that the rate of her promotions at McClelland and Stewart far outpaced her salary increments.

Porter grew increasingly proficient and, within two years of her hiring, she had gained McClelland's full confidence. He described her as "mature ... [and] exceptionally valuable. She works very hard, is conscientious, but more important than anything else she knows what publishing is all about."[27]

By 1973, Porter had "mastered the ... business"[28] and had risen to the position of editorial director. That February, when McClelland asked if "one good editor [could] replace the work of 2 juniors," she provided a detailed analysis of the needs of her department and offered to "put a budget together fairly quickly."[29] Porter's answer was firm, however – "We have had a number of discussions on this point and I have made my opinion fairly clear. We publish too many books to be able to eliminate any one of the 'bodies' currently in the Editorial Department"[30] – precisely the sort of response one might expect from an editor who was initiated into Canadian publishing at McClelland and Stewart, under the inimitable stewardship of Jack McClelland. Porter had become a leader in her own right.

Five years later, in 1978, McClelland expressed his admiration for Porter in a characteristically frank letter: "you have more aptitude for the publishing field than anyone I have ever met and I think my opinion is corroborated by the respect in which you are held by so many authors and by so many international publishers."[31] Although he was not above teasing her – he regularly pointed to her native "Hungarian tendency to shade the truth a little when it's convenient" – McClelland valued Porter's directness and trusted her "good editorial gut instincts."[32]

For her part, Porter once joked that mastering the art of drinking vodka martinis had been a greater challenge than learning the intricacies of Canadian publishing. In truth, she was contented and stimulated at McClelland and Stewart, where her talents – identified by Sylvia Fraser as "a hard edge, determination and ability"[33] – were appreciated. Porter "loved the work" and felt "very lucky ... I worked night and day and would have worked an extra two or three hours a day, if there had been another two or three hours a day to give. Weekends didn't exist. I was just really excited about being there and working with the authors ... There was a sense of being able to influence the way things happened – to change them."[34] McClelland and Stewart was the ideal training ground for Porter, an exceptional editor whose efforts did indeed help "change" Canada's literary landscape.

Seal Books

In 1967, when she moved to London and first entered publishing, Porter joined a field historically dominated by men. On the surface, as she traversed the globe in pursuit of editorial opportunities, it might have appeared that she paid little heed to the gender inequity in publishing. That she was cognizant, however, of her gendered position in the highly competitive book trade may be gleaned from her early ambition, which led her first from Cassell to Collier Macmillan and from there to McClelland and Stewart, where she decided to carve a niche for herself in the Canadian company.

In fact, archival evidence suggests that Porter saw herself as part of a new generation of publishing women who were moving into senior editorial and executive positions. Of special interest is a newspaper article, which she clipped and saved, that described editors Betty Prashker and Patricia Soliman of the New York publishing company Coward, McCann and Geoghegan.[35] Prashker managed to have both a family and a career in publishing – she went on to become associate publisher and vice-president of Doubleday, and then vice-president and editor-in-chief of Crown Publishing – and Soliman rose to the position of president and publisher of Coward, McCann and Geoghegan, and later became associate publisher and vice-president of Simon and Schuster. Prashker and Soliman may have become role models for Porter, who sought similar opportunities in Toronto.

The path was especially difficult for a woman who wanted children. McClelland, for instance, was so worried when Porter married in 1972 that he gave her a wedding gift of two large brandy snifters: one filled with birth control pills, the other with condoms.[36] It was a stunt, but his message was clear: he did not want her to get pregnant and possibly leave her job. When she gave birth to her first child in 1973, McClelland arrived at the hospital with a boxful of manuscripts. Since she was "sitting there anyway," he asked, "why don't you read them?";[37] he could not fathom that she "might want some time off."[38] Porter returned to work just three weeks later. Often, she brought her daughter to the office and occasionally McClelland watched the baby while Porter was in meetings. Porter also worked in the evenings, after her daughter was asleep. In fact, during her tenure at McClelland and Stewart, almost all her publishing decisions were made "late at night."[39] Once she had a second child in 1977, life became even more complicated. She tried staying home full-time to look after her daughters, but soon grew bored. Porter was torn. She wanted time to raise her children – she enjoyed "motherhood, which came easily to me"[40] – but also longed for the excitement of publishing. Finally, at McClelland's urging, she accepted a promotion that seemed to offer a viable compromise and became president and editor-in-chief of Seal Books.

In 1977, in partnership with the New York–based company Bantam Books, McClelland and Stewart had launched Seal Books as a new mass-market subsidiary. In January 1979, the chance to head Seal Books appealed to Porter for two key reasons. First, it brought her new authority, since she represented 51 per cent of Seal Books under the joint banner of McClelland and Stewart and Bantam Books. Second, she acquired greater autonomy over her work schedule, which gave her flexibility to meet the competing demands of family and career.

Porter's "overwhelming memory" of the period when her daughters were young is one of "guilt"[41] for wanting a stimulating and challenging position. Other mothers wondered openly how she could leave her children while she worked, which only fuelled her self-reproach. Moreover, when her eldest child clung to her legs as she left the house each morning, she felt "selfish"; Porter had internalized an unfair set of expectations, resulting in an uneasy sense of "competition between my kids and my job."[42]

Over the course of her career, Porter worked alongside women who also became important figures in Canadian publishing. At McClelland and Stewart they included editors Linda McKnight, Lily Poritz Miller, and Ellen Seligman. Later, under her own direction, Key Porter Books employed several notable women, among them editors Phyllis Bruce, Clare McKeon, and Susan Renouf. Porter also counted prominent journalists and social activists

Doris Anderson and June Callwood as close friends. Despite these examples of successful professional women, she came to realize that she "could not have it all."[43] Although she believed women could balance "a career and a marriage," for Porter "the real issue was the conflict between work and motherhood."[44] In practice, she never resolved that conflict, but self-awareness proved invaluable as she consciously charted a career path that blended professional opportunity with time for family.

From her office on St Clair Avenue East, Porter managed Seal Books with her usual flair. She handled the budget, liaised with members of the board of directors, implemented plans for growth, and oversaw the prestigious Seal Books First Novel Award, valued at $50,000 Canadian. With the promise of hardcover publication by McClelland and Stewart in Canada, Little, Brown in the United States, and André Deutsch in the United Kingdom, the award elicited much new writing.[45]

But the position did not hold Porter's interest for long. By 1981, she was "bored witless" and no longer having "any real fun"[46] at Seal, which lost money "almost from the start."[47] As MacSkimming explains, Bantam retained "control over pricing, distribution, even cover design,"[48] and the American partner's service fees were taxing. Seal did not answer Porter's needs after all.

Restlessness drove her to explore new opportunities outside of McClelland and Stewart, the firm that had welcomed her in 1969 as an editor and where Porter had learned to navigate the exciting but treacherous terrain of Canadian publishing. In an attempt to forestall her departure and facilitate her desire "to get into full-scale book publishing in Canada," which he knew to be her "first love,"[49] McClelland tendered the unlikely offer to sell Porter his publishing company for the sum of 1 million dollars. Though she "like[d] pushing boulders uphill,"[50] Porter was not willing to assume the significant financial liabilities enumerated openly in McClelland's letter of offer. Neither further cajoling nor cautionary tales of publishing woe could alter Porter's growing certainty that she ought to strike out on her own. Finally, on 31 March 1982, she resigned from Seal Books and McClelland and Stewart.

In fact, McClelland's fervour had fired Porter's desire to start her own firm. She had succumbed to publishing's "addictive" appeal: work that was "fast-moving and demanding, where you're constantly dealing with myriad problems coming at you from all directions and averting any number of catastrophes in a single day."[51] On the "very sad occasion" of her departure from the company, McClelland acknowledged that Porter had "been absolutely fantastic. Your contribution as an active officer at M&S and then at Seal has been incredible."[52]

When she assumed the helm of Seal Books, Porter had also partnered with Michael de Pencier of Key Publishers[53] to form Key Porter Books. In doing so, she became the first woman to co-found a publishing company devoted to Canadian literary non-fiction. The decision to specialize in works of non-fiction served to differentiate Key Porter from McClelland and Stewart. Although McClelland regretted that the two firms were not associated, Porter would not risk alienating her closest colleague by treading on his commercial ground. Several months after leaving Seal, in the fall of 1982, she assumed the lead as publisher of Key Porter.

CBC producer Geraldine Sherman once ascribed Porter's work ethic to her "central European fatalism ... that disbelief in the continuity of good fortune. It makes her work hard and enjoy life enormously."[54] But Porter's drive was also boosted by McClelland, whose nationalist vision and passion for publishing she embraced as her own.

Authors' Advocate

Porter formed the belief that "writers are extraordinary people"[55] at McClelland and Stewart, where she worked closely and effectively with Canadian authors. There she also learned that "without authors, there would not be a book business. If you are in the shoe business, you don't have to worry too much about individuals. But in this industry, you are as good as the books you publish, and that means the authors."[56] Thus, Porter's open defence of poet Earle Birney and prose writer Farley Mowat, as well as her endorsement of individual writers such as Margaret Laurence, Allan Fotheringham, and Sylvia Fraser, stemmed from both admiration and economic necessity.

Porter's outsider status – she was born in Budapest in 1943, escaped the Hungarian Revolution in 1956 by immigrating with her divorced mother to New Zealand, worked in London and New York in 1967, and travelled to Peru prior to settling in Toronto in 1968 – gave her a unique perspective on Canadian literature. Porter responded to the writing of Canada as anything but parochial or dull. As a woman who initially felt "out of sync with the world around [her] ... a stranger ... [who sought] ways to fit in,"[57] she was excited by the literature she read as part of her immersion in Canadian culture. At the same time, having been raised within a strong-minded, literary family and mentored by self-proclaimed nationalist Jack McClelland, Porter felt confident in her own judgment and in her high opinion of Canadian writers.

Porter's vocal support for Canadian authors – a by-product of her wish to see them achieve recognition in their own country – was balanced by her capacity to forge interpersonal relationships, which meant that she was charged with handling McClelland and Stewart's most troublesome writers. Hence, it was by design that she came to work closely with poet Earle Birney, one of the more captious writers on McClelland and Stewart's list.

In a series of aggressive letters, the poet complained bitterly about the terms of his publishing contracts, delayed page proofs, and the publicizing of his books.[58] Birney also nursed his anger over two errors: the faulty insertion of three lines in "Maritime Faces" when it appeared in his *Selected Poems 1940–1966* (1966) and the misattribution of lines quoted from his poem "Arrivals" in a 1971 pictorial calendar produced by McClelland and Stewart.

Porter served as intermediary between Birney and McClelland, whose conflicting points of view regularly threatened to dissolve their long association. To McClelland, Birney was a "pain in the ass"[59] who wasted much of Porter's time. With Porter, however, Birney was polite and amenable; he was also one of her greatest admirers. Through skilful peacemaking, Porter calmed poet and publisher alike.

Porter remained connected to Birney until his death in 1995, when she was moved to defend him in the pages of the *Toronto Star*. An obituary by Philip Marchand, which disparaged Birney as a minor poet who "enjoyed life too much to devote himself wholeheartedly to his chosen art,"[60] so puzzled Porter that she wrote a corrective letter to the editor of the newspaper. Porter chastised Marchand for suggesting that major poets were only "those who sacrificed everything – even possibly their sex lives – in pursuit of the Muse."[61] The rebuke was her final show of support for Birney and an example of her willingness to publicly vindicate Canadian writers.

Her early relationship with the "feisty and combative"[62] Farley Mowat grew into one of the more meaningful connections, and one of the most public, of Porter's career. Soon after she arrived at McClelland and Stewart, Porter was introduced to Mowat via his manuscript *Sibir: My Discovery of Siberia* (1970), which described the author's travels in the Soviet Union during the Cold War. At first, they did not see eye to eye: "He was as much in love with Russians as I was terrified of their brutality. I was a survivor of the 1956 Hungarian Revolution, he of the Second World War, when the Russians were allies."[63] Not surprisingly, Porter and Mowat "fought and argued, yelled at and harangued each other,"[64] and eventually "retired into sullen silence."[65] The silence did not last, however; they soon put aside their differences and continued to work together as editor and author.

Porter came to appreciate Mowat as "the quintessential storyteller"[66] who loved to entertain his readers. She counted herself among his fans and formed a warm alliance with the writer. Moreover, in 1987, two years after Jack McClelland sold his firm to Avie Bennett and retired from publishing, Mowat left McClelland and Stewart and joined Key Porter Books out of regard for Porter. As his publisher, Porter grew even closer to Mowat; he was a prominent author on Key Porter's list, which also included the work of his wife, Claire Mowat.

In 1996, the year after she publicly chided Philip Marchand for his unflattering assessment of Birney, Porter found herself backing Mowat in a clash with freelance journalist John Goddard. Goddard's scathing cover article in the May 1996 issue of *Saturday*

Night – accompanied by an image of Mowat with an elongated Pinocchio nose – exposed inconsistencies in Mowat's *People of the Deer* (1952), *The Desperate People* (1959), and *Never Cry Wolf* (1963), and accused the author of misrepresenting the federal government's role in the famine among Keewatin Caribou Inuit in the late 1940s and in the management of the wolf population in the North.[67] When Porter learned of Goddard's impending attack on Mowat, she jokingly threatened *Saturday Night* editor Kenneth Whyte: were he to publish "'anything nasty about Farley' she would call in her husband, libel lawyer Julian Porter."[68] Given her public profile, the comment circulated widely in the media and brought nearly as much attention to Porter as Goddard's article did to Mowat, but the clamour served only to solidify their bond and intensify Porter's affection for Mowat.[69]

When Porter retired from publishing, Mowat claimed it was his doing: "I wore her out!" he declared.[70] Yet it was the opposite. In looking back, Porter was proud "to have a chance ... to say, 'Well, I haven't done much, but I have worked with Farley Mowat,' that's a great thing. If that's all that goes on my tombstone, I haven't done badly."[71]

In fact, Porter never missed a chance to defend Canadian authors. At a private cocktail party in Vancouver, for instance, when she heard a woman say "that Canada [had] produced no writers of international quality," Porter was "outraged" and "yelled at her ... [that] she wouldn't know quality if she tripped over it."[72] In May 1980, during the National Book Festival, a weeklong public celebration held at Toronto's Harbourfront Centre, she declared novelist Margaret Laurence a hero – as editor at McClelland and Stewart, Porter had worked with Laurence – and claimed that Canada needed more such leaders.

The same assertiveness led her to pursue journalist Allan Fotheringham for Key Porter Books. In 1982, within two years of having first approached Fotheringham through a terse letter that read, "Dear Mr. Fotheringham. I think you have a book in you. Next time in Toronto, call me for lunch. Anna Porter,"[73] she had published *Malice in Blunderland, or, How the Grits Stole Christmas*, Key Porter's first best-selling title and the first of Fotheringham's six books to be issued by the press.[74]

Porter's investment in Sylvia Fraser's *The Book of Strange*, first published by Doubleday Canada in 1992, demonstrated her passion for Canadian writers and her zeal for publishing. A fierce tenacity propelled her efforts to expand into the American market with Fraser's book. First, she purchased separate American rights to the work and gave it a new title, *The Quest for the Fourth Monkey: A Thinker's Guide to the Psychic and Spiritual Revolution*. She then hired a New York firm to publicize the book and made it the focal point of Key Porter's exhibit at the American Booksellers Association annual convention (now BookExpo). Finally, she claimed to have spent $20,000 promoting the first printing: a quality paperback of 15,000 copies, issued by Key Porter Books in 1994. That *Toronto Star* columnist Beverley Slopen was authorized to report on this extraordinary push to break into the American market is a prime example of Porter's audacity and desire to be seen publicly as an advocate for Canadian writers.[75]

Public Advocacy

Porter also campaigned on behalf of the wider publishing community. Soon after joining McClelland and Stewart, she learned how much domestic publishers were hindered in their attempts to make Canadian books available to a national readership. The key difficulties they faced – a relatively small population dispersed over a vast country, the high cost of manufacturing and distributing books in Canada, and the behemoth south of the border that easily infiltrated the local market for English-language books – were new to Porter. She was moved to address the systemic inequity – linked to historically weak copyright protection for Canadian publications – plaguing the local publishing industry.

Out of a belief in publishing as an essential cultural enterprise whose products reflected a country back to its citizens – she learned this from her maternal grandfather Vili Rácz, a magazine publisher in Budapest who was jailed as a dissident during the Hungarian Revolution[76] – Porter openly defended the efforts of Canadian publishers.

She was deeply troubled by shrinking government support for publishing. In July 1996, for example, in response to the bankruptcy and closure of Coach House Press, one of the country's premier small presses, often cited for launching the literary career of Michael Ondaatje, Porter insisted that Canadian publishing was "facing a major crisis."[77] The closure was precipitated by Ontario government cutbacks, which resulted in a 74 per cent reduction in funding to Coach House and severe losses to other publishing houses. Key Porter, for one, was forced to cancel its fall fiction list.[78]

Porter accepted some responsibility for the lack of understanding that led to the drastic cuts. She admitted, for instance, that domestic publishers had "done a really crappy job of explaining how this industry works ... and what government funding and policy has accomplished [for publishers and readers] in this country."[79] Regardless, she argued that publishing, which produced the historical and intellectual record of the country, ought to benefit from the same kind of subsidies or "regulatory schemes" that ensured the profitability and longevity of "the oil and cable industries,"[80] for example.

Although Porter was familiar with the economic challenge of making books in an inhospitable domestic environment, amid an ever-increasing threat of foreign takeover, it was Jack McClelland's struggles to sustain his firm that best exemplified to her the difficulties facing all Canadian publishers. Publicly, she lauded McClelland's "patience" and "endurance,"[81] which she put on view in *Imagining Canadian Literature*, a selection of Jack McClelland's letters edited by Sam Solecki and published by Key Porter Books in 1998 as a testimonial to the publisher's genius and tenacity.

Diminishing government investment and the foreign acquisition of Canadian publishing companies continued to rankle Porter, whose knowing voice dominated the media, even after she sold Key Porter Books and retired from publishing in 2005.[82] In a 2011 *Globe and Mail* article, for instance, she asked pointedly: "How did people get the [false] idea that there are electrified fences against foreign investment in Canadian literature?"[83] Porter openly decried the presence of foreign-owned publishers in Canada and saw clearly that it was nothing less than "our future as a distinct cultural entity"[84] that was at stake if further foreign investment was permitted. The rise of international publishing conglomerates and recent amalgamations, such as Penguin Random House Canada (in 2012), confirms her belief that Canadian publishing and literary culture remain exceedingly vulnerable.

World conflict has also elicited an urgent response from Porter, whose foundational belief in the right of individuals to live free of discrimination and fervent attachment to democratic values grew out of her own experience as a youth in Hungary during the tumultuous postwar period and the knowledge she later acquired about the fate of Hungarian Jews during the Second World War.

As a young activist, for example, Porter tried to enlist in the Israeli army at the start of the Six-Day War in 1967, but was rebuffed.[85] In April 2002 – by then she was more realistic but no less resolute – Porter took part in a protest outside the French consulate in Toronto denouncing a series of recent attacks against Jews in France. As a writer, she has not hesitated to take up her pen to denounce anti-Semitism. Along with journalist Arlene Perly Rae and writer/broadcaster Irshad Manji, she wrote a *Toronto Star* opinion piece titled "A Call to Arms on Anti-Semitism," which exhorted Canada to sponsor a 2004 United Nations resolution condemning "a centuries-old racism directed against Jews."[86] Sponsorship would reinforce Porter's idea of Canada based on its "diversity, our embrace of universal human rights and our determination to combat racism of all kinds."[87]

For Porter, publishing was her way of serving the country and writing continues to be her way of reaching readers. Since 2002, in the pages of *Maclean's*, the *Globe and Mail*, and the *Toronto Star*, she has published articles and book reviews that deal especially with events arising in Israel and Central Europe, which she generally reads through the lens of a question that preoccupies her mind: "What does a moral person do when faced with injustice?"[88] She has probed the Israeli-Palestinian conflict; political instability in Chechnya, Georgia, Germany, and Poland; and human rights offences against the Roma in the Czech Republic and Hungary, as well as in Canada.

Porter's books extend her journalism and look deep into the historic events etched into her consciousness. They also reflect a desire to unearth the valiant individuals – like her publisher grandfather Vili Rácz, who once gave refuge to persecuted Jews – whose actions have a positive shaping influence during turbulent times. *Kasztner's Train: The True Story of Rezso Kasztner, Unknown Hero of the Holocaust* (2007), for example, uses interviews with survivors to tell the full story of Hungarian-Jewish lawyer Rezsö Kasztner (also known as Rudolf Kastner), who saved the lives of more than 1,600 Jews during the Second World War.

The legacy of the Holocaust fuels *The Ghosts of Europe: Journeys through Central Europe's Troubled Past and Uncertain Future* (2010), which also relies on interviews – with writer and former Czech president Václav Havel, Hungarian writer György Konrád (also known as George Konrad), and Polish journalist and former dissident Adam Michnik, among others – in its analysis of the changed politics and culture of Central Europe. As Porter once explained: "coming from a country where freedom of speech was a serious problem and writers tended to be imprisoned ... I have always valued the freedom to ask writers, 'what is on your mind,' even if it's critical of ... government."[89]

That Porter is also outspoken on the issue of freedom of speech is not surprising for a writer so invested in exposing historical wrongs and political corruption. Thus, in 2011 she felt impelled to publish a *Maclean's* exposé on Hungary's new media legislation.[90] Porter objected to the power given to a media council, wholly made up of members of the ruling party, that had the authority to judge compliance with rules, renew or refuse licences, and levy fines of up to $950,000. For Porter, the heightened restrictions and surveillance brought back the ignominy felt by her grandfather under an earlier regime of control, when he was a publisher of magazines in the interwar period.

Through her work with a number of cultural agencies, Porter has demonstrated her lifelong commitment to the advancement of reading, writing, and freedom of expression. She has served on the board of directors of the Canada Council for the Arts and PEN Canada,[91] national organizations that support artistic work, advocate on behalf of writers, and promote the vital importance of art to the culture and economy of Canada, as well as countries worldwide. Currently, she is a member of the advisory council of CODE, the Canadian Organization for Development through Education, which supports literacy in Canada and around the globe. She serves on the Toronto Public Library Foundation governor's council, a group of ambassadors for and advisers to the TPL, and on the board of directors of Word on the Street, an annual literary event in Toronto. In addition, she has juried the Scotiabank Giller Prize (in 2012), the British Columbia National Award for Canadian Non-Fiction (in 2014), and the National Business Book Award (since 2015).

Porter's knowledge and expertise in the field of culture have been of particular value to government. Her experience in publishing led to her chairing a special working group on Canadian content and culture as part of the federal government's 1995 Information Highway Advisory Council. The group concluded that "government must act to ensure that when we look into the electronic mirror, we see a Canadian face,"[92] and made twenty key recommendations. Among the more far-sighted were the need to retain a policy of protection for Canadian culture in relation to emerging technologies and to digitize the contents of libraries, archives, and public art galleries to ensure broad access to all collections.

In 2003, Prime Minister Jean Chrétien's Task Force on Women Entrepreneurs solicited input from Porter.[93] Pleased to offer her view of conditions affecting businesswomen in Canada, Porter was characteristically frank and cogent in outlining several issues for consideration. She knew, for instance, that "the single greatest challenge" facing women entrepreneurs was securing investment funding: "My own experiences with banking have been horrendous, somewhat exacerbated by the fact that banks are allergic to the publishing business as well as to dealing with women entrepreneurs."[94] From her perspective, the lack of financing also prevented women entrepreneurs from either innovating or expanding their businesses. That "male customers view women in business as, at best, an anomaly"[95] was an additional hurdle. As these comments reveal, Porter was always cognizant of the presence of gender bias in the business sphere. What they further show is the clear thinking and bold determination that helped mitigate the effect of such bias on her publishing career.

In retrospect, Porter's personal decision in 1969 to join McClelland and Stewart had broader implications, for it signalled the undeniable rise of women as career professionals in Canadian trade publishing. Two such women were Louise Dennys and Cynthia Good, who, like Porter, also started off as editors. All three went on to achieve prominence as publishers, at Lester and Orpen Dennys (now at Penguin Random House Canada), Penguin Books Canada, and Key Porter Books, respectively.

Porter has been recognized for her early vision and subsequent accomplishment. For "bringing Canadian titles to the attention of the international market place" she was invested as an Officer of the Order of Canada in 1992. She received the Order of Ontario in 2003. And for laying "the foundations of the Canadian publishing industry, from the 1960s to 1985," she was one of twelve pioneering women to accept the Association of Canadian Publishers President's Award in 2011.[96]

As these honours attest, Porter has brought positive change to Canada's cultural sphere. She did so purposefully: by editing and publishing this country's writers; by advancing the cause of Canadian publishing; by fighting ongoing discrimination and exposing racist practices through her writing; and by defending free speech through PEN and other artistic organizations. For half a century, Anna Porter has made it her business to speak out on behalf of culture in Canada and democratic rights worldwide.

chapter seven

The "Grande Dame" of Literary Agents: Bella Pomer

A clear path leads from Sybil Hutchinson, who helped James Reaney achieve considerable fame, to Bella Pomer (1926–), a similarly enterprising literary agent who eventually saw her most prominent client, Carol Shields, win international acclaim.

In 1978, following seven years as subsidiary rights manager for the Macmillan Company of Canada, Pomer left her secure position and established the Bella Pomer Literary Agency. At the time, there were few literary agents in Canada, but Pomer was undaunted by the prospect of entering a burgeoning field that soon was dominated by a cluster of women based in Toronto. Along with Nancy Colbert, Beverley Slopen, and Lucinda Vardey, who also formed agencies in the 1970s, Pomer spearheaded a business model for agency work in this country.

Pomer's competence and knowledge of the publishing business earned her a reputation as a straightforward and resolute agent. Over the course of her career, she helped consolidate the role of the professional literary agent in Canada by mediating with editors and publishers and effecting significant improvement in conditions for authors. She fought to place the work of Canadian writers with domestic and international publishers, negotiated improved publishing contracts and royalty advances, and promoted Canadian authors at home and around the globe.

Macmillan Company of Canada

Bella Pomer's career ambitions grew out of a love of books. As a child, she was an avid reader – the library was a second home and her "window on the world."[1] Every two days, from the age of nine to twelve, she borrowed books from her local branch of the Toronto Public Library, located at the corner of Queen and Lisgar Streets. She also attended the Saturday morning story hour at the Boys and Girls House on College Street (now the Lillian H. Smith branch of the Toronto Public Library).

At the Boys and Girls House, Pomer (née Lieberman) came under the formative influence of popular storyteller and librarian Alice Kane. Kane "specialized in singling out children in need of special attention" and Pomer "was taken under Kane's wing after returning a book her puppy had chewed up."[2] Kane took Pomer "to her heart," as she did "with children ... generation after generation";[3] she guided Pomer's reading and gave her roles in dramatizations of fairy tales. Soon, Pomer formed a "very happy relationship with the remarkable librarian."[4]

After graduating from Parkdale Collegiate Institute, Pomer studied English for two years at the University of Toronto, but left in 1945 to marry clothing importer Harold Pomer. While raising their daughters full-time, she wrote the odd film review and kept an index for the *Canadian Forum*.

Gradually, she became more publicly engaged and by 1971 Pomer was a member of the advisory board of the Canadian Writers' Guild, a precursor to the Writers' Union of Canada (founded in 1973). On behalf of the guild, she attended the Ontario Royal Commission on Book Publishing – the same commission that heard Eleanor Harman's brief on the challenges facing scholarly publishers in the province. Pomer had her own suggestion for the commission. She "proposed a special tax on books not produced in Canada of ... a few cents a book. Part of the funds [collected] ... could then be used to promote Canadian talent."[5] Pomer's nascent desire to assist Canadian writers hinted at her future as a literary agent.

Pomer's attendance at the commission proved fortuitous. In the audience on 16 April 1971 was Hugh Kane, Alice Kane's brother, who was then president of the Macmillan Company of Canada – in 1969, Kane had left McCelland and Stewart to head Macmillan. As a youth, Pomer had met Hugh Kane at library events, where he often helped Alice Kane, and over the years she had maintained contact with both brother and sister. In the spring of 1971, at the time of the commission, Pomer was looking for a job; her daughters were teenagers and she had more free time. She broached the subject with Hugh Kane, who promptly invited her to lunch and asked if she would like to handle subsidiary rights for Macmillan. Pomer gladly accepted his offer of a part-time position, to begin in the fall of 1971.

In 1971, Kane's firm was struggling financially. The recent cancellation of provincial textbook grants and the deregulation of approved titles for Ontario classrooms meant that Macmillan, much like Clarke, Irwin, received far fewer contracts to publish textbooks, formerly the source of substantial revenue that helped bolster the company and sustain its trade publishing programs.

Kane sought wider distribution for Macmillan's titles as a means of increasing the company's profits, but he faced a serious hurdle. World rights were still outside the reach of Canadian publishers. In fact, for much of the twentieth century, the American and British publishers who held sway over English-language publishing worldwide regularly demanded North American and world rights, and "typically viewed Canada's market as part of their own."[6] Thus, as Jessica Potter and James H. Marsh explain, domestic publishers could not "secure profits from subsidiary rights, and were, in effect, forced to operate only inside Canada,"[7] always a relatively small market.

Although she was hired to expand Macmillan's market, Pomer was doubly disadvantaged: she knew little about Canadian publishing and even less about the uncharted terrain of subsidiary rights. To "get her bearings"[8] and learn the trade, she "read every issue of *Publishers Weekly* from cover to cover" and it remained her "Bible"[9] throughout her career. She also had the much-needed support of Hugh Kane, who sent her to New York to meet with publishers, editors, and executives of the Book-of-the-Month

Club and *Reader's Digest*. Soon, Pomer acquired the knowledge and the connections necessary to negotiate international rights. Macmillan's "gentlemanly"[10] approach to these transactions – the company claimed just 10 per cent of the income from the rights it controlled – also eased her way.

As she worked to place Macmillan titles with publishers in the U.S. and the U.K., and to sell paperback rights and secure translation rights, Pomer's part-time position grew into a full-time job. Her first five years at Macmillan were "wonderful"; by 1976, however, she was less "eager to get down there in the morning, not wanting to go in to the office."[11] Maclean Hunter had purchased the company three years earlier and the culture of Macmillan gradually had shifted away from literary titles to commercial books. Moreover, under the new president, George Gilmour, Pomer was regarded as a "junior"[12] member of the firm. There were no prospects for advancement, no opportunities to take courses to boost her learning.

Pomer grew increasingly dissatisfied and eventually felt blocked. When her husband finally suggested that she leave her position in the fall of 1978 to start her own agency, she leapt at the chance. She had, in effect, "learned to be an agent"[13] by managing subsidiary rights for Macmillan.

The Role of an Agent

Unlike Sybil Hutchinson, who conducted her agency from home while she was a full-time editor at the Book Society, Pomer was a career agent and one of the first to devote herself to such work. Pomer was like most literary agents, George Fetherling explains, "veterans of major publishing houses – usually of the firms' marketing arms though sometimes of editorial departments."[14] She set up her agency at a time when writing and publishing in Canada were expanding. Pomer saw opportunity in the growing interest in Canadian authors, both locally and globally, and seized the occasion to capitalize on that curiosity. Her efforts to broaden markets for Canadian writers, grow their readership, and strengthen their earnings proved beneficial to her clients and her agency alike.

As Mary Ann Gillies shows in *The Professional Literary Agent in Britain, 1880–1920*, the emergence of the literary agent wrought significant and irrevocable changes in the publishing industry. Agents brought a new professionalism to the business of authorship that changed author-publisher relationships. By the 1920s and 1930s in Britain and the United States, literary agents – who "were almost always men" – had "prompted a radical shift in the balance of power in publishing."[15] As influential middlemen, agents effectively "destabilized the author-publisher dyad"; they "undermined publishers' traditionally dominant position by forcing them to expose their activities to [the] public scrutiny ... of authors and agents. They [also] helped authors empower themselves – by assisting them in their fights for better financial terms and more control over their literary property."[16]

The literary agent was slower to emerge in Canada, where, as Lorraine York explains, "professionalization of the writing life"[17] came late, hindered by a comparatively small market and the unavailability of subsidiary rights. Although Hutchinson and Molinaro established the first successful commercial literary agency in 1950, it was not until the 1970s that agents began to increase in number. These agents, as Frank Davey points out, "helped to internationalize Canadian writing, it being more lucrative for both writer and agent to place a manuscript first with an American publisher, and to split off the Canadian rights for separate sale and thus better domestic royalties."[18] Very soon, agents' efforts to secure improved publishing contracts helped transform publishing practice and the culture of authorship in Canada.

The rise of Canadian agents, Lecker notes (citing Paul Litt's summary in volume 3 of *History of the Book in Canada*), owes much to the "mini-explosion in Canadian book publishing during the 1970s and 1980s" that followed the Massey Commission, which reported on the state of Canadian culture in 1951, and the creation of the Canada Council for the Arts in 1957. The founding of several publishing houses that came of new federal funding was a great boon to authors. The expansion of publishing companies also fostered a more competitive industry. In this new "highly commercialized environment," agents "played a key role in promoting and protecting writers' interests."[19]

Most of Canada's first agents were women, an indication of their wider participation in the general workforce by the later decades of the twentieth century and their heightened presence in the book trade in particular. Collectively, the entrepreneurial women who established literary agencies in Toronto faced the challenge of carving a niche for themselves within the domain of publishing. Individually, each embraced the chance to operate independently and to represent her own clients. Although annual earnings fluctuated, professional autonomy and absorbing work offered great recompense.

The New York–based agent Joseph Regal once defined his role as "one-third lawyer, one-third editor, and one-third schmoozer, with a little bit of psychologist thrown in."[20] The Bella Pomer papers, held at the University of Toronto's Thomas Fisher Rare Book Library, corroborate Regal's description of the multifaceted agent. Like Regal and other literary agents who undertook a broad range of activities on behalf of their clients, Pomer occupied the complex position of an intermediary figure who dealt in books as cultural products and sought financial gain from those same products. Thus, to adopt York's view of the successful agent, she was at once a "literary" and a "business" person[21] – a professional with an aesthetic appreciation for the books she marketed.

A consideration of literary agents' activities shows the degree to which their work straddles the cultural and economic spheres. Surprisingly, York confirms, the "variegated nature"[22] of agency work has changed little over time. Remarkable continuity exists "between what literary agents do today and what they did a century ago, notwithstanding the tremendous changes in the communications technologies they rely on to conduct their day-to-day business."[23] Based on their wide knowledge of the publishing industry, agents match manuscripts with editors and publishers; negotiate advantageous contracts; and oversee the production process, from submission to publication of a manuscript. They provide short- and long-term advice to authors; handle sales of serial, foreign, and translation rights; and manage finances by collecting statements, maintaining records, distributing royalty payments, and deducting their own fees.[24] Often, they offer editorial advice.

Agents also function interpersonally by safeguarding authors' privacy, shielding them from distractions and intrusions, and by extending emotional support – functions that go beyond most standard literary and business relationships and mark the uniqueness of the agent-author association. York notes that personal relationships are, in fact, "fundamental to the profession."[25] Indeed, the most successful agent-author tie is based on a sense of connection that forms early and is sustained over time, often developing into what is commonly understood to be friendship. Thus, the agent-author relation is nuanced, a potentially strong "amalgamation of friendly advocacy and promotion of business interests."[26]

Despite the influence of literary agents on shifts and developments in Canadian publishing practice, scholarship has paid scant attention to their intermediary function in the literary marketplace and has focused instead on foreign representation of Canadian authors. Clarence Karr's publishing study of early Canadian fiction writers, for example, discusses the role of agents, such as New York–based Paul Reynolds, in furthering the career of Arthur Stringer. Misao Dean and Linda M. Morra, respectively, examine Sara Jeannette Duncan's affiliation with the renowned British agency A.P. Watt and Company, and Jane Rule's disagreements with two of her New York–based agents, Willis Kingsley Wing and Kurt Hellmer. JoAnn McCaig's *Reading in Alice Munro's Archives* and Lorraine York's *Margaret Atwood and the Labour of Literary Celebrity* each probe the productive connection between a writer and her literary agent: Munro's association with New York–based Virginia Barber and Atwood's alliance with California-based Phoebe Larmore, as well as a number of other agents.[27] The fact that York opens her pioneering study of Atwood's celebrity authorship with a chapter on the writer's professional relationships with her agents signals their foundational role in literary production.

Pomer was herself a pivotal figure. She understood the interdependence of agent and author, and knew that her success hinged on the gains she achieved for her clients. Thus, as she carefully guided the career trajectories of others, she deliberately charted her own rise as a professional agent.

Bella Pomer Literary Agency

Gillies describes two ways in which British agent A.P. Watt established a "public persona" – his "most important public relations job"[28] – when he was starting out in the 1870s. First, he created "a public presence in the publishing world, getting his name known among the editors and publishers who made the decisions about what would appear in print."[29] Second, he reached "beyond the circle of writers he knew from his own business and social life ... to attract a large enough pool of author-clients to place his agenting business on firm financial ground."[30]

A century later, when Pomer set up a home office on Shallmar Boulevard in mid-town Toronto – she moved to St Clair Avenue West in 2005 – she was cognizant of the same need to build a reputation as an essential member of a publishing community that had yet to recognize literary agents. Like Watt and other agents who followed his lead, she placed advertisements to promote her services and woo new clients. To broaden her professional reach – through her work at Macmillan, she already knew many editors and publishers in Canada and the United States – she joined the Book Publishers' Professional Association and the Independent Literary Agents Association. She also attracted a small circle of Macmillan authors – Constance Beresford-Howe, Pauline Gedge, and Ken Mitchell – as her first clients; since the company no longer employed someone to handle subsidiary rights, they sought Pomer's representation.

These small beginnings in 1978 laid the foundation for Pomer's agency and, within two years, skill and drive led to her first international success.[31] In 1980, she placed Pauline Gedge's historical novel *Child of the Morning* (published by the Macmillan Company of Canada in 1977) with Balland, a small Paris publisher. Although it won Alberta's Search-for-a-New-Novelist competition, the work had had little success in Canada. French readers, however, were entranced by Gedge's tale of Hatshepsut, one of Egypt's two female pharaohs, and the novel quickly became a bestseller in France.

As Pomer once recalled, Gedge's novels were "totally popular in France, Germany, and Spain right from the start."[32] Gedge went on to become a commercial success, netting the bulk of her income from "international sales."[33] In fact, from 1980 onward, she was Pomer's "steadiest earner,"[34] which served author and agent alike. Gedge could devote herself to writing full-time, while Pomer acquired credibility and a financial base for her agency.[35] Of all her clients Pomer grew closest to Gedge, forming a partnership founded on their shared first triumph as agent and author.

Pomer had another early success with H.R. Percy's second novel, *Painted Ladies*. By the time Percy contacted Pomer, the work had been "shelved for almost a year."[36] The agent read it, "thought it was wonderful," and believed "Lester & Orpen Dennys would be the perfect publisher. The first reader of *Painted Ladies* [indeed] reported that it was the best manuscript she'd seen in years. The rest, as they say, is history."[37] History was kind to Percy, whose *Painted Ladies* – no longer an abandoned manuscript – "took off."[38] It was short-listed for the Governor General's Literary Award in 1983, proving Pomer both an excellent judge of fiction and a sharp literary agent.

Pomer's auspicious placement of *Child of the Morning* and *Painted Ladies* set the stage for incremental success. She felt "charged" and decided to push hard with "literary writers."[39] Since she always appreciated literary fiction, Pomer was pleased to represent Matt Cohen, Jack Hodgins, and Carol Shields, who were among her long-standing clients.

By representing literary authors, Pomer acquired significant "symbolic capital" – to invoke Pierre Bourdieu's conceptual understanding of "a reputation for competence and an image of respectability and honourability"[40] – among writers, publishers, editors, and other agents. With the exception of Shields, these writers did not markedly boost Pomer's income, but they did provide prestige and respect – benefits that were not lost on the strategic agent who successfully negotiated the cultural and economic hierarchies of the writing and publishing worlds.

Figure 7. Bella Pomer, March 1982

Matt Cohen

Matt Cohen sought Bella Pomer's help in expanding his international readership, and so she set out to try to place his fiction in the United States and Britain. When her valiant efforts did not produce the desired results, agent and author were both disappointed. Regardless, their relationship was always professional, occasionally playful, and never dishonest. It showcased Pomer's advocacy, persistence, and firm belief in Cohen's writing. It also revealed her integrity and the challenges she faced when a valued author – who could not know the many ways in which she campaigned on his behalf – did not feel adequately supported by his agent.

Matt Cohen signed on with Pomer's agency in 1987. Author and agent were in regular communication via mail, as well as telephone; since Cohen lived in mid-town Toronto, he could telephone his agent at will without incurring long-distance charges.

Pomer soon proved her mettle with Cohen's novel *Emotional Arithmetic*. In October 1989, she received two bids to issue the work, one from Anna Porter at Seal Books (in 1987, when he retired from publishing, Jack McClelland had sold his 75 per cent interest in Seal to Key Porter Books) and another from Louise Dennys at Lester and Orpen Dennys. She accepted Dennys's offer and, one year later, when Lester and Orpen Dennys brought out *Emotional Arithmetic*, the agent celebrated the book's publication. She was also proud to have placed the novel with a press known for its "respected list with nothing substandard on it – they are like Knopf or Farrar [Straus and Giroux in the U.S.]."[41]

Having secured Canadian publication by a highly reputable publisher, Pomer sought similar publication in the United States. Between October 1989 and September 1991, she submitted *Emotional Arithmetic* to no fewer than thirty-three American publishing companies without success.

Pomer did not take rejection lightly. She kept circulating Cohen's novel, and mounted a campaign of resistance. A strongly worded letter to Nan Talese, senior vice-president of Doubleday who criticized *Emotional Arithmetic*, showed Pomer as Cohen's staunch ally:

> It certainly startled me to find you commenting so negatively on Matt's writing. The few U.S. editors who have seen EMOTIONAL ARITHMETIC have declined it because they prefer plot-driven novels, or because they were simply not carried away by this novel. Each has, however, had high praise for the quality of the writing ...
>
> It would be a dull world if we all liked the same writers, and heaven knows this is a subjective business we are in, but the words "the writing is not up to what I expect" are not what I expect to hear in a decline for a writer such as Matt Cohen.[42]

In defending her client, Pomer championed Cohen's novel, as well as his reputation as a writer of "quality" fiction. Moreover, by suggesting that authors "such as Matt Cohen" deserved careful consideration and should not be dismissed lightly, Pomer was affirming the cultural value of Cohen's serious fiction – a notion that underwrote her firm response to Talese, as well as her continued efforts to place Cohen's work.

Pomer's persistence finally resulted in an offer to publish *Emotional Arithmetic* from St Martin's Press in New York. When that offer was subsequently withdrawn, agent and author were frustrated. Later, they were mollified when St Martin's issued an American edition of the novel in 1995.

By 1997, Pomer had grown despondent over her inability to place Cohen's fiction in Britain. When editor Penelope Hoare of the London publishing house Sinclair-Stevenson rejected Cohen's novel *Last Seen*, published by Knopf Canada in 1996, Pomer did not hold back: "You cannot imagine how disappointed I was to receive ... your decline of ... LAST SEEN. It makes one despair, really, when one hears, 'I love this novel, and so do all the other people who have read it' ... [I]f you cannot find a way to publish a book you love I don't know what the answers are!"[43] Pomer was forced to concede that British publishers did not see Cohen's fiction as "marketable" – they appeared to favour "brand new writers, preferably young, without hampering track records of low sales."[44]

Pomer may have been discouraged by the lack of international interest in Cohen's writing, but she was not defeated. The challenge only drove her to strike harder in the Canadian market, as was the case in 1999, when she tried to negotiate the simultaneous publication of the novel *Elizabeth and After* and the short story collection *Getting Lucky*. Louise Dennys, who had joined Knopf Canada as publisher in 1991, was interested in both titles, but unsure about releasing the two books in one year. Finally, Pomer and Dennys found "a way to work this out":[45] Knopf Canada issued *Elizabeth and After* in 1999 – the novel won the Governor General's Literary Award for fiction – and *Getting Lucky* in 2000.

Their joint professional concerns may have been serious, but Cohen and Pomer also shared lighthearted exchanges. Teddy Jam,

Cohen's alter ego and the pseudonym under which he published ten children's books, brought out Pomer's playful side. Since Teddy Jam's true identity was not known publicly – it was only revealed after Cohen's death – Pomer was sworn to secrecy and she faithfully maintained the deception. As H.J. Kirchhoff quipped in the *Globe and Mail*, "nobody knows who he really is except his agent, Bella Pomer, and she's not telling."[46]

In a letter to Cohen, Pomer counselled Teddy Jam, who was thinking of writing a mystery: "detective fiction with a hook of locale, ethnicity, an inside look at a profession or unknown 'world' ... stands the best chance ... He should not, however, expect to make a fortune."[47] She went on to ask, "Who will Teddy's sleuth be? If he wants to take a crack at it to amuse himself (though heaven knows, he's got plenty to do!) I certainly consider myself expert enough in this genre ... to be able to let him know if his series is going to work, but he'll have to write one first, and believe it or not, a good mystery isn't all that easy to toss off!"[48] Pomer's expertise came from representing a number of mystery writers, including Lyn Hamilton, Medora Sale, and Eric Wright.

When Teddy Jam declined her offer of assistance, Pomer asked Cohen to convey a message: "Please tell Teddy I'm rather hurt that he should feel so shy with me after all this time. Makes me feel like an object instead of a person. But I'll do my best not to take it personally – I realize how jittery these reclusive types can be."[49] Pomer's delight in Cohen's ruse and his Teddy Jam persona affirmed her "personal relationship"[50] with the author. She was not only Cohen's advocate; she was also his accomplice.

Pomer's good will was tested, however, when Cohen refused to follow protocol regarding foreign publication. Pomer maintained connections with sub-agents around the world, individuals with whom she had established stable alliances based on reliability and trust. She also had links to international publishers. Once, Cohen spurred his Dutch translator, Peter Bergsma, to submit *The Bookseller* – the novel was issued by Knopf Canada in 1993 – to publisher Eva Cossée in Amsterdam. When Cohen informed Pomer of the move, she was agitated. As the agent explained, the matter should have been handled by her own sub-agent in the

Netherlands, Klaasje Mul. Untroubled by Pomer's dismay, Cohen asserted his prerogative to act independently.

On another occasion, Cohen directed Pomer to accept an offer from a Polish publisher to issue *The Bookseller*. Pomer did not put much faith in "the publisher in question, which used to be state-owned, has been in difficulty since going private and is ... a poor payer of advances and royalties ... I had that with one publisher in Greece and don't want to go through it again. Not much point in getting published if you don't get anything!"[51] Cohen countered that he stood to benefit by broadening his readership and was willing to forfeit royalty payments to gain a Polish audience. He infuriated Pomer by ignoring her sensible advice founded on past experience. The agent was "steamed,"[52] but wisely deferred their discussion of Polish publication to a later date. Though Pomer could not always avoid professional conflict – particularly with Cohen – she tried to face it with composure and tact.

Their association was further strained, however, when Pomer's frank assessment of Cohen's short stories drew the author's ire. As York confirms, "some of the agent's work ... intersect[s] with that of the editor"[53] and editorial review was part of Pomer's service to Cohen. In April 1996, after reading several of Cohen's stories, she offered an unequivocal critique: "[I] can't figure out what you're doing here ... they seem too cut up, jumping around, and though enlivened by many very clever bits here and there, seem to have little humanity or central focus. I guess I'm just not a post-modern[ist] or de-constructionist ... but I've always loved your stories, so I'm disappointed."[54]

Not surprisingly, Cohen refuted Pomer's comments and alleged that she never liked his short fiction, despite her claim to the contrary. Cohen's response grated on Pomer, who felt she had been misunderstood. With uncharacteristic force, she announced that she was "offended" at his "suggestion that I only like stories of yours that are 'straight'; this has never been true. The stories you sent me just weren't there yet; they were disjointed, unfinished, unfocused. However weird, stories do need a centre and I think you were just enjoying playing around."[55]

Cohen was convinced that Pomer did not appreciate his short fiction and, though he conceded that short stories were difficult to sell in a market that favoured the novel, he resented the need to defend them to his agent. A disappointed Cohen proposed that he reclaim his stories and try to place them without Pomer's help.

After quiet reflection, Pomer reacted more typically and with restraint. She agreed to return Cohen's stories and admitted that he was "quite right. You should not have to 'defend' your stories to me."[56] She also confessed to not being "able to pinpoint [exactly] what gives me a problem with these [stories]" and apologized "for any grief my remarks have caused you."[57] Pomer's conciliatory approach – one aspect of her skill as an agent – marked this exchange with Cohen.

Unfortunately, Cohen's dissatisfaction grew and no amount of reassurance on Pomer's part – "the writing in your novels often takes my breath away"[58] – could restore the former tenor of their relationship. In early 1999, Cohen chose to terminate his agency agreement with Pomer and offered two reasons for his decision: he did not believe his work was earning sufficient income, either for himself or his agent, and he did not feel fully supported by Pomer.

Pomer was not surprised by Cohen's resolve; she had known "for some time that you're not happy with my work on your behalf."[59] Although she accepted the break, she felt compelled to answer his two main points. First, she saw Cohen's financial situation as similar to "most of my writers" and, "without modesty, I think I'm worthy my keep for all of them, and for you, too."[60] Second, often in the past Cohen had not only solicited Pomer's editorial input, he had accepted her "honest" advice.[61]

The end was not all gloom, however, since Cohen hoped Pomer would remain Teddy Jam's agent. Mischievous, even as their professional association was ending, Pomer answered: "Matt, it goes without saying that we remain friends. All the same, I can't see my way clear to representing Teddy Jam if I'm not representing his friend Matt Cohen; I'm sure that if we put our heads together we can figure out some way to keep him incognito."[62]

The agency agreement between Cohen and Pomer came to a formal close in April 1999, although Pomer handled translation rights to Cohen's novels until 1 March 2000; on that date, all rights transferred to his new literary agent, Anne McDermid. McDermid, unfortunately, never got a chance to work with Cohen, for he was diagnosed with lung cancer in spring of 1999 and died later that year on 2 December.

Cohen's death, following a rapid and unexpected decline, shocked and saddened Pomer. Cohen had not reached the height of literary success both he and his agent had envisaged, but Pomer did see his work published in Canada and the United States, translated into Dutch, French, and German, and – just prior to his untimely death – win national recognition with the Governor General's Literary Award. Moreover, Pomer never ceased to admire both the quality of Cohen's prose and the integrity of his artistic vision. She was delighted when the film version of *Emotional Arithmetic*, starring Christopher Plummer and Susan Sarandon, premiered at the Toronto International Film Festival in 2007. With a keen sense of triumph, she recalled that *Emotional Arithmetic* was the first novel she had placed for Cohen in 1990.

In early June 1999, when she first learned of his illness, Pomer wrote to Cohen: "I wish you'd call *me*, though what we'd find to say … I'd probably cry. I just find myself wanting to reach out and touch you … It's been a lot of years, Matt, and you must know how very fond I am of you."[63] More than a decade later, in a 2012 interview, Pomer laughingly recounted that Cohen "was high maintenance and he fired me, but we had a strong connection."[64] The tie between agent and author was akin to a long friendship – despite its rough patches, good feeling prevailed.

Jack Hodgins

Bella Pomer's representation of Jack Hodgins was different in character but equal in duration to that of Cohen. Pomer helped Hodgins in a number of ways. She assessed his writing and negotiated with his editor/publisher Douglas Gibson, sought to widen his domestic audience, and tried to place his fiction with international publishers. At the same time, she gave Hodgins the emotional support he required and appreciated.

Hodgins knew Pomer from her years at the Macmillan Company of Canada. In the 1970s, Macmillan had published his first books:

the short story collection *Spit Delaney's Island* (1976) and the novel *The Invention of the World* (1977). During a visit to Toronto in the early 1980s, Hodgins contacted Pomer to ask if she would take him on as a client. At the time, he had a secure publisher in Macmillan and an established relationship with editor Douglas Gibson. Pomer suggested that an agent based in New York might be better placed to help him gain access to the American market. Hodgins took Pomer's advice and enlisted the services of a New York agent, but eventually was disappointed by her lack of initiative.

In August 1988, having decided to seek a new agent, Hodgins wrote to Pomer. Two years earlier, Hodgins had left Macmillan to follow Gibson, who had moved to McClelland and Stewart. Hodgins now sought a broad readership for *The Honorary Patron*, a novel published in 1987 under Gibson's editorial imprint – it was awarded the Commonwealth Literature Prize – and *Left Behind in Squabble Bay*, a children's book published in 1988, and he hoped Pomer would agree to represent him.

Pomer responded to Hodgins's letter with an enthusiastic telephone call confirming their agency agreement. The author was delighted to have Pomer's support and promised to neither pester nor direct her, but to keep in touch regularly. He was affable and thankful, two traits that won the respect of Pomer and set the tone for a friendly alliance that grew more genial over time.

Geographic distance may have helped preserve the integrity of communication between Hodgins and Pomer. Hodgins lived at the far end of the country on Vancouver Island, where he was professor of creative writing at the University of Victoria from 1983 to 2002. To contact his agent, he relied on correspondence and occasional long-distance telephone calls, which were costly since they could go on for "as much as 40 minutes."[65]

From the start of their professional agreement, Pomer was much more than an agent who only handled commercial matters; she was also one of Hodgins's first readers. He solicited her editorial response to his work and received her candid analysis without ire or defensiveness. In fact, the sort of frank appraisal that angered Cohen had the opposite effect on Hodgins, who valued Pomer's commentary.

For her part, Pomer was always "glad to read anything"[66] Hodgins sent her, but was governed by the belief that she served the author's best interests by acknowledging inferior work, encouraging him in his craft, and refusing to let good will dictate the agent-author exchange, which sometimes called for unpleasant truths and difficult discussions. Thus, the desire to maintain positive relations with Hodgins did not prevent Pomer from voicing her strong opinions about his fiction.

Less than one year into their agency agreement, in May 1989, for example, Pomer provided an unflattering assessment of the story "Letter to Venice": "This is not up to your standard. It reads like a first draft, the germ of a story. Edna is all on one note, far too much of a caricature to interest the reader, and the first-person voice is also one not-very-interesting note. The story is flat, all on the surface, without texture and nuance, Jack."[67] Hodgins was not put off by Pomer's criticism. Instead, he was spurred to revise the story.

A four-page response to *The Macken Charm*, published by McClelland and Stewart in 1995, confirmed that Pomer was both an incisive reader of fiction and dedicated to Hodgins. In a letter dated 8 March 1994, she addressed nine questions sent earlier by Hodgins to help guide her reading of the novel. Pomer claimed to be a subjective "reader rather than an editor,"[68] but her detailed comments suggested otherwise.

Pomer explained why some characters lacked interest, pointed to inconsistencies in characterization and plot development, and noted problems in time frame and narrative structure. She highlighted "practical matters," such as errors in pagination, shifts in tenses, and the "difficult" and "expensive" process of acquiring permission to cite song lyrics in fiction, but she also commended Hodgins's effective use of the flashback and his achievement in writing a universal "rite of passage novel."[69] Rather than impose her views on the author, Pomer counselled Hodgins to trust his "gut" – "ignore anything you don't 'feel' is something that needs attention."[70]

It was with a similar show of integrity and commitment that Pomer twice read 1998's *Broken Ground* in draft form and made recommendations that brought Hodgins to see his novel anew. Initially, she advised him to comb "for small things"[71] in the first third and to substantively revise the final third of the novel. Her second reading addressed narrative perspective and characterization – Johanna, for example, seemed to have "lost some of the vividness and strength she had in the last draft – perhaps you've pruned a bit too much?"[72] As she had done previously for *The Macken Charm*, she also provided a list of inconsistencies and queries of a practical nature. Pomer dismissed her own editorial efforts – "I wasn't really reading with a pencil in my hand; more important to get the sweep!"[73] – but archival evidence shows that she devoted time and energy to reading and commenting on Hodgins's novel.

In fact, Pomer was as much editor as agent to Hodgins, whose willingness to accept criticism may have stemmed from a general uneasiness about his writing. A nagging feeling that he was valued less than other authors issued under Douglas Gibson's imprint exacerbated his self-doubt. Hodgins's sense of neglect was justified, for Gibson was an inattentive editor. Routinely preoccupied, he was an irregular correspondent and frustratingly indecisive. In face-to-face meetings, Hodgins was soothed and beguiled by Gibson's natural charm, but such encounters were infrequent, given the distance that separated Toronto and Victoria. The impression that he was "a 'second-class citizen' at McClelland & Stewart"[74] persisted, and Hodgins was driven to seek Pomer's help in negotiating the firm's "caste system for its authors."[75]

Pomer intervened on a number of issues, both small and large. Hodgins's 1992 travel book, *Over 40 in Broken Hill: Unusual Encounters in the Australian Outback*, co-published by McClelland and Stewart and University of Queensland Press, included advertisements for other Douglas Gibson Books, even though the clause allowing for such notices had been removed from the publication contract. In a letter to Gibson, Pomer stressed: "Jack feels strongly about this and is not pleased."[76]

In the same letter, Pomer complained about the unconscionable delay in issuing a contract for *A Passion for Narrative: A Guide for Writing Fiction*, finally published in 1993. "Despite a number of reminders ... by phone which you failed to respond to," it took Gibson "a full year"[77] to make an offer on a book he had prompted Hodgins to write. Since "everything to do with his projects is allowed to drag on for so long," Pomer warned that Hodgins could "end up a disgruntled author who wants to turn elsewhere."[78]

Early on, Pomer correctly discerned a "pattern"[79] in Gibson's indifferent behaviour. Thus, she was always poised to prod Gibson into action, even when she knew he resented "the machinations"[80] of an agent. In truth, Pomer regretted the adversarial relationship and would have preferred an easy connection with Gibson, who was both editor and publisher to Hodgins, a complex position that gave him undue advantage over the author. There were even times when Gibson sacrificed the aesthetic concerns of an editor to the marketing needs of a publisher. In lieu of *The Macken Charm*, for example, he proposed the generic title "Occasions of Life," which Pomer denounced as "downright embarrassing ... It sounds like non-fiction, and self-help at that."[81]

Problems between Hodgins and Gibson escalated at the close of 1997. The author was anxious to receive a contract for *Broken Ground*, but Gibson had not yet committed to publishing the novel. Hodgins also hoped to specify plans for promotion and publicity in the publishing contract for *Broken Ground*, since he believed his books were not advertised as widely as many other McClelland and Stewart titles. Pomer was more realistic and assured Hodgins that "*all* publishers have to be dragged kicking and screaming to print advertising."[82] At the same time, she was growing increasingly certain that Gibson was not doing enough to advance Hodgins's career and was not the sort of "good fiction editor"[83] he needed. She thought Hodgins should "walk away"[84] from McClelland and Stewart.

As Hodgins's agent, situated outside the dyadic relationship of author-publisher, Pomer could act boldly when necessary. Thus, on 8 January 1998, she delivered an ultimatum: if Gibson could not agree to undertake "a publishing campaign" to promote and publicize *Broken Ground*, then "Jack himself has said ... he doesn't want you to publish" the book.[85] Pomer's tactic worked; the novel was published later that year and promoted to satisfy Hodgins. Moreover, it won British Columbia's Ethel Wilson Fiction Prize in 1999, which generated precisely the sort of publicity Hodgins had been seeking. In the end, Pomer was elated. Her efforts on Hodgins's behalf had paid off handsomely.

Pomer always was cognizant of Hodgins's changeable relationship with Gibson. What she wanted for the author, in addition to proper compensation and "better positioning" in the international market, was "a first-rate editor"[86] who would provide the full attention his writing deserved. She reminded Hodgins that John Pearce of Doubleday Canada had long been interested in his work; she also recommended Douglas and McIntyre and HarperCollins Canada for their excellent fiction lists. But despite a troubled history with Gibson, who retired from publishing in 2008, Hodgins did not choose to sever ties with his long-time editor/publisher and, to this day, he remains a McClelland and Stewart author.

Not only did Pomer help scale the rocky terrain of Hodgins's relationship with Gibson, she was also his sounding board and a source of emotional support. As he had originally promised, Hodgins wrote to Pomer regularly. In long, confessional letters, he discussed current and future projects; his ongoing frustration with McClelland and Stewart; the pleasures of a 1995 trip to Melbourne, Australia, where he was fêted as a visiting writer; and his contrasting lack of recognition in Canada. He also shared worries about advancing his career and achieving financial security. Hodgins regarded his letters as "meditation[s]"[87] – a place to clarify his thoughts – written as much for himself as for Pomer.

In the privacy of correspondence, Hodgins voiced a deep insecurity about his work. In 1996, for example, when *The Macken Charm* was not short-listed for literary prizes, he questioned the quality of the novel. Distressed by Hodgins's "lack of confidence,"[88] Pomer tried to boost his morale: "I can understand you feeling despondent ... but you mustn't allow yourself to think it wasn't 'good enough.' It simply didn't get the credit it deserved. It's difficult just now to be a white male writer of a 'certain age' ... when all the attention is on new voices, particularly if they are women or ethnic. It is too bad, but it can't last forever, I keep telling myself."[89]

Outwardly, Pomer's statement might seem at odds with the fact that she represented so many women writers whose work she admired. Here, though, her first concern was to convey her regard for Hodgins's fiction. Moreover, in sharing her hard-won knowledge that publishing was governed, in large part, by cultural trends that were both variable and unpredictable and did not always favour the authors she represented, Pomer hoped to comfort Hodgins.

In 2001, Pomer penned a similarly consoling letter when *Broken Ground* was not considered for national awards: "I know how hard it is to accept ... but Jack, it happens a lot to other wonderful writers like yourself. You aren't alone in this."[90] Pomer knew that citing such trends would offer little solace, but was equally aware of Hodgins's great need for reassurance, which she proffered willingly throughout their association.

Pomer's connection with Hodgins was personal and therapeutic, to invoke Regal's description of the agent as a "bit of psychologist."[91] She offered sympathy in the form of private condolences when Hodgins's beloved father died after a prolonged illness: "I'm so very sorry to hear about your father. It's a blow even when expected."[92] When a friend could not grasp the meaning of the book title *Broken Ground*, Pomer counselled Hodgins to lay aside his "doubts": the lack of understanding was "inane" and "no one who reads the book could possibly mistake the connection between the title and the content."[93] Her criticism of Hodgins's friend was meant to help the writer regain perspective and equilibrium.

Hodgins's qualms were quieted by Pomer's faith in his writing, as well as her determination to advance his career. To generate interest in his work, Pomer sent excerpts from Canadian book reviews to her various sub-agents. She also promoted Hodgins's fiction annually at the Frankfurt Book Fair and tried to place it with international publishers.

When McClelland and Stewart handled American and British distribution – often without benefit to the company itself – Pomer gave it "full marks for trying"[94] to secure foreign publication of Hodgins's titles, since she knew how "tough" it was "to place quality fiction by mid-career [Canadian] writers in the U.S.,"[95] and that breaking "into the U.K. [was] worse even."[96] At the same time, she always sought to soften the blows of international rejection. When, for instance, *Broken Ground* did not find favour with either American or British publishers, she explained that Americans were less interested in the novel's depiction of the First World War than their own

"Civil War, WW2, Korea and ... Vietnam";[97] moreover, Canada was not a "sexy ... literary address ... for most U.S. and U.K. publishers."[98]

Even her connection with New York editor Ann Close of Knopf did not result in American publication of *Broken Ground*, which was rejected by as many as thirty-six U.S. publishing houses. Finally, after trying unsuccessfully to place Hodgins's "wonderful novels" with international publishers "large and small," Pomer felt "defeated ... it beats me why there have been no takers."[99] Douglas Gibson addressed the same puzzle in his 2011 memoir, where he posits the general perception of Hodgins as "a regional writer"[100] whose work was specific to Vancouver Island as one reason why the novels may not have had a broader reach.

The agency agreement between Pomer and Hodgins came to a gradual end that was free of rancour. Hodgins first hinted at change in June 2001, when he asked Pomer, who had exhausted her list of American contacts, if McClelland and Stewart might be able to place *Broken Ground* in the United States. Several years earlier, in fact, a frustrated Pomer, feeling she had made little difference to his career and earnings, had offered to stop representing Hodgins. At the time, the author convinced her to remain his agent and together they went on to celebrate the rise of Hodgins's literary reputation in Canada.

Eventually, however, both came to a clearer view of their arrangement. Hodgins was not actively seeking a new agent, but he felt demoralized by the lack of international interest in his books and could no longer justify Pomer's labour on his behalf. On 13 November 2001, in a letter to Pomer that was true to both his generous nature and their amicable connection, Hodgins terminated their long-standing agreement. Rather than complain, he thanked the agent for her patience, support, and energetic vision, and acknowledged her extraordinary efforts over thirteen years.

The letter saddened but did not surprise Pomer, who was both "deeply disappointed" and baffled by the lack of response to Hodgins's work, which had not "been for want of trying"[101] to attract foreign publishers. The 1990s, as she recalled in 2015, was a difficult decade "to get the least bit of attention in the U.S., U.K., and Europe for writing coming out of Canada."[102]

Despite the mutual decision to end their agency agreement, Pomer was dejected by her failure to bring Hodgins real financial gain. What she did provide was editorial advice, professional mediation, and a willing ear, all of which Hodgins appreciated. Still, Pomer's incapacity to increase Hodgins's visibility and literary income rankled. Today, she continues to feel "disappointed ... that despite my utmost efforts, his books ... didn't 'travel' outside of Canada."[103]

Carol Shields

The agency agreement between novelist Carol Shields and Bella Pomer lasted twenty years, from 1982 to 2002, during which time Shields "had extraordinarily close contact with her agent,"[104] as Catherine Hobbs notes. Pomer's vision and tenacity helped shape Shields's career, the high point of which was the publication in 1993 of *The Stone Diaries*. In fact, Shields became Pomer's best-known client and won the international acclaim that eluded both Matt Cohen and Jack Hodgins.

Shields's first literary agent, like Hodgins's, was based in New York. By 1980, Shields had published two volumes of poetry – *Others* (1972) and *Intersect* (1974) – and two novels – *Small Ceremonies* (1976) and *The Box Garden* (1977) – but had yet to establish a literary reputation. Hence, when Virginia Barber offered her representation, Shields happily accepted. Barber, who already represented Alice Munro and Rudy Wiebe, had a strong interest in Canadian writers. From 1980 to 1981, Barber tried to expand Shields's readership, but was unable to place her early novels and short fiction in the United States. Very soon, according to Pomer, Barber withheld "the moral support that comes from liking what a person has written" and grew "dismissive" of Shields.[105]

Pomer and Shields met in the spring of 1981 at the annual meeting of the Writers' Guild of Alberta, where they both had been invited to lead workshops. During a seminar, when she was seated beside Shields in the audience, Pomer saw a chance to say how much she admired Shields's writing and that she "would be delighted"[106] to become her agent. Pomer's timing was impeccable. Shields was already looking for a new literary agent and was pleased to learn of Pomer's interest. By March 1982, having terminated her agency agreement with Virginia Barber, Shields had signed on with Pomer.

Pomer and Shields communicated via correspondence and long-distance telephone calls. From 1980 to 2000, Shields lived in Winnipeg, where both she and her engineer husband, Donald Shields, taught at the University of Manitoba. The couple retired to Victoria in 2000 and they also maintained a second home in Montjouvent, France. Thus, Pomer and Shields met infrequently, usually when the author visited Toronto.

Pomer responded to Shields's creative vision, in particular her capacity to draw complex female characters. Soon, the appeal of Shields's work extended to the author herself, whose charming manner delighted Pomer. Shields, too, had a warm feeling for Pomer, but her initial need for emotional support diminished over time and the friendly tie between author and agent finally gave way to a more professional alliance.

Over the course of two decades, Pomer assisted Shields in various ways. She offered career guidance, especially in the early years of their association; provided editorial advice; marketed individual stories; sought foreign publication of Shields's work; negotiated with publishers and agents; and guarded the author's privacy.

Immediately, Pomer began to pay special attention to the "trajectory of the writer's career" and was "thinking forward"[107] to Shields's next work. A practical realist, she recognized Shields's narrative strengths and directed her to concentrate on writing novels, which brought her more public notice than short stories. To retain "the discerning audience capable of appreciating your subtlety, delightful comedy and remarkable ability to illuminate human experience," she also nudged Shields towards writing that was "taut and sharp."[108]

From the start, Shields drew on Pomer's editorial skill, confirming York's view that the agent's "concern for the shape of the [author's] career easily shades into aesthetic response to the work."[109] Pomer proceeded with caution, however, and set clear editorial parameters: "I'm absolutely ruthless about pruning where it's needed, as you'll no doubt see ... In the end it is you alone who decides on such [editorial] comments and suggestions as I do make."[110] Since editorial "comments," no matter how benignly delivered, could lead to hurt feelings, the agent hoped to forestall potential conflict. Pomer also knew that Shields needed an agent whose first priority was to advance her career. Thus, Pomer wisely downplayed her secondary role as critical reader.

Pomer's assessment of a short story early in 1983, soon into her agreement with Shields, showed her characteristic frankness. She found the piece "fuzzy," lacking both interest and a "sense of illumination."[111] In contrast, "The Next Best Kiss" was stronger – it had "some rather hummocky bits as well as lovely gold nuggets"[112] – while "Weather" required "little copyediting changes" to make it "crisper."[113] She also admired the "exquisite"[114] scene between the two women in "The Scarf," although she recommended revising its narrative voice for consistency, and loved the existential quality of "The Orange Fish."

Pomer admitted to having "blind spots, like everyone else,"[115] and did not expect Shields to yield to her view "unless what I say strikes some chord of agreement."[116] Often, her comments resonated with the author, who happily heeded Pomer's suggestions.

Pomer understood that the New York market was paramount and regularly submitted Shields's work to the *New Yorker*, the premier magazine for short fiction. She hoped "to crack them one day"[117] with a story by Shields – fellow Canadians Mavis Gallant and Alice Munro rose to fame in the pages of the *New Yorker* – but was realistic in her aspirations and warned the author against unchecked optimism. In the end, despite Pomer's persistent attempts, Shields's fiction did not appear in the magazine.

A break did come, however, with the publication of *The Stone Diaries*. When Random House of Canada issued the novel in 1993 – eleven years after Shields first signed on with Pomer's agency – the response was immediate. Critics and readers alike were intrigued by the novel's structure and captivated by it elusive protagonist, Daisy Goodwill Flett. The work won universal acclaim and Pomer celebrated Shields's victory: "What we have all hoped for has happened – you are *in demand*."[118] She coaxed Shields to promote the novel in the United States, where it appeared under the Viking Penguin imprint, even as she understood the author's need for quiet time and replenishment. Pomer's pleas were not self-motivated. This was Shields's public moment and the agent was loath to see her squander the chance to solidify a career so long in the making: "In the beginning, it took excruciating effort to get promotion opportunities for you in the U.S. Now that you've reached this very welcome stage, I feel you mustn't miss this opportunity."[119]

Pomer knew to profit by this "welcome stage" in the writer's career. She worked closely with editor Mindy Werner of Viking Penguin and sub-agent Carole Blake of the Blake Friedmann Agency, respectively, to orchestrate American and British publication of all of Shields's books and to ensure that each received individual attention. She also negotiated with other sub-agents to arrange foreign publication of Shields's work, which increased exponentially in the wake of *The Stone Diaries*.[120]

Long-awaited success brought Pomer and Shields closer. When *The Stone Diaries* was short-listed for Britain's Booker Prize (now the Man Booker Prize), Pomer travelled to London in October 1993 to attend the awards gala in support of her star client. The novel lost out to Roddy Doyle's *Paddy Clarke Ha Ha Ha*, but the agent's presence at "the stellar event"[121] gave Shields "courage and balance" and the dinner Pomer hosted at Boyds gave them both a chance to unwind after "the Booker experience."[122]

Soon there was cause for full celebration, for *The Stone Diaries* received the Governor General's Literary Award for fiction. In May 1995, when the novel was awarded the Pulitzer Prize, family obligations prevented Pomer from attending the luncheon ceremony at Columbia University, but her feeling of joy on behalf of Shields carried all the way from Toronto to New York.[123] By the end of that year, *The Stone Diaries* had sold close to 600,000 copies in the United States alone,[124] which delighted author and agent alike.

Eventually, the excitement surrounding *The Stone Diaries* subsided and Shields faced uncertainty, a feeling she conveyed to her agent. As always, Pomer was supportive: "Carol, what you were saying about not knowing how many more novels you have in you, that's not an unexpected reaction to the enormous success of DIARIES ... I can't imagine that you will stop writing; if the books need to be spaced further apart, there's nothing wrong with that, either."[125] There is no doubt that Pomer's representation of Shields, whose "literary prominence [eventually] provided enormous symbolic capital," helped establish her own "primacy in the ... literary agency business."[126] But, as her comment reveals, Pomer was much more than a professional who shared in Shields's triumph; she was also an ally and an attentive listener.

Pomer was a strong defender of Shields. In 1985, when Shields's story "Flitting Behaviour" was rejected by *Toronto Life*, Pomer took editor Jocelyn Laurence to task: "To be amusing and ironic is not at all incompatible with being serious. Obviously, you didn't like the story, and that, of course is your prerogative."[127] George Woodcock's "dismal review" of *The Stone Diaries* prompted a heated letter to the editor of *Quill and Quire*: "It was a blow to see ... [Shields's] book in the hands of a reviewer who has no understanding of her strengths at all. 'Craftsmanly' indeed! What a put-down."[128] Shortly afterward, she pressed president Douglas Pepper of Random House of Canada: "The Christmas gift season's coming up, and Carol is slipping a little on the G[lobe] & M[ail] list. A shot in the arm is what's needed now"[129] for *The Stone Diaries*.

In the same way that she mediated the relationship between Jack Hodgins and Douglas Gibson, Pomer interceded between Shields and Stoddart Publishing. In the 1980s – long before the success of *The Stone Diaries* – Pomer had brokered Stoddart's publication of two works by Shields: the short story collection *Various Miracles* (1985) and the novel *Swann: A Mystery* (1987). *Swann* was Shields's first book to receive wide public acclaim – it won the Arthur Ellis Award and was short-listed for the Governor General's Literary Award – but Pomer claimed it was not adequately publicized.

Although Shields had a good working relationship with Stoddart editor Ed Carson, Pomer was convinced that the firm had "mishandled" the promotion of *Swann*, which sold "2000 copies or less"[130] in its first year. In 1988, she deemed the sales record unacceptable "for a book everyone agrees is special in more ways than one," and averred that Stoddart was not "comfortable handling ... quality or upmarket fiction."[131]

Required by contract to offer Stoddart Shields's next book, Pomer demanded a timely response to the short story collection *The Orange Fish*. At the same time, she made it clear that the author intended to sever ties with the company: "Most publishers recognize that if a writer doesn't want to stay, it's better to let ... her go – it doesn't promise much for the next book or relationship when one side wants a divorce."[132]

Pomer's strategy worked. After one week of deliberation, Stoddart declined to issue *The Orange Fish*. Now Shields was free to publish with Random House of Canada, where she could continue working with Carson who had moved to the firm in 1985. At Random House, which issued *The Orange Fish* in 1989, Shields became a valued author who was treated "as a treasure."[133] In 1994 Carson left for HarperCollins, but by then Shields felt a deep loyalty to Random House and chose to remain with the company.

Meanwhile, Stoddart continued to be a source of irritation. Only belatedly did Shields discover the publisher had altered the subtitle on the paperback publication of *Swann* from *A Mystery* to *A Literary Mystery*. Moreover, since Stoddart did nothing to promote *Various Miracles* and *Swann*, bookstores rarely stocked the titles. In 1993, as soon as *The Stone Diaries* received the Governor General's Literary Award, Pomer wrote to Stoddart, urging him to publicize Shields's backlist: "I hope your sales people are actively 'selling' SWANN and VARIOUS MIRACLES rather than merely passively sitting back and waiting for orders to come in."[134] Jack Stoddart Jr, however, ignored her plea.

Pomer and Shields were baffled. They could not comprehend the publisher's refusal to capitalize on Shields's new popularity in the wake of *The Stone Diaries*. They were also "distressed by the virtual burial"[135] of *Various Miracles* and *Swann*, especially since advertising "would have given the two titles a profile and tripled"[136] the books' modest sales.

Stoddart's passivity, which may have been deliberate, had the effect of provoking Shields's ire and increasing her desire to reclaim her titles. In January 1995, at the request of Shields and Pomer, Random House of Canada made an offer to purchase outright Stoddart's stock of *Various Miracles* and *Swann*, with no further costs to the firm or future royalty payments. It was only Shields's willingness, however, to pay "an additional $5,000 to have the contracts assigned to Random [House of] Canada" – a willingness born of exasperation – that finally brought the majority of "her books under one roof"[137] and an end to her bondage to Stoddart.[138] Later that year, when both books were issued under the Random House imprint, Shields and Pomer celebrated their joint achievement of having rescued two of the author's earlier works and ensuring their longevity. Together, they recognized the protracted battle with Stoddart as a defining feature of their relationship.

Shields acknowledged Pomer as her champion and constant source of support. At the same time, however, she focused on the financial side of their arrangement and often raised economic concerns with her agent. Gender may have played a role here, for Shields might have worried that a personal bond of friendship with her female agent could hamper their professional negotiations. Thus, she made the early decision to deal openly with financial issues and to be forthright in all monetary discussions.

Periodically, for example, Shields disputed Pomer's right to her agency fee. Such questioning gave rise to tension that would soon subside, only to recur when the author next raised the matter of financial obligation to her agent. In each instance, Pomer, though well aware that "agencies are dicey when it comes to income"[139] and that "quality fiction," in particular, was "not something that pays off in the short run,"[140] provided requisite clarification and retained her businesslike composure. Even so, the repeated strain led to eventual rupture.

A first clash occurred in February 1985 when Pomer expected a commission from Shields's second-prize winnings in a CBC short story contest. As she had done in the past, Shields had voluntarily submitted "Flitting Behaviour" – the same story rejected by *Toronto Life* – to the CBC competition. In Pomer's view, such contests were "publicized, glamourized markets which pay a slightly higher fee than usual and provide extra promotion and publicity ... but they are markets nonetheless."[141] Shields disagreed, however, and did not accede to Pomer's request for a commission. Instead, she asked that their agency agreement differentiate clearly between literary prizes and markets.

In May 1986, Pomer provided a rationale for requesting a commission on prospective funding from the Foundation to Underwrite New Drama for Pay Television (now the Harold Greenberg Fund). Since she had broached the idea of a film version of *Swann* with Shields, and then met with foundation chair Phyllis Yaffe to discuss the project, Pomer believed she ought to be "compensated for my initiatives."[142] Many years later, however, when Shields wrote the screenplay for *Swann* – eventually released in 1996 as a film starring Brenda Fricker and Miranda Richardson – Pomer once again had to petition the author for a commission.

In 1995, when Shields agreed to extend a film option on her 1992 novel *The Republic of Love* without Pomer's knowledge, the agent was forced to remind the author that documents requiring a signature ought to go through her agency. Pomer wanted to verify what Shields "may be signing and agreeing to ... [since] I rarely find that anything drawn up by a lawyer doesn't require some change of wording."[143]

After she read a screenplay for *Larry's Party* (1997) – the novel won the U.K.'s Orange Prize (now the Women's Prize for Fiction) and France's Prix de Lire – Shields sought a consulting fee and was disappointed to learn that Pomer had neglected to secure remuneration for her consultancy work. Pomer assumed responsibility for the oversight and offered to pay the author herself, but Shields was not inclined to forgive the error.

Shields often granted rights to anthologists and publishers, a practice that annoyed Pomer, who preferred to vet all permission requests. As she explained in 1999: "I'm not trying to earn myself an extra dollar here, I just worry that you may unwittingly grant rights that conflict with other licenses we grant for your work."[144] In fact, as Shields's agent, it was Pomer's duty to attend to such details. That she felt the need to justify her aims to Shields signalled the deteriorating rapport between agent and author.

By late 2000, Shields was growing impatient with her agent, likely the result of incremental tension over financial matters. Moreover, in 1998 she had been diagnosed with breast cancer and a new awareness of her own mortality had led to a preoccupation with the international publication of her final novel *Unless*, the literary legacy she would leave her readers, as well as the financial legacy she would leave her family. This was a trying phase in Shields's personal life; it was also a challenging period in her association with Pomer, the limits of which were tested over the next two years.

In May 2001, in "response to various comments"[145] made by Shields and the intimation that she had mishandled the American publication of *Larry's Party* – although it won the National Book Critics Circle Award, the novel did not sell widely in the United States – Pomer was impelled to correct a false impression of her agency work. In an expansive email, she explained first that she did not do "lunch," which usually "turn[ed] out to be ¾ social chitchat"; she chose, rather, to promote Shields's books at annual book fairs in Frankfurt and London and among publishers in New York. Second, she cited *Publishers Weekly* and publishers' catalogues as more valuable sources than the *New York Times Book Review* for "what's being published and how." Third, she noted that her 15 per cent commission fee was standard among literary agents. Fourth, she tried to calm Shields's "anxiety" about her literary legacy, which was "lasting." Finally, since Shields worried that Pomer had neither a business partner nor a plan for the future of her agency should she decide to retire, she confirmed her intention to remain active for the foreseeable future, although she was not taking on new clients.[146]

Pomer's careful clarification, elicited by Shields's concern for the future and worry that her agent was not doing enough to advance international publication of her books, quieted the author, but her uneasiness soon resurfaced. In June 2002, she felt it fair to ask Pomer to absorb all postal costs previously passed on to the author. The agent's response – an explanation that she only sought reimbursement for international postage and books purchased – did not satisfy Shields, so Pomer acquiesced for the sake of their relationship.

The following month brought the charge that Pomer was not proactively trying to place *Unless* with foreign publishers, even though she had scored an extraordinary coup by securing Canadian and British royalty advances of "well into six figures"[147] from Random House of Canada and Fourth Estate, respectively. *Unless* had just been issued in Canada and the U.K. and was already circulating among publishing houses, but Shields was frustrated – no doubt feeling the pressure of time during the final year of her life.[148] Pomer was hurt and confused by the accusation. She was also angry: how could Shields question her commitment after so many years of dedicated labour? The end of their association was in sight.

As she told Shields, Pomer knew herself to be "an excellent agent" who had earned her reputation for being "enormously effective."[149] She was also "an ardent fan" of Shields's work and her proponent, having represented the author for many "lean"[150] years prior to the triumph of *The Stone Diaries*. By June 2002, however, Pomer suspected that Shields had come to question her expertise and "begrudge" her "share of this success."[151] Although she felt "affection," "respect," and solicitude for the author, especially in light of her "fight with this dreadful disease,"[152] Pomer could not forestall the close of their agency agreement.

In late June, Pomer asked to visit Shields in Victoria; she hoped a face-to-face exchange might re-establish their bond. Shields, however, had already made the decision to terminate her twenty-year agreement with Pomer, which she did over the telephone on 2 July 2002 and confirmed by letter twelve days later. Shields contended that Pomer's commission was high and her efforts to secure international publication and film rights to her books unsatisfactory. The facts countered her allegations, but the personal connection between Pomer and Shields – the core of their agent-author relationship – had been strained beyond repair. Pomer had no choice; she accepted Shields's decision and formally agreed to a termination date of 30 September 2002. Deeply pained by their parting, she regretted the loss of a writer whose stellar career she had helped shape and whose friendship she still prized.

Over the course of their long association, Pomer and Shields had successfully resolved their disagreements. Moreover, during

Shields's final months, as her health deteriorated, Pomer had maintained constant contact, offering comfort and professional support. She knew, for example, how important it was for Shields to stay connected to her readers and had arranged publicity for *Unless* via telephone interviews from her home in Victoria. Thus, Pomer was saddened by the abrupt and irrevocable turn in their relationship.

Yet she remained a champion of Shields. Pomer was "heartbroken" when *Unless* was short-listed for the Giller Prize (now the Scotiabank Giller Prize) but did not win the award. She wrote to Shields on 6 November 2002 to say the "Giller choice ... should have been you."[153] That note, and Pomer's warm hug at the Giller Prize gala in Toronto, touched Shields deeply. Their professional tie may have been severed, but their personal connection endured.

When Shields died on 16 July 2003, several months after they reunited briefly at the Giller Prize celebration, Pomer experienced a profound sense of loss. Not only did she mourn the death of a great writer whose work she knew intimately, she grieved the rupture of her past close relationship with Shields.

Pomer regarded the agent-author alliance as "a business marriage" that was "personal."[154] At any one time, she represented approximately thirty writers and, to varying degrees, she felt connected to each of her clients.[155] Authors relied not only on her professional expertise; they also responded to her vital personality, straightforward manner, and persistence – "When I really believe in something, I just keep on trying."[156] For Matt Cohen, Jack Hodgins, Carol Shields, and her many other clients, Pomer always expended her best effort, even when perseverance did not achieve the desired results.

Through her successful representation of authors and her vigorous marketing strategies, Pomer "developed a reputation for professionalism, integrity, and intelligence."[157] She began attending the Frankfurt Book Fair in the 1970s, "when no one wanted anything to do with Canadian writers."[158] The Buchmesse, which dates back to the fifteenth century, has always been, as Louise Dennys describes it, "the fast-beating heart of international publishing ... a bazaar, a souk – thousands of excited publishers buying and selling the country-rights to their authors' works"[159] – and Pomer participated annually. She regularly attended the London Book Fair and occasionally BookExpo. In addition, she frequently travelled to New York to meet with publishers and editors and to visit the Canadian consulate, where she boosted her clients whose titles were issued under American imprints.

By transforming "book deals into business transactions,"[160] as Stephen Smith notes, Pomer succeeded in altering publishers' negative perception of agents. With understanding and skill, she brokered better terms and royalty advances for her clients. She also sold their work to publishers outside of Canada. Such intervention brought "industry-wide changes to [domestic] publishing contracts"[161] and helped reform past practices that favoured publishers over authors.

Often, Pomer was called upon to share her knowledge and expertise. From 1979 to 1993, she served as a rights consultant to the Toronto Public Library, and, from 1982 to 1988, she was a foreign rights representative for the University of Toronto Press. In 1989, she led a workshop at the annual meeting of the Writers' Guild of Alberta, in which she advised attendees on how to secure agency representation. In the early 1990s, at Douglas Gibson's behest, Pomer reviewed McClelland and Stewart's publishing contract and provided a five-page detailed report that responded to each of its twenty-three clauses – her clients' contracts received similar scrutiny. Her comments reflected her vast experience as a shrewd negotiator who did not hesitate to raise objections when appropriate, as well as her guiding impulse to protect the rights of authors.

Pomer operated independently throughout her career – she worked alone, handled her own bookkeeping, and only later hired a part-time assistant to help with clerical tasks and mailing manuscripts – but she exerted influence as "one of Toronto's top agents."[162] In 1994, after more than fifteen years in the business, she admitted "there was a great deal of resentment among publishers when agents began to establish themselves ... It's quite a turnaround now, because you have publishers who won't look at anything unless it comes from an agent."[163] Lecker confirms Pomer's view: "the kind of literature that gets presented to Canadian publishers is the direct result of decisions made by a small group of people, again and again."[164] That Canada's literary agents – just "thirty or so" in number[165] – now wield significant power is due, in part, to Pomer's leadership.

When editor William H. New was preparing his 2002 *Encyclopedia of Literature in Canada*, he thought Pomer ideally suited to write the entry on literary agents, but she was too busy to "do an adequate job of it."[166] In fact, judging from her archival correspondence, Pomer was both an expert agent and a proficient writer; had she accepted New's invitation, her submission would surely have been much more than "adequate."[167]

Many colleagues recognized Pomer as a talented agent, but she was best known to Beverley Slopen, a fellow agent, journalist, and friend. One year, during the Frankfurt Book Fair, Pomer and Slopen shared a hotel room. At the end of each day, "they brought in food, put their feet up," and discovered they enjoyed the bustle of the fair much more in one another's company.[168] From that point forward, they travelled together to both the Frankfurt and London Book Fairs, shared living quarters, and soon developed a deeper friendship, free of professional competition. In a 1996 piece in the *Toronto Star*, Slopen lauded Pomer as one of Canada's "'hot' author representatives."[169]

Pomer's capacity for friendship was, in fact, one of her greatest strengths. It shaped her relationships with authors, enlivened her professional connections with publishers, editors, and agents, and influenced her success. By 2000, after twenty-two years as a literary agent, Pomer was regarded as the "*grande dame* of the Canadian scene."[170] She was still active and enjoying her "wonderful career," feeling "lucky to have stumbled into it."[171] In truth, Pomer was no stumbler. Always self-aware and deliberate – even as a young girl devoted to the library – she forged an accomplished career, the best part of which "was being able to place books well."[172]

As Lorraine York observes, in the past two decades, as publishers have adopted austerity measures and stripped themselves of in-house editors, the literary agent has come to replace the editor as "the primary source of consistency for authors."[173] In reality, only a practised agent like Pomer could substitute for an editor, and "consistency" was but one feature of her fidelity to authors. She was also their public advocate and private confidante, one who provided the direction and support they most needed.

Conclusion

The severing of professional ties between Bella Pomer and Carol Shields, followed mere months later by Shields's death, seemed to coincide – as if by design – with a series of events that shook the Canadian publishing industry to its core. The first of these was the sale in June 2000 of 25 per cent of McClelland and Stewart to the American publisher Random House, with the remaining 75 per cent of the company donated to the University of Toronto. Random House of Canada, then "the strongest player in the market," undertook responsibility for running the firm, which it did by overseeing McClelland and Stewart's "sales, distribution, accounting, and financial management."[1] Meanwhile, the university agreed to safeguard the Canadian focus of the storied company. For owner Avie Bennett this unusual arrangement was advantageous. It allowed him to divest himself of McClelland and Stewart while retaining his nationalist profile.

Publicly, the bipartite transfer of McClelland and Stewart was presented as a viable plan and a benevolent gesture. Bennett's move even received the blessing of two of the press's most celebrated writers, Margaret Atwood and Michael Ondaatje. The storyline changed radically in 2012, however, the year McClelland and Stewart was fully absorbed by Random House (now Penguin Random House Canada, an amalgamation that is owned jointly by the international conglomerate Bertelsmann and Pearson). Though deeply disturbed by the loss, the wider publishing community was not surprised. The earlier partial sale of Canada's most treasured publisher to an

American firm had already shown that federal officials were willing and able to bypass existing legislation to allow the foreign purchase of a domestic publishing company. As journalist Elaine Dewar disclosed in 2017, the details surrounding the acquisition were even more disturbing than they first appeared. In truth, Random House had been given de facto control in 2004 – eight full years before the complete transfer of the firm – and since that time McClelland and Stewart had been Canadian in name alone.[2]

The unloading of McClelland and Stewart was followed by the merger in August 2001 of Canada's two mega bookstore chains, Chapters and Indigo, which, for all intents and purposes, resulted in Chapters/Indigo acquiring a monopoly over book sales in this country. Further, by granting premium shelf space solely to books whose publishers could afford large promotional costs, Chapters/Indigo further delimited the range and number of books available to the Canadian reading public. The closure of many independent bookstores that lacked the financial resources needed to compete with the marketing strategies deployed by the big-box chain – among them Montreal's long-standing Double Hook (1974–2005), which had stocked only Canadian titles – helped strengthen Chapters/Indigo's hold on bookselling across the land.

It was the 2002 collapse of Stoddart Publishing and its distribution arm, General Distribution Services, however, that dealt the most devastating blow to the industry. As MacSkimming explains, General "handled order fulfillment for some 200 other publishers, sixty-two of them Canadian [including small literary presses], and processed $87 million in annual sales."[3] The company faced cash flow problems, due in large part to massive returns from Chapters/Indigo – legally, booksellers have up to one year to return unsold books for credit – and the bankruptcy of its Arizona-based financial lender, Finova. It then received a loan guarantee in the amount of $4.5 million from the Department of Canadian Heritage, but Stoddart could not rally and General Publishing, "the company that held all of Jack Stoddart's publishing interests, 85 percent owned by him personally,"[4] finally filed for bankruptcy protection.

In chronicling the fall of Stoddart's publishing empire in *The Perilous Trade*, MacSkimming emphasizes the plight of small literary presses whose books were locked away in the outsized warehouse rented by General Distribution Services. Prevented by law from accessing their books, which were deemed property of the insolvent General, publishers had neither inventory nor cash at hand. The situation was ruinous and, while the Department of Canadian Heritage, the Canada Council for the Arts, and the Ontario government eventually provided financial assistance to rescue the ailing publishers, the foundering of General had both immediate and lasting effects. Authors, editors, book designers, printers, and booksellers lost revenue. Independent publishers like Montreal's Véhicule Press and Regina's Coteau Books suffered most, however. Not only had they forfeited books and income; they now knew the hard truth of their extreme vulnerability.[5]

Also in 2002, the internet retailer Amazon.com, founded in Seattle in 1994 by Jeff Bezos, initiated its now firmly established practice of selling books priced in Canadian dollars and shipping them from Canadian booksellers. Amazon, which was already servicing Canadian readers through its American website, soon cut deeper into the business of domestically owned bookstores, both the giant chain Chapters/Indigo and the small independent shops.[6]

Later that same year, in cold November 2002, the federal government sanctioned the sale of yet another Canadian publisher to an American firm – this time it was Distican that went to Simon and Schuster – providing further evidence of its laissez-faire approach to international competition and its general readiness to contravene its own long-standing laws preventing foreign ownership of Canadian publishing companies.

Macfarlane, Walter and Ross was the next casualty. An esteemed publisher of non-fiction, the firm was created in 1988 by principals John Macfarlane, Jan Walter, and Gary Ross, in partnership with Stoddart Publishing. In 1999, when he purchased the company from Jack Stoddart, Avie Bennett brought Macfarlane, Walter and Ross to McClelland and Stewart. In 2000, however, Macfarlane, Walter and Ross was transferred along with McClelland and Stewart to Random House. Then, three years later, when its sales were judged weak, Macfarlane, Walter and Ross was closed down – and the decision to do so was made not by Random House officials, but by McClelland and Stewart publisher himself, Douglas Gibson.[7]

It was only recently that the publishing community had absorbed the fact that Bennett had relinquished McClelland and Stewart to the care of Random House. Now it was being forced to accept the disappearance of Macfarlane, Walter and Ross, another well-established and distinguished firm. For the general public, it was unsettling to learn of the loss of another Canadian company. For those in publishing, however, it was an even more disturbing – and by now all-too-familiar – scenario.

Anna Porter's decision to retire from publishing underlined the extraordinary effort required – and the depletion it engendered – to sustain a Canadian company in the new global marketplace of the twenty-first century. In 2004, Porter sold "a majority interest"[8] in Key Porter Books, the company she had formed in 1979 and had run since 1982, to the book distributor H.B. Fenn. Over the next eight months, she helped transition Key Porter to Fenn. Then, in 2005, she left publishing and returned to writing.

Porter, who had always been more roused than taxed by the challenges of publishing, was finally flattened. As she explained to MacSkimming, "The nail in the coffin of my publishing career was the G[eneral] D[istribution] S[ervices] fiasco ... Key Porter lost about $750,000 after the emergency assistance trickled down from government ... it's a difficult business at the best of times, and frankly I'd lost heart."[9] Porter was genuinely disheartened: "You've poured your heart and soul into creating all these books, and you think your inventory is worth something, until your bankers tell you it's nothing except a colossal drain on the company. It's enough to make you weep."[10] It took seven more years before Fenn made the ultimate decision to suspend Key Porter's operations. In January 2011, its coffin was shut tight forever and Porter was left to mourn the demise of her creation.

Fenn's own bankruptcy closure, coming one short month after it dissolved Key Porter Books, points to today's radically altered publishing landscape, which bears little resemblance to the domestic publishing scene of the last century. Today, almost all the imprints that dominate this volume have either disappeared or have been subsumed by other companies. Only the scholarly publishers Oxford University Press Canada and the University of Toronto Press survive. Instead, merged companies and global conglomerates, in particular the German-owned Bertelsmann, have gained a near monopoly over Canadian publishing. Competition, which would otherwise indicate a healthy market for books, is thus severely curtailed, resulting in lower authors' advances.

The current publishing climate, run on a strict business model, rewards star authors and those with a proven track record of successful sales. Although independent presses remain open to new voices, once they achieve some renown, Canadian authors – who cannot be faulted for doing so – often decamp for larger publishing houses, with their promise of wider audiences and a greater financial return on writerly investment. Small domestic publishers simply cannot compete with international conglomerates, which have economic clout and a large capacity for digital marketing and author promotion.

Moreover, e-books, which were only on the horizon in 2002, the year Pomer and Shields parted ways, are now fully integrated into twenty-first century book production. It is a fact that digital publishing, in tandem with digital marketing, have transformed – many might say eased – the way books now reach readers.[11]

Ironically, many of these irrevocable changes came about largely as a result of the successful project of twentieth-century Canadian publishing. It can be argued, in fact, that recent moves by multinational consortiums to acquire Canadian imprints – their drive for market expansion and commercial dominance notwithstanding – shows the degree to which domestic publishing came of age during the last century.

This maturing, my research reveals, was facilitated in no small way by the leading roles played by several Toronto women who were well placed in Canadian publishing. As cultural workers, whose orientation I have interpreted as broadly feminist, these women publishers, editors, executives, and literary agents were catalysts for change: their own interventions helped transform the practice of publishing and the concomitant culture of authorship in Canada.

When Irene Clarke co-founded Clarke, Irwin in 1930, for example, she did more than expand the number of Canadian-owned publishing companies. She demonstrated one woman's willingness to assume the fiscal and administrative responsibilities known to all publishers. Under her direction, Clarke, Irwin grew into a publisher of note that issued educational books for Canadian students and trade titles that reflected the nation back to its readers. When necessary, she also engaged publicly with issues affecting domestic publishers. In the late 1960s, as we have seen, she criticized the Ontario government's implementation of changes that sharply impacted educational publishers.

Men and women alike noticed Clarke's capacity for leadership. The latter, in particular, looked to her as an example of someone who built a successful career in publishing. That she offered guidance to some, including the Macmillan Company of Canada's Gladys Neale, as well as editors Eleanor Harman and Sybil Hutchinson, underscores the collaborative nature of bookmaking – a fact further borne out by the intersecting career paths traced in this study.

Clarke's determination to publish the work of Emily Carr was another example of the kind of support she extended to women, in this case a writer whose earliest prose sketches bolstered Clarke's hopes for an expansive national literature. In championing the painter-turned-writer, Clarke also displayed a far-sighted grasp of Carr's significance for future generations of Canadian readers.

Eleanor Harman and Francess Halpenny were not present at the founding of the University of Toronto Press, but they were vital to the rise of Canada's first scholarly publisher. Individually, each brought executive skill and scholarly insight to her respective position; jointly, they established the press's standards for editorial excellence.

Administrative expertise led Harman up the ranks of the University of Toronto Press. As deputy to director Marsh Jeanneret, she was responsible for overseeing the day-to-day operations of the press's editorial, design and production, sales, and warehousing departments. An adept manager who was both detail- and goal-oriented, Harman relished all aspects of her supervisory role.

Harman derived particular satisfaction, however, from her editorial projects. Her work on individual manuscripts inspired her top initiatives: the house organ *Press Notes from the University of Toronto Press* and *Scholarly Publishing: A Journal for Authors and Publishers*. The first reflected her dual executive and editorial commitment to the University of Toronto Press, while the second showed her ambition to reach a broad audience seeking analysis of the nature of scholarly editing and publishing. As the founding editor of both vehicles, Harman enlarged the list of journals issued by the press. At the same time, she was instrumental in disseminating knowledge of a specialized field she herself was newly charting.

If Harman was the executive heart of the University of Toronto Press, Halpenny formed its editorial core. Halpenny was a meticulous scholarly editor who deployed her intelligence and writerly skill in various ways: by working closely with authors on manuscripts that covered a diverse range of disciplines; by serving as general editor of *The Dictionary of Canadian Biography/Dictionnaire biographique du Canada* for nearly two decades; and by publishing academic articles that addressed many facets of scholarly editing.

For Halpenny, the work of editing was more than fulfilling; it grew into a calling. Hence, she believed it was her professional responsibility, first, to develop the principles of scholarly editing, and then to explain the importance of editing to the scholarly enterprise. Both her in-house achievements and scholarly work validated the role of the editor and the purpose of editing; they also served to secure a place for the University of Toronto Press among the top academic publishers in North America.

Another publishing hub was McClelland and Stewart, where editors soaked up the nationalist culture of the press and, through their work with authors and their manuscripts, fostered the rise of Canadian literature. Sybil Hutchinson, for example, profiled noteworthy poets in the Indian File books, an influential series she conceived for the firm. Moreover, as an early advocate for the immigrant writer Henry Kreisel, the avant-garde novelist Sheila Watson, and the innovative poet and playwright James Reaney – each of whom went on to achieve literary acclaim – Hutchinson proved to be sophisticated in literary taste and prescient in editorial judgment. She may not have seen eye to eye with publisher Jack McClelland, but her editorial efforts advanced the reputation of his company and its writers.

Claire Pratt followed Hutchinson's lead as both a series and manuscript editor. Her editorial contributions to the New

Canadian Library evinced an intuitive apprehension of the historic significance of the paperback reprint series – even as it was establishing itself as the first source for Canadian literary titles – and her regard for originary texts. She brought the same editorial integrity to her work with journalist Peter C. Newman, novelist Margaret Laurence, and poet Irving Layton. Pratt's scrupulous manuscript editing was welcomed by Newman; her discerning assessment of Laurence's earliest writing gave the author critical insight and valued encouragement; and her conscientious handling of his books, as well as her frank but sympathetic response to his verse, boosted Layton, too. Pratt's editorial diplomacy smoothed the way to publication. Her approach also fostered each writer's loyalty, which was a great benefit to McClelland and Stewart.

Hutchinson and Pratt brought an understanding of Canadian writing to McClelland and Stewart. Anna Porter, on the other hand, arrived at a time of growth for the press, but with little knowledge of the Canadian literary field. Through hands-on work, she developed a critical appreciation for local writing and became a proficient editor.

Temperamentally, Porter was suited to the hive of activity at McClelland and Stewart. She assessed countless submissions and worked effectively with poet Earle Birney and prose writer Farley Mowat. She also embraced the enthusiasm and nationalism of Jack McClelland and became an ardent proponent of the literature she soon claimed as her own. The connection between McClelland and Stewart and Porter proved mutually rewarding. While she lent the firm her managerial and editorial skill and went on to head its mass-market subsidiary, Seal Books, Porter gained a mastery of publishing and formed lasting professional alliances.

It should be noted that Jack McClelland was not the only publisher to influence Porter. By co-founding Key Porter Books in 1979 and setting out as Canada's first female publisher of literary non-fiction, Porter was also following the example of publisher Irene Clarke, who, five decades earlier, had broken new ground for women by establishing Clarke, Irwin.

McClelland and Stewart also provided the basis for Hutchinson's groundbreaking agency work. Poets Robert Finch and James Reaney, who were featured in McClelland and Stewart's Indian File series, became clients when Hutchinson established herself as a literary agent. Her interventions on behalf of Finch and Reaney were much more than attempts to secure their financial well-being; they were mediating efforts on the part of a dauntless agent – whose role was altogether new to Canadian publishing – to represent the authors' best interests.

Nearly three decades after Hutchinson embarked as an agent, Bella Pomer started her own agency as a way to move forward with autonomy in the field of publishing. When she left her position as subsidiary rights manager at the Macmillan Company of Canada to set up her Toronto office, Canadian literature was gaining wider recognition and writers were seeking greater advantage through improved publishing contracts. Pomer provided the help they needed to effect such positive change and, in the process, firmly established herself as a professional agent.

In total, Pomer represented roughly thirty authors. She found an international audience for the work of Pauline Gedge. She placed Matt Cohen's fiction in Canada and the United States and saw it receive the Governor General's Literary Award. She negotiated with publisher Douglas Gibson on behalf of Jack Hodgins and celebrated his winning the Ethel Wilson Fiction Prize. And she helped Carol Shields build a triumphant career and achieve international recognition. That writers and publishers alike saw her as an unwavering and polished intermediary confirms the degree to which Pomer had a hand in consolidating the agent's central role in Canada's literary marketplace, which continues to this day.

In fact, this volume owes much to Pomer, who, by granting access to her archival papers, made it possible for me to feature the professional literary agent in this study of publishing women. Pomer made it less of a challenge to locate "accurate ... data describing the presence of women in Canada's literary history,"[12] the difficulty Carole Gerson faced in researching women involved in print culture. Like Gerson, I was spurred on by a scarcity of information and resolved to comb the available resources for missing details. I was determined to do what Alistair McCleery has done for Allen Lane, the founder of Penguin Books: to study "the human figure ... [in] book history ... whose individual decisions made a difference and whose career merits rigorous ... scrutiny."[13] The result is this retrospective analysis – born of archival discoveries, enlightening interviews, and fortuitous secondary findings – of seven women who worked in mainstream publishing and whose individual accomplishments stand in for a lack of comprehensive data describing women's broad participation in twentieth-century Canadian publishing.

It is my hope that this volume, which elucidates the vision and influence of leading figures,[14] will suggest further avenues of enquiry into the sphere of women and publishing. In fact, one of the not-so-tacit aims of this book has been to indicate how much research needs to be done if we are to fully grasp the complexity of women's role in publishing, the nature of their cultural work, and the extent to which their ingenuity and energy have been fundamental to building, refining, and sustaining this country's ever-changing book trade.

Notes

Introduction

1. Howsam, "Thinking Through the History of the Book."
2. William H. (Bill) Clarke, personal interview, 23 September 2010.
3. Gerson, "Women and Print Culture" 356.
4. Gerson, *Canadian Women in Print* 4.
5. Gerson references these women in "Women and Print Culture" 356.
6. Leroux 82.
7. The source for these details is Leroux 82–3.
8. Nelson 224.
9. Leroux 83.
10. Gerson, "Publishing by Women" 319.
11. See Cooper, "'Out of a Cardboard Box beside Our Bed like a Baby'" 291–306.
12. See Clark, "'A Grand Old House'" 51–90.
13. Clark, "'A Grand Old House'" 53.
14. Clark, "'A Grand Old House'" 86.
15. Clark, "'A Grand Old House'" 86.
16. Audley 99.
17. Parker, "The Struggle for Literary Publishing" 8.
18. Parker, "The Struggle for Literary Publishing" 9.
19. Parker, "The Struggle for Literary Publishing" 9.
20. Lorimer 84.
21. King 28.
22. Donnelly, "Jack McClelland."
23. Donnelly, "Jack McClelland."
24. Donnelly, "Jack McClelland."

25 In 2000, Random House of Canada acquired 25 per cent of McClelland and Stewart. Twelve years later, it secured the remaining 75 per cent and assumed ownership of the company. For a full account of the machinations behind the transfer of McClelland and Stewart to Random House, see Dewar, *The Handover*.
26 MacLaren, "Canadian Book History" 805.
27 See Panofsky, *The Literary Legacy*.
28 See Parker, "The Sale of Ryerson Press" 7–56.
29 King 230.
30 Donnelly, "Jack McClelland."
31 MacSkimming, *The Perilous Trade* 310.
32 Dan Levant qtd in Gold 543.
33 Publishers William Blackwood, Richard and George Bentley (father and son), and Daniel and Alexander Macmillan (brothers) in the United Kingdom; Alfred A. Knopf and Richard L. Simon and M. Lincoln ("Max") Schuster in the United States; and John and Jack McClelland (father and son) in Canada.
34 Publishers William Clarke of Clarke, Irwin, Marsh Jeanneret of University of Toronto Press, Mel Hurtig of Hurtig Publishers, and Robert Lecker of ECW Press, and editors Kildare Dobbs of the Macmillan Company of Canada, John Metcalf of the Porcupine's Quill and more recently of Biblioasis, and Douglas Gibson of McClelland and Stewart; publishers Lorne Pierce of Ryerson Press, John Morgan Gray of the Macmillan Company of Canada, Jack McClelland of McClelland and Stewart, and editor William Toye of Oxford University Press Canada. See [Clarke], *William Henry Clarke, 1902–1955*; Jeanneret, *God and Mammon*; Hurtig, *A Twilight in the Country*; Lecker, *Dr. Delicious*; Dobbs, *Running the Rapids*; Metcalf, *An Aesthetic Underground*; Gibson, *Stories about Storytellers*; Newfeld, *Drawing on Type*; Campbell, *Both Hands*; Panofsky, *The Literary Legacy of the Macmillan Company of Canada*; King, *Jack, a Life with Writers*; Panofsky, "'A Press with Such Traditions'" 7–29; Solecki, ed., *Imagining Canadian Literature*; and Davis and Morra, eds., *Margaret Laurence and Jack McClelland, Letters*.
35 See Halpenny, "100 Books for 100 Years" 57–93; L. Lewis, *Love, and All That Jazz*; and Porter, *In Other Words*.
36 M.L. MacDonald 139.
37 See Galarneau and Gallichan, "Working in the Trades" 80–6; Leroux, "Printers: From Shop to Industry" 75–87; Burr and Leroux, "Working in the Printing Trades" 358–68; Fleming, "The Binding Trades" 101–6; Gerson, "Women and Print Culture" 354–60; Gerson, "Publishing

by Women" 318–22; Burr, "Defending 'The Art Preservative'" 47–73; M.L. MacDonald, *"The Montreal Museum, 1832–1834"* 139–50; Irvine, *Editing Modernity*; and Hammill, *Literary Culture and Female Authorship in Canada*.

38 See *Canada's Early Women Writers*; *Database of Canada's Early Women Writers*; Pike, "A Selective History of Feminist Presses and Periodicals in English Canada" 209–18; Niedzwiecki, "Print Politics"; Kim "The Politics of Print"; T.E. Jordan, '"Branching Out"; Gerson, *Canadian Women in Print 1750–1918*; York, *Literary Celebrity in Canada* and *Margaret Atwood and the Labour of Literary Celebrity*.
39 Long xx.
40 Darnton 76.
41 Nash 267.
42 See Bourdieu, *Distinction*.
43 Howsam, "In My View" [1]. See also Sarah Werner's response to Howsam, "Weaving a Feminist Book History."
44 Howsam, "Women in Publishing" 67.
45 Travis 276.
46 See Travis 275–300.
47 See Murray, *Mixed Media*. In analysing women's participation in print culture of the Romantic period, Michelle Levy also considers the importance of gender. See Levy, "Do Women Have a Book History?"
48 Gerson, "Project Editing in Canada" 73.
49 Gerson, "Project Editing in Canada" 73.
50 Gerson, *Canadian Women in Print* 198.
51 Rimstead 176.
52 Gerson, *Canadian Women in Print* 198.
53 Murray 23.
54 Gerson, *Canadian Women in Print* xi.
55 Murray 215.
56 Gerson, *Canadian Women in Print* 198.
57 Nelson 224.
58 Lownsbrough 51.
59 Adachi M3.
60 Gerson, *Canadian Women in Print* 197.
61 Liz Calder qtd in Adachi M3.
62 Toller, "The Pink Ghetto" 14.
63 Two notable articles that focus on the Victorian period are Fredeman, "Emily Faithfull and the Victoria Press" 139–64; and Stone, "More Light on Emily Faithfull and the Victoria Press" 63–7.

64 See *Modernist Archives Publishing Project*.
65 *Women in Publishing*.
66 See Wood, "A Touch of Frost." I am grateful to Rex Williams for bringing this article to my attention. See also J. Lewis, *Penguin Special*. The Eunice Frost Papers are held in Special Collections, University of Bristol Library.
67 Exceptional Women in Publishing (website).
68 See *Women in Book History Bibliography*.
69 See Danky and Wiegand, eds., *Women in Print*.
70 Jordan and Patten 13.
71 Jordan and Patten 11.
72 Jordan and Patten 11.
73 Morra, *Unarrested Archives* 178.
74 Morra, *Unarrested Archives* 178.
75 Hobbs, "Personal Ethics" 187.
76 Hobbs, "Personal Ethics" 187.
77 John W. Irwin, email to author, 2 December 2008.
78 See Lennox and Panofsky, eds., *Selected Letters of Margaret Laurence and Adele Wiseman*.
79 Jaillant.
80 Baron 251.
81 Kelly.
82 Jaillant.
83 Jaillant.
84 Morra, *Unarrested Archives* 178.
85 Archival sources are cited in the Selected Bibliography.
86 Lopez 98.
87 Jaillant.
88 Long xx.
89 Travis 293.
90 Long xx.

1. "Exceptional in building a Canadian company": Irene Clarke

1 Neale 38.
2 Howsam, "In My View" 2.
3 For a brief overview of the firm, see Donnelly, "A History of Clarke, Irwin & Company Limited" iii–xi.
4 William Arthur Deacon qtd in "Clarke, Irwin" 153.
5 MacSkimming, *The Perilous Trade* 15.

6 Neale 38.
7 Dennys 235.
8 Neale 38.
9 William H. (Bill) Clarke, personal interview, 23 September 2010.
10 Neale 38.
11 MacSkimming, *The Perilous Trade* 72.
12 Neale 38.
13 William H. (Bill) Clarke, personal interview, 23 September 2010.
14 William H. (Bill) Clarke, personal interview, 23 September 2010.
15 William H. (Bill) Clarke, personal interview, 23 September 2010.
16 William H. (Bill) Clarke, personal interview, 23 September 2010.
17 Alden Nowlan qtd in Toner 198.
18 I. Clarke, "Address by Irene Irwin Clarke in Convocation Hall" 22.
19 Surridge and Derry, eds. 145.
20 Irene Clarke to Piers Raymond, 24 January 1958, box 1, file 23, CI fonds, Mills Memorial Library, MU.
21 Fulford 6.
22 William H. (Bill) Clarke, personal interview, 23 September 2010.
23 William H. (Bill) Clarke, personal interview, 23 September 2010.
24 MacSkimming, *The Perilous Trade* 17.
25 Donnelly, "A History of Clarke, Irwin & Company Limited" v.
26 Parker, "The Struggle for Literary Publishing" 9.
27 Irene Clarke to Willis Kingsley Wing, 22 November 1955, box 1, file 15, CI fonds, Mills Memorial Library, MU.
28 Lecker, "Canadian Authors and Their Literary Agents" 116.
29 MacSkimming, personal interview with William H. Clarke, 21 January 1999, p. 20, Roy MacSkimming fonds, Mills Memorial Library, MU.
30 Parker, "The Sale of Ryerson Press" 31.
31 Clark, "'A Grand Old House'" 86.
32 Donnelly, "Clarke, Irwin."
33 Donnelly, "Clarke, Irwin."
34 Donnelly, "Clarke, Irwin."
35 The third Marchbanks title is *Samuel Marchbanks' Almanack* (Toronto: McClelland and Stewart, 1967), and the third Salterton title is *A Mixture of Frailties* (Toronto: Macmillan Company of Canada, 1958).
36 See Gratien Gélinas, *Bousille et les Justes* (1959), *Tit-coq* (1948), and *Hier, les enfants dansaient* (1968).
37 See *New Canadian Library Collecting* blog for a complete list of titles in Clarke, Irwin's Canadian Paperback series.
38 Neale 38.

39 Tippett 256.
40 Morra, *Unarrested Archives* 66.
41 Irene Clarke to Ralph Hancox, 31 May 1972, box 103, file 2, CI fonds, Mills Memorial Library, MU.
42 Dimson 67.
43 Brydge 5.
44 Tippett 256.
45 Brydge 7.
46 Davies 18.
47 W.H. Clarke to Eric Brown, 16 June 1941, National Gallery of Canada.
48 Irene Clarke to Ralph Hancox, 31 May 1972, box 103, file 2, CI fonds, Mills Memorial Library, MU.
49 Tippett 265.
50 Tippett 265.
51 Irene Clarke to Ralph Hancox, 31 May 1972, box 103, file 2, CI fonds, Mills Memorial Library, MU.
52 Brown and Robertson, *Sunday Supplement*.
53 Bill Clarke to G.W. Stewart, 16 August 1974, box 103, file 3, CI fonds, Mills Memorial Library, MU.
54 Clarke also oversaw publication of Carr's *Growing Pains*; *A Little Town and a Little Girl*; an abridged version of *Klee Wyck*; *The Heart of a Peacock*; *Pause: A Sketch Book*; *An Address*; and *Fresh Seeing*.
55 Irene Clarke to Ina Uhthoff, 18 January 1967, box 4a, file 31, CI fonds, Mills Memorial Library, MU.
56 Clarke references her "114 letters from Emily Carr" (their current location is unknown) in a letter to Russell E. Smith, 29 September 1961, box 19, file 17, CI fonds, Mills Memorial Library, MU. Irene Clarke to Ralph Hancox, 31 May 1972, box 103, file 2, CI fonds, Mills Memorial Library, MU.
57 Dimson 67.
58 Morra, ed., *Corresponding Influence* 165, 245, 249, 267.
59 Morra, ed., *Corresponding Influence* 202, 215, 248.
60 Irene Clarke to the Canada Council for the Arts, 31 October 1967, box 26a, file 1, CI fonds, Mills Memorial Library, MU.
61 Irene Clarke to Bill Clarke, [April 1954], box 75, file 3, CI fonds, Mills Memorial Library, MU.
62 Irene Clarke to *Victoria Daily Times*, 23 October 1966, box 4a, file 31, CI fonds, Mills Memorial Library, MU.
63 "Mrs. Clarke Opens Emily Carr Show" 6.
64 Irene Clarke to Ina Uhthoff, 18 January 1967, box 4a, file 31, CI fonds, Mills Memorial Library, MU.

65 Irene Clarke to Ina Uhthoff, 18 January 1967, box 4a, file 31, CI fonds, Mills Memorial Library, MU.
66 Irene Clarke to Emily Carr, [July 1944], MS-2763, box 2, file 10, Emily Carr papers, British Columbia Archives.
67 "Mrs. Clarke Opens Emily Carr Show" 6.
68 Donnelly, "Clarke, Irwin."
69 Newman 34.
70 Donnelly, "Clarke, Irwin."
71 MacSkimming, *The Perilous Trade* 302.
72 Donnelly, "Clarke, Irwin."
73 Donnelly, "Clarke, Irwin."
74 "Irene Irwin Clarke, 83" A28.
75 "Irene Irwin Clarke: Publisher" D9.
76 William H. (Bill) Clarke, personal interview, 23 September 2010.

2. A "Principal Architect" of the University of Toronto Press: Eleanor Harman

1 Montagnes, "In Tribute" 8–9.
2 Jeanneret, *God and Mammon* 48.
3 Montagnes, "In Tribute" 9.
4 Deacon, "The Fly Leaf," 23 February 1946: 8.
5 Eleanor Harman qtd in Deacon, "The Fly Leaf," 23 February 1946: 8.
6 Eleanor Harman to Francess Halpenny, 9 August 1973, FGH fonds, UTA.
7 MacSkimming, *The Perilous Trade* 92.
8 Deacon, "The Fly Leaf," 5 December 1942: 8.
9 Barrett.
10 Clark, "The Rise and Fall" 229.
11 Clark, "The Rise and Fall" 229.
12 MacSkimming, *The Perilous Trade* 94.
13 MacSkimming, *The Perilous Trade* 95.
14 "Three Heads" 18.
15 "Three Heads" 18.
16 "Three Heads" 20, 18.
17 Jeanneret, *God and Mammon* 16.
18 "Three Heads" 20.
19 Deacon, "The Fly Leaf," 10 December 1949: 14.
20 Jeanneret, *God and Mammon* 17.
21 Brown, Harman, and Jeanneret, *The Story of Canada*.
22 Jeanneret, *God and Mammon* 17.

23 "Three Heads" 20.
24 Deacon, "Introduces Younger Readers" 12.
25 Deacon, "Introduces Younger Readers" 12.
26 Deacon, "Critical Comments" 10.
27 Maurice Lebel qtd in Deacon, "The Fly Leaf," 24 January 1953: 22.
28 Harman took a particular interest in historic women. In 1966, she published a book chapter on the five women (known as the "Famous Five") whose landmark efforts led to the legal recognition in 1929 of women as "persons" eligible to sit in the Canadian Senate. See her "Five Persons from Alberta" 158–78. Harman may have felt a kinship with Henrietta Muir Edwards who, prior to marriage, was involved in publishing. In 1878, the sisters Henrietta and Amelia Muir opened the Montreal Women's Printing Office on Bleury Street. The shop employed women and issued the newspaper *Woman's Work in Canada* (Gerson, *Canadian Women in Print* 9–10). Three public sculptures commemorate the "Famous Five": Barbara Paterson's identical sculptures on Parliament Hill in Ottawa and Olympic Plaza in Calgary, and Helen Granger Young's sculpture on the grounds of the Manitoba Legislature in Winnipeg. See www.famou5.ca.
29 For recent analyses of the content of *The Story of Canada* and other textbooks, see Igartua, "What Nation, Which People?" and Carmen Poole, "'Not of the Nation'" 81–102.
30 Montagnes, "University of Toronto Press" 1148.
31 MacSkimming, *The Perilous Trade* 93.
32 Floyd Chalmers qtd in Jeanneret, *God and Mammon* 156.
33 MacSkimming, "Francess Halpenny interview, 23 October 1998," Roy MacSkimming fonds, Mills Memorial Library, MU.
34 François Charles Archile Jeanneret qtd in MacSkimming, *The Perilous Trade* 96.
35 MacSkimming, *The Perilous Trade* 92.
36 Qtd in Jeanneret, *God and Mammon* 117.
37 L. Lewis 195.
38 MacSkimming, *The Perilous Trade* 97.
39 L. Lewis 174.
40 L. Lewis 173.
41 Jeanneret, *God and Mammon* 238.
42 Jeanneret, *God and Mammon* 237.
43 MacSkimming, *The Perilous Trade* 110.
44 Jeanneret, *God and Mammon* 57.
45 Jeanneret, *God and Mammon* 75.
46 Jeanneret, *God and Mammon* 75.

47 Macleod 103.
48 Macleod 103.
49 Jeanneret, *God and Mammon* 136.
50 Jeanneret, *God and Mammon* 136.
51 Jeanneret, *God and Mammon* 132.
52 Jeanneret, *God and Mammon* 132.
53 Jeanneret, *God and Mammon* 35.
54 Jeanneret, *God and Mammon* 162.
55 Jeanneret, *God and Mammon* 221.
56 MacSkimming, *The Perilous Trade* 104–5.
57 Eleanor Harman qtd in Jeanneret, *God and Mammon* 153.
58 MacSkimming, *The Perilous Trade* 102.
59 Jeanneret's claim that the John Stuart Mill "mega project" was one of Canada's "great international scholarly contributions" (*God and Mammon* 288, 170) remains true today.
60 Eleanor Harman to Barbara Plewman, 7 September 1965, UTP fonds, UTA.
61 L. Lewis 174.
62 MacSkimming, *The Perilous Trade* 92.
63 Harman, Review of *The Building of the House*, 98–9.
64 Harman, "Ghost Writing" 10.
65 Harman, "A Reconsideration" 150, 152.
66 Harman, "Copy Editing" 133.
67 Harman, "A Reconsideration" 151.
68 Harman, "A Reconsideration" 151.
69 Harman, "A Reconsideration" 151.
70 Deacon, "Far-Flung English" 25.
71 Harman, "Copy Editing" 133–4.
72 Jeanneret, *God and Mammon* 237.
73 Harman, "Hints on Proofreading."
74 Eleanor Harman to Paul Arthur, 15 February 1963, UTP fonds, UTA.
75 Eleanor Harman qtd in Deacon, "The Fly Leaf," 1 November 1952: 13.
76 Jeanneret, *God and Mammon* 251.
77 Jeanneret, *God and Mammon* 252.
78 MacSkimming, *The Perilous Trade* 110.
79 Jeanneret, *God and Mammon* 252.
80 Eleanor Harman to Francess Halpenny, 17 February 1960, FGH fonds, UTA.
81 Eleanor Harman to Francess Halpenny, 17 February 1960, FGH fonds, UTA.
82 Jeanneret, *God and Mammon* 252.
83 Harman, "University Press Association."
84 Stursberg.

85 Harman, "Royal Commission."
86 Harman, "AAUP Meets."
87 Harman, "Buchmesse."
88 Harman, "Buchmesse."
89 For a full study of Pierce's editorial career, see Campbell, *Both Hands*.
90 All citations are taken from Lagacé, "The Art of Editing."
91 Harman, "Hints on Proofreading."
92 Eleanor Harman to Harold Kurschenska, 29 August 1961, UTP fonds, UTA.
93 Webb 166.
94 Jeanneret, *God and Mammon* 255, 253.
95 Jeanneret, *God and Mammon* 253.
96 Jeanneret, *God and Mammon* 253.
97 Jeanneret, "Editorial" 4.
98 Jeanneret, *God and Mammon* 255, 254.
99 MacSkimming, *The Perilous Trade* 111.
100 Harman and Montagnes x.
101 Pascoe 89.
102 Rohmann.
103 Gregor.
104 Tarver 563. See Halpenny, "The Thesis and the Book" 3–10.
105 Jeanneret, *God and Mammon* 255.
106 Jeanneret, *God and Mammon* 257.
107 "Ernst and Ernst Report" 1.
108 Lowman 4.
109 Harman, "Commission" 1.
110 Harman, "Commission" 12.
111 Harman, "Commission" 12.
112 Harman, "Commission"'13.
113 Harman, "Commission" 12.
114 Harman, "Founding a University Press" 58.

3. The "Editorial Conscience" of the University of Toronto Press: Francess Halpenny

1 Haycock 27.
2 Mavor Moore to Francess Halpenny, 16 October 1987, file 3, FGH fonds, UTA.
3 Maude.
4 Francess Halpenny qtd in Haycock 27.
5 Francess Halpenny qtd in Carey D5.

6 MacSkimming, "Francess Halpenny interview, 23 October 1998," Roy MacSkimming fonds, Mills Memorial Library, MU.
7 Francess Halpenny qtd in Haycock 27.
8 Jeanneret, *God and Mammon* 64.
9 Halpenny, "Education and Training" 165.
10 MacSkimming, "Francess Halpenny interview, 23 October 1998," Roy MacSkimming fonds, Mills Memorial Library, MU.
11 MacSkimming, "Francess Halpenny interview, 23 October 1998," Roy MacSkimming fonds, Mills Memorial Library, MU. Vis-à-vis gender, see Wright, *The Professionalization of History in English Canada*.
12 Jeanneret, *God and Mammon* 64–5.
13 On the University of Toronto Press, see Harman, "Founding a University Press" 19–58; Jeanneret, *God and Mammon*; Kachergis, ed., *One Book/Five Ways*; Macleod, "Proper Care and Work Well Done"; Montagnes, "University of Toronto Press" 1148–9; and Halpenny, "100 Books for 100 Years" 57–93.
14 Francess Halpenny qtd in Haycock 28.
15 Francess Halpenny qtd in Haycock 28.
16 Francess Halpenny to Robin P. Hoople, 4 March 1971, FGH fonds, UTA.
17 Halpenny, "An Editorial Career."
18 Halpenny, "The Scholarly Books" 61.
19 Halpenny, "Living a Project" 209.
20 See, for example, the following articles by Halpenny: "The Scholarly Books of the University of Toronto Press" 59–62; "A Canadian Publishing Programme"; "University Presses" 110–14; "The Editor on His Campus" 370–76; "Responsibilities of Scholarly Publishers" 223–31; "Living a Project" 204–20; and "100 Books for 100 Years" 57–93.
21 Francess Halpenny to Raymond A. Anselment, 23 December 1976, B87-0051/049, FGH fonds, UTA.
22 Halpenny, "100 Books" 61.
23 Halpenny, "The Scholarly Books" 59.
24 Halpenny, "100 Books" 87.
25 Halpenny, "Shall We Join" 50.
26 Halpenny, "The Editorial Function" 71.
27 Francess Halpenny qtd in Haycock 27.
28 Halpenny, "Responsibilities" 227.
29 Cullen 4.
30 Halpenny, "The Editorial Function" 67.
31 Halpenny, "The Editorial Function" 70.
32 Halpenny, "'Responsibilities" 227.

33 Isay 253.
34 Isay 253.
35 Halpenny, "Shall We Join" 50.
36 Halpenny, "The Editorial Function" 71.
37 MacSkimming, "Francess Halpenny interview, 23 October 1998," Roy MacSkimming fonds, Mills Memorial Library, MU.
38 Halpenny, "Shall We Join" 50.
39 Halpenny, "100 Books" 65.
40 Francess Halpenny to Robert MacGregor Dawson, 26 August 1947, B87-0051/026, FGH fonds, UTA.
41 Eleanor Harman qtd in Jeanneret, *God and Mammon* 145.
42 Sarah Dawson to Francess Halpenny, 23 November 1958, FGH fonds, UTA.
43 Halpenny, "100 Books" 66.
44 Robert MacGregor Dawson qtd in Harman, "Founding a University Press" 53.
45 Halpenny, "100 Books" 82.
46 Halpenny, "100 Books" 82.
47 Halpenny, "In Tribute" 28.
48 See. Halpenny, "In Tribute: Russell Harper" 28.
49 "Francess Georgina Halpenny" B19.
50 MacSkimming, "Francess Halpenny interview, 23 October 1998," Roy MacSkimming fonds, Mills Memorial Library, MU.
51 See Shipton, "An Academic Rock Star's Advice for Editors."
52 See Halpenny, "'The Ethics of Editing"; "Submitting a Manuscript"; "An Editorial Career"; and J.C.J., "House Style"; "The Collection and the Book"; and "[SIC]."
53 See Halpenny, ed., *Editing Twentieth-Century Texts* and *Editing Canadian Texts*.
54 Francess G. Halpenny, personal interview, 21 May 2008.
55 Francess Halpenny qtd in Hampton 10.
56 Jeanneret, *God and Mammon* 176.
57 Halpenny, "Twenty Years" 200.
58 In the 1950s and 1960s, Nicholson's bequest was supplemented by funding from the Ford Foundation, the Canada Council for the Arts, and Canada's Centennial Commission. In March 1973, an additional grant from the Canada Council in the amount of $307,240 further expanded the work of the DCB/DBC.
59 Halpenny, "Teaching History with the DCB," B2000-0023/006, FGH fonds, UTA.
60 Jeanneret, *God and Mammon* 285.

61 Jeanneret, *God and Mammon* 285.
62 Jeanneret, *God and Mammon* 285.
63 Jeanneret, *God and Mammon* 282, 286.
64 Haycock 27.
65 Jeanneret, *God and Mammon* 285.
66 Halpenny, "Men in History."
67 Halpenny, "Men in History."
68 Halpenny, "Men in History."
69 Halpenny, "Men in History."
70 Halpenny, "Conference on Literary Biography," B2000-0023/006, FGH fonds, UTA.
71 Halpenny, "Conference on Literary Biography," B2000-0023/006, FGH fonds, UTA.
72 Halpenny, "Research – Problems and Solutions" 39, 42.
73 Halpenny, "Research – Problems and Solutions" 37.
74 Halpenny, "Research – Problems and Solutions" 37.
75 Jeanneret, *God and Mammon* 283.
76 To date, volumes 1 to 15 of the DCB/DBC have been published. Volumes 16 to 22 are in preparation.
77 Halpenny, "Teaching History with the DCB," B2000-0023/006, FGH fonds, UTA.
78 Francess Halpenny qtd in Carey D5.
79 Halpenny, "Convocation Address, Carleton University, 1991," B2000-0023/005, FGH fonds, UTA.
80 Rutherford 199.
81 Moore 34–5.
82 Qtd in Hampton 10.
83 "Francess Halpenny Awarded Molson Prize."
84 "UBC Medal Honours Editor."
85 Halpenny, "Teaching Publishing" 75.
86 Francess Halpenny qtd in Haycock 61.
87 See Halpenny, "Twenty Years of Canadian Biography" 193–201.
88 Halpenny, "Help the Humanities" A6.
89 Halpenny, "Help the Humanities" A6.
90 Halpenny, "The Humanities in Canada" 161.
91 Halpenny, "Convocation Address, University of Toronto, 1994," B2000-0023/005, FGH fonds, UTA.
92 Halpenny, "100 Books" 87.
93 Langan.

4. "She knew the business ... and the Canadian literary market": Sybil Hutchinson

1. Earle Birney to Ralph Gustafson, 22 May 1942, MSS 6, MSS 6/1–6/2, box 2, file 68, Ralph Gustafson literary papers, US.
2. See Sybil Hutchinson, "Kettleful of Sunshine" 2–8; and "Second Sight" 77–83.
3. Sybil Hutchinson, Report on "72 Under the 0" by Allan Stratton, [14 July 1978], AFC 18, JR fonds, WU.
4. Birney 99.
5. Sybil Hutchinson to Ralph Gustafson, 29 October 1942, MSS 6, MSS 6/1–6/2, box 2, file 68, Ralph Gustafson literary papers, US.
6. Birney 99.
7. Sybil Hutchinson to Bill McConnell, 8 February 1973, box 57, file 1, Book Society of Canada fonds, MU.
8. Birney 138.
9. [Clarke], *William Henry Clarke, 1902–1955*.
10. John W. Irwin, personal interview, 21 August 2013.
11. Speller 3–4. See also Sandra Campbell, *Both Hands*; and MacLaren, "'Significant Little Offerings" 9–49.
12. Speller 4.
13. Daniells, *Deeper into the Forest*, dust jacket.
14. Campbell 58.
15. Speller 4.
16. Sybil Hutchinson to Henry Kreisel, 12 July 1946, MSS 59, box 1, file 7, HK fonds, UM.
17. Gray 35.
18. Sybil Hutchinson to Henry Kreisel, 12 July 1946, MSS 59, box 1, file 7, HK fonds, UM.
19. Sybil Hutchinson to Henry Kreisel, 8 April 1948, MSS 59, box 1, file 7, HK fonds, UM.
20. Kreisel 70.
21. Sybil Hutchinson to Henry Kreisel, 7 May 1948, MSS 59, box 1, file 7, HK fonds, UM.
22. Sybil Hutchinson to Henry Kreisel, 7 May 1948, MSS 59, box 1, file 7, HK fonds, UM.
23. Sybil Hutchinson to Henry Kreisel, 3 May 1948, MSS 59, box 1, file 7, HK fonds, UM.

24 Sybil Hutchinson to Henry Kreisel, [May 1948], MSS 59, box 1, file 7, HK fonds, UM.
25 Sybil Hutchinson to Henry Kreisel, 26 August 1948, MSS 59, box 1, file 7, HK fonds, UM.
26 Sybil Hutchinson to Henry Kreisel, [October 1948], MSS 59, box 1, file 7, HK fonds, UM.
27 Sybil Hutchinson to Henry Kreisel, 29 September 1948, MSS 59, box 1, file 7, HK fonds, UM.
28 Sybil Hutchinson to Henry Kreisel, 8 February 1949, MSS 59, box 1, file 7, HK fonds, UM.
29 Sybil Hutchinson to Henry Kreisel, 14 April 1949, MSS 59, box 1, file 7, HK fonds, UM.
30 Sybil Hutchinson to Henry Kreisel, 8 February 1949, MSS 59, box 1, file 7, HK fonds, UM.
31 Sybil Hutchinson to Henry Kreisel, 17 February 1949, MSS 59, box 1, file 7, HK fonds, UM.
32 Sybil Hutchinson to Henry Kreisel, 10 August 1960, MSS 59, box 1, file 7, HK fonds, UM.
33 Kreisel 71.
34 Kreisel 70.
35 Kreisel 70.
36 Kreisel 70.
37 Sybil Hutchinson to Sheila Watson, 26 January 1949, Sheila Watson Archives, John M. Kelly Library, University of St Michael's College, UT.
38 Sybil Hutchinson to Sheila Watson, 26 January 1949, Sheila Watson Archives, John M. Kelly Library, University of St Michael's College, UT.
39 Jack Eric Morpurgo qtd in "Professor Jack Morpurgo."
40 Sybil Hutchinson to James Reaney, 30 December 1977, JR fonds, WU.
41 Sybil Hutchinson to Sheila Watson, 26 January 1949, Sheila Watson Archives, John M. Kelly Library, University of St Michael's College, UT.
42 Sybil Hutchinson to Sheila Watson, 20 April 1950, Sheila Watson Archives, John M. Kelly Library, University of St Michael's College, UT.
43 St Onge 23.
44 King 25–6.
45 King 35.
46 King 40.
47 Sybil Hutchinson to Henry Kreisel, 14 April 1950, MSS 59, box 1, file 7, HK fonds, UM.

214   Notes to pages 100–6

48 Sybil Hutchinson to Henry Kreisel, 14 April 1950, MSS 59, box 1, file 7, HK fonds, UM.
49 Sybil Hutchinson to Sheila Watson, 20 April 1950, Sheila Watson Archives, John M. Kelly Library, University of St Michael's College, UT.
50 Sybil Hutchinson to Henry Kreisel, 1 June 1950, MSS 59, box 1, file 7, HK fonds, UM.
51 Sybil Hutchinson to Henry Kreisel, 1 June 1950, MSS 59, box 1, file 7, HK fonds, UM.
52 Harman, "A Reconsideration" 151.
53 Harman, "A Reconsideration" 151.
54 Sybil Hutchinson to A.L. Pattee, 26 March 1962, box 56, file 27, Book Society of Canada fonds, MU.
55 Sybil Hutchinson to Peter J. Feteris, 11 July 1973, box 57, file 8, Book Society of Canada fonds, MU.
56 Sybil Hutchinson to David Chestnut, 4 January 1973, box 57, file 8, Book Society of Canada fonds, MU.
57 Sybil Hutchinson to Patricia McDonough, 22 October 1973, box 57, file 8, Book Society of Canada fonds, MU.
58 John C.W. Irwin qtd in John W. Irwin, personal interview, 21 August 2013. John W. Irwin suspects Hutchinson may have had Asperger Syndrome.
59 John W. Irwin, personal interview, 21 August 2013.
60 For Lecker's full discussion of Hedges, Southam, and de Merian, see "Canadian Authors and Their Literary Agents, 1890–1977" 93–120. Lecker further likens earlier interventions by Toronto editors Edward Caswell, Carl Eayrs, and Donald French to those generally undertaken by literary agents.
61 Sybil Hutchinson to Alice Cameron Brown, 30 January 1952, MSS 105, box 7, file 5, Alice Cameron Brown fonds, UM.
62 Sybil Hutchinson to James Reaney, 21 October 1971, JR fonds, WU.
63 Sybil Hutchinson to R. Shipley, 29 August 1977, JR fonds, WU.
64 Sybil Hutchinson to Alice Cameron Brown, 4 September 1953, 105, box 7, file 5, Alice Cameron Brown fonds, UM.
65 Sybil Hutchinson to Alice Cameron Brown, 4 December 1954, 105, box 7, file 5, Alice Cameron Brown fonds, UM.
66 Sybil Hutchinson to Alice Cameron Brown, 22 December 1953, 105, box 7, file 5, Alice Cameron Brown fonds, UM.
67 Inkster.
68 Inkster.

Notes to pages 106–15   215

69 Inkster.
70 Inkster.
71 Sybil Hutchinson to Ralph Gustafson, 21 November 1949, MSS 6, MSS 6/1–6/2, box 2, file 68, Ralph Gustafson literary papers, US.
72 Susan Wallace and her husband, James Stewart Reaney, are James Reaney's literary executors. Together, they maintain the website jamesreaney.com.
73 York, *Margaret Atwood* 54.
74 Sybil Hutchinson to Earle Toppings, 6 October 1967, JR fonds, WU.
75 Sybil Hutchinson to Robert N. Hinitt, 27 April 1967, JR fonds, WU.
76 Sybil Hutchinson to James Reaney, 15 May 1969, JR fonds, WU.
77 Sybil Hutchinson to H.N. Bawden, 6 March 1969, JR fonds, WU.
78 Sybil Hutchinson to Donald Sutherland, 16 August 1971, JR fonds, WU.
79 Sybil Hutchinson to James Reaney, 4 August 1971, JR fonds, WU.
80 Sybil Hutchinson to James Reaney, 4 August 1971, JR fonds, WU.
81 Sybil Hutchinson to Donald Sutherland, 26 August 1971, JR fonds, WU.
82 Sybil Hutchinson to Donald Sutherland, 26 August 1971, JR fonds, WU.
83 Sybil Hutchinson to David Robinson, 8 February 1972, JR fonds, WU.
84 Sybil Hutchinson to Press Porcépic, 6 December 1977, JR fonds, WU.
85 Sybil Hutchinson to Richard Nielsen, 16 March 1978, JR fonds, WU.
86 Jack McClelland to Sybil Hutchinson, 17 January 1977, JR fonds, WU.
87 Sybil Hutchinson to Earle Birney, 24 March 1987, Box 237, Earle Birney papers, Thomas Fisher Rare Book Library, UT.
88 Susan Reaney, email to author, 19 February 2014.
89 Sybil Hutchinson to Tim Inkster, 12 December 1982, box 20, file 6, Robert Finch papers, Thomas Fisher Rare Book Library, UT.

5. A "tremendous job of editing": Claire Pratt

1 Brandeis, "Claire Pratt" 13.
2 Pratt contracted polio at the age of four and the disease had a major impact on her life. It led to complications such as infection, countless surgeries, and protracted periods of recuperation.
3 Claire Pratt diary, 9 April 1959, box 17, file 1, MCP fonds, E.J. Pratt Library, VU.
4 Claire Pratt diary, 16 February 1961, box 17, file 1, MCP fonds, E.J. Pratt Library, VU.
5 Pratt, ed., *Viola Whitney Pratt: A Testament of Love* 52.
6 Claire Pratt diary, 16 February 1961, 22, box 17, file 1, MCP fonds, E.J. Pratt Library, VU.

7 Claire Pratt diary, 17 March 1960, box 17, file 1, MCP fonds, E.J. Pratt Library, VU.
8 Claire Pratt diary, 5 April 1958, box 17, file 1, MCP fonds, E.J. Pratt Library, VU.
9 Claire Pratt diary, 19 June 1961, box 17, file 1, MCP fonds, E.J. Pratt Library, VU.
10 Pratt, ed., *Viola Whitney Pratt: A Testament of Love* 49.
11 Friskney 150.
12 See Friskney, *New Canadian Library*.
13 Friskney 150.
14 Claire Pratt to Douglas Lochhead, 8 January 1960, series Cae, box 12, file 26, M&S fonds, Mills Memorial Library, MU.
15 Claire Pratt to Malcolm Ross, 14 September 1960, series Cae, box 12, file 26, M&S fonds, Mills Memorial Library, MU.
16 Claire Pratt to A.M. Klein, 15 May 1961, series Cae, box 12, file 1, M&S fonds, Mills Memorial Library, MU.
17 These include Frances Brooke's *The History of Emily Montague* (ed. Mary Jane Edwards, 1985); Catharine Parr Traill's *Canadian Crusoes* (ed. Rupert Schieder, 1986); James De Mille's *A Strange Manuscript Found in a Copper Cylinder* (ed. Malcolm Parks, 1986); John Richardson's *Wacousta* (ed. Douglas Cronk, 1987); Susanna Moodie's *Roughing It in the Bush* (ed. Carl Ballstadt, 1988); Rosanna Leprohon's *Antoinette de Mirecourt* (ed. John C. Stockdale, 1989); Thomas McCulloch's *The Mephibosheth Stepsure Letters* (ed. Gwendolyn Davies, 1990); Julia Catherine Beckwith Hart's *St Ursula's Convent* (ed. Douglas G. Lochhead, 1991); John Richardson's *The Canadian Brothers* (ed. Donald Stephens, 1992); Thomas Chandler Haliburton's *The Clockmaker, Series One, Two, and Three* (ed. George L. Parker, 1995); Catharine Parr Traill's *The Backwoods of Canada* (ed. Michael A. Peterman, 1997); and William Kirby's *Le Chien d'or* (ed. Mary Jane Edwards, 2012).
18 Bowering 1199. See Brandeis, "Claire Pratt: Art and Adversity" 3–28 and "The Graphic Work of Claire Pratt" 29–33.
19 Gustafson, *Rivers Among Rocks*, colophon.
20 Claire Pratt to Jack McClelland, 2 April 1962, series Cae, box 20, file 22, M&S fonds, Mills Memorial Library, MU. See Speller, "Frank Newfeld and McClelland & Stewart's Design for Poetry Series" 3–36.
21 Jack McClelland to Claire Pratt, [January 1961], series Cae, box 12, file 5, M&S fonds, Mills Memorial Library, MU.
22 Jack McClelland to Claire Pratt, [January 1961], series Cae, box 12, file 5, M&S fonds, Mills Memorial Library, MU.

23 E.J. Pratt (1882–1964) thrice won the Governor General's Literary Award for poetry: for *The Fable of the Goats and Other Poems* (1937), *Brébeuf and His Brethren* (1940), and *Towards the Last Spike* (1952). From 1929 to 1955, Viola Whitney Pratt (1892–1984) was editor of *World Friends*, a monthly magazine for children published by the Woman's Missionary Society of the United Church of Canada.
24 Claire Pratt to Stanley Knowles, 24 January 1961, series Cae, box 12, file 5, M&S fonds, Mills Memorial Library, MU.
25 Claire Pratt to Stanley Knowles, 24 January 1961, series Cae, box 12, file 5, M&S fonds, Mills Memorial Library, MU.
26 Stanley Knowles to Claire Pratt to Stanley Knowles, 31 January 1961, series Cae, box 12, file 5 M&S fonds, Mills Memorial Library, MU.
27 Jack McClelland to Claire Pratt, [1961], series Cae, box 12, file 5, M&S fonds, Mills Memorial Library, MU.
28 Claire Pratt to Peter Newman, 15 August 1963, series Cae, box 12, file 60, M&S fonds, Mills Memorial Library, MU.
29 Claire Pratt to Peter Newman, 27 August 1963, series Cae, box 12, file 60, M&S fonds, Mills Memorial Library, MU.
30 Peter Newman to Claire Pratt, 18 August 1963, series Cae, box 12, file 60, M&S fonds, Mills Memorial Library, MU.
31 Peter Newman to Claire Pratt, 15 September 1963, series Cae, box 12, file 60, M&S fonds, Mills Memorial Library, MU.
32 Peter Newman to Claire Pratt, 15 September 1963, series Cae, box 12, file 60, M&S fonds, Mills Memorial Library, MU.
33 Claire Pratt to Peter Newman, 19 October 1963, series Cae, box 12, file 60, M&S fonds, Mills Memorial Library, MU.
34 Claire Pratt to Peter Newman, 19 October 1963, series Cae, box 12, file 60, M&S fonds, Mills Memorial Library, MU.
35 Peter Newman to Claire Pratt, 20 October 1963, series Cae, box 12, file 60, M&S fonds, Mills Memorial Library, MU.
36 Claire Pratt to Peter Newman, 19 October 1963, series Cae, box 12, file 54, M&S fonds, Mills Memorial Library, MU.
37 Claire Pratt to W.L. Morton, 20 November 1963, series Cae, box 12, file 55, M&S fonds, Mills Memorial Library, MU.
38 Claire Pratt to W.L. Morton, 9 March 1964, series Cae, box 12, file 55, M&S fonds, Mills Memorial Library, MU.
39 Claire Pratt to Henry Kreisel, 9 April 1964, series Cae, box 12, file 6, M&S fonds, Mills Memorial Library, MU.
40 Pratt, ed., *Viola Whitney Pratt: Papers and Speeches* 163.

41 Claire Pratt, Reader's Report, 18 February 1963, series Cae, box 12, file 7, M&S fonds, Mills Memorial Library, MU.
42 Claire Pratt to Margaret Laurence, 20 February 1963, series Cae, box 12, file 7, M&S fonds, Mills Memorial Library, MU.
43 Claire Pratt to Jack McClelland, 25 July 1963, series Cae, box 12, file 7, M&S fonds, Mills Memorial Library, MU.
44 Margaret Laurence's Manawaka series comprises four novels – *The Stone Angel* (1964), *A Jest of God* (1966), *The Fire-Dwellers* (1969), and *The Diviners* (1974) – and the short story cycle *A Bird in the House* (1970).
45 Irving Layton to Claire Pratt, [December 1958], series Cae, box 12, file 11, M&S fonds, Mills Memorial Library, MU.
46 Claire Pratt to Irving Layton, 18 December 1958, series Cae, box 12, file 11, M&S fonds, Mills Memorial Library, MU.
47 Irving Layton to Claire Pratt, 26 December 195[8], series Cae, box 12, file 11, M&S fonds, Mills Memorial Library, MU.
48 Irving Layton to Claire Pratt, 26 December 195[8], series Cae, box 12, file 11, M&S fonds, Mills Memorial Library, MU.
49 Irving Layton to Claire Pratt, 10 March 1959, series Cae, box 12, file 11, M&S fonds, Mills Memorial Library, MU.
50 Irving Layton to Claire Pratt, 10 March 1959, series Cae, box 12, file 11, M&S fonds, Mills Memorial Library, MU.
51 Irving Layton to Claire Pratt, 10 March 1959, series Cae, box 12, file 11, M&S fonds, Mills Memorial Library, MU.
52 Mount 200.
53 Irving Layton to Claire Pratt, 9 January 1960, series Cae, box 12, file 9, M&S fonds, Mills Memorial Library, MU.
54 [Claire Pratt] to Irving Layton, 9 January 1961, series Cae, box 12, file 9, M&S fonds, Mills Memorial Library, MU.
55 Claire Pratt to Irving Layton, 12 January 1961, series Cae, box 12, file 9, M&S fonds, Mills Memorial Library, MU.
56 Irving Layton to Claire Pratt, [March 1961], series Cae, box 12, file 9, M&S fonds, Mills Memorial Library, MU.
57 Layton 173.
58 Claire Pratt to Irving Layton, 22 February 1961, series Cae, box 12, file 9, M&S fonds, Mills Memorial Library, MU.
59 Claire Pratt to Irving Layton, 1 March 1961, series Cae, box 12, file 9, M&S fonds, Mills Memorial Library, MU.
60 Irving Layton to Claire Pratt, 10 March 1961, series Cae, box 12, file 9, M&S fonds, Mills Memorial Library, MU.
61 Claire Pratt to Jack McClelland, 16 January 1964, series Cae, box 11, file 21, M&S fonds, Mills Memorial Library, MU.

62 Mount 201–2.
63 Claire Pratt to Irving Layton, [September 1962], series Cae, box 12, file 10, M&S fonds, Mills Memorial Library, MU.
64 Irving Layton to Claire Pratt, 17 September 1962, series Cae, box 12, file 10, M&S fonds, Mills Memorial Library, MU.
65 Irving Layton to Claire Pratt, 6 January 1964, series Cae, box 11, file 21, M&S fonds, Mills Memorial Library, MU.
66 Irving Layton to Claire Pratt, 15 January 196[4], series Cae, box 11, file 21, M&S fonds, Mills Memorial Library, MU.
67 Claire Pratt to Irving Layton, 21 May 1964, series Cae, box 11, file 21, M&S fonds, Mills Memorial Library, MU.
68 Irving Layton to Claire Pratt, 23 May 1964, series Cae, box 11, file 21, M&S fonds, Mills Memorial Library, MU.
69 Jack McClelland to Irving Layton, 17 January 1964, series Cae, box 11, file 21, M&S fonds, Mills Memorial Library, MU.
70 Jack McClelland to Irving Layton, 17 January 1964, series Cae, box 11, file 21, M&S fonds, Mills Memorial Library, MU.
71 Claire Pratt to Irving Layton, 9 June 1964, series Cae, box 11, file 21, M&S fonds, Mills Memorial Library, MU.
72 Irving Layton to Claire Pratt, 14 June 1964, series Cae, box 11, file 21, M&S fonds, Mils Memorial Library, MU.
73 Jack McClelland to Claire Pratt, 14 September 1970, series C, box 2, file Pratt: Transmittals, M&S fonds, Mills Memorial Library, MU.
74 Jack McClelland to Anna Szigethy, 7 October 1970, series C, box 2, file Pratt: Transmittals, M&S fonds, Mills Memorial Library, MU.
75 Claire Pratt qtd in Brandeis, "Claire Pratt" 15.

6. Publishing "Maestro" and Cultural Advocate: Anna Porter

1 Porter has published four crime novels, *Hidden Agenda*, *Mortal Sins*, *The Bookfair Murders*, and *The Appraisal*; two memoirs, *The Storyteller: Memory, Secrets, Magic and Lies,* and *In Other Words: How I Fell in Love with Canada One Book at a Time*; a popular work, *Vampires: From Vlad Drakul to the Vampire Lestat*, released under the name Anna Szigethy and co-authored with Anne Graves; and three works of non-fiction, *Kasztner's Train: The True Story of Rezso Kasztner, Unknown Hero of the Holocaust*, *The Ghosts of Europe: Journeys through Central Europe's Troubled Past and Uncertain Future,* and *Buying a Better World: George Soros and Billionaire Philanthropy*. She is also co-editor with Marjorie Harris of *Farewell to the 70s: A Canadian Salute to a Confusing Decade* and editor of *Jack McClelland: The Publisher of Canadian Literature*.

2 Porter, "I'm All Right" 49.
3 Porter, "A Canadian Education" 104.
4 Porter, "A Canadian Education" 104–5.
5 Porter, "A Canadian Education" 116.
6 Porter, "Farley Mowat" 329.
7 Robert Fulford qtd in Lownsbrough 64. Two years earlier, Key Porter Books had published Robert Fulford's *Canada: A Celebration*.
8 Porter, "The Master Storyteller" 316.
9 Anna Porter qtd in MacSkimming, "*The Perilous Trade* Conversations" 76.
10 Anna Porter to Jack McClelland, 4 February 1974, series A, box 68, M&S fonds, Mills Memorial Library, MU. See Doug Michel and Bob Mellor, *Left Wing and a Prayer: Birth Pains of a World Hockey Franchise* (Ottawa: Excalibur Sports Publications, 1974).
11 Anna Porter to Jack McClelland, et al., 26 September 1973, box Ja11, file 45, M&S fonds, Mills Memorial Library, MU. *The National Parks of Canada* by Kevin McNamee and J.A. Kraulis (Toronto: Key Porter Books, 1994) was among the books Porter later published.
12 Anna Porter to Jack McClelland, 10 January 1975, M&S fonds, Mills Memorial Library, MU.
13 Anna Porter to Jack McClelland, 16 October 1973, series A, box 51, file 29, M&S fonds, Mills Memorial Library, MU.
14 Jack McClelland to Anna Porter, 17 October 1973, series A, box 51, file 29, M&S fonds, Mills Memorial Library, MU.
15 Anna Porter to Jack McClelland, 31 July 1973, M&S fonds, Mills Memorial Library, MU.
16 Anna Porter to Jack McClelland, 31 July 1973, M&S fonds, Mills Memorial Library, MU.
17 Jack McClelland to Anna Porter, 10 August 1973, M&S fonds, Mills Memorial Library, MU.
18 Anna Porter, personal interview, 25 October 2013.
19 Jack McClelland to Anna Porter, [5 October 1973], M&S fonds, Mills Memorial Library, MU.
20 Five of Dennis Lee's children's books later appeared under the Key Porter imprint: *Bubblegum Delicious* (2000); *The Cat and the Wizard* (2001); *Garbage Delight: Another Helping* (2002); *So Cool* (2004); and *Silverly/Good Night, Good Night* (2006).
21 Jack McClelland to Anna Porter, 15 March 1974, series A, box 68, M&S fonds, Mills Memorial Library, MU.
22 Anna Porter to Jack McClelland, 26 February 1974, series A, box 68, M&S fonds, Mills Memorial Library, MU.

23 Jack McClelland to Anna Porter, 5 March 1974, series A, box 68, M&S fonds, Mills Memorial Library, MU.
24 Jack McClelland to Anna Porter, 5 March 1974, series A, box 68, M&S fonds, Mills Memorial Library, MU.
25 Sylvia Fraser qtd in MacSkimming, *The Perilous Trade* 153.
26 MacSkimming, *The Perilous Trade* 152.
27 Jack McClelland to Larry Ritchie, 21 March 1971, M&S fonds, Mills Memorial Library, MU.
28 Donaldson 26.
29 Anna Porter to Jack McClelland, 16 February 1973, M&S fonds, Mills Memorial Library, MU.
30 Anna Porter to Jack McClelland, 16 February 1973, M&S fonds, Mills Memorial Library, MU.
31 Jack McClelland to Anna Porter, 14 September 1978, box 38, file 16, M&S fonds, Mills Memorial Library, MU.
32 Kome 38d.
33 Sylvia Fraser qtd in Allemang 36.
34 Anna Porter qtd in MacSkimming, "*The Perilous Trade* Conversations" 76, 77.
35 See box 2CA50, file 1978, 2nd and 3rd accruals, M&S fonds, Mills Memorial Library, MU.
36 Anna Porter, personal interview, 25 October 2013.
37 Anna Porter, personal interview, 25 October 2013.
38 Anna Porter qtd in Toller, "A Fine Balance" 12.
39 Anna Porter, personal interview, 25 October 2013.
40 Anna Porter, personal interview, 25 October 2013.
41 Anna Porter, personal interview, 25 October 2013.
42 Anna Porter, personal interview, 25 October 2013.
43 Anna Porter, personal interview, 25 October 2013.
44 Anna Porter, personal interview, 25 October 2013.
45 MacSkimming, *The Perilous Trade* 157.
46 Anna Porter qtd in MacSkimming, "*The Perilous Trade* Conversations" 78.
47 MacSkimming, *The Perilous Trade* 156.
48 MacSkimming, *The Perilous Trade* 157.
49 Jack McClelland to Anna Porter, 10 July 1981, M&S fonds, Mills Memorial Library, MU.
50 Anna Porter to Jack McClelland, 7 July 1982, M&S fonds, Mills Memorial Library, MU.
51 Anna Porter qtd in MacSkimming, *The Perilous Trade* 411.
52 Jack McClelland to Anna Porter, 31 March 1982, M&S fonds, Mills Memorial Library, MU.

53 Key Publishers issued the magazines *Canadian Business*, *Canadian Geographic*, *Toronto Life*, *Quill and Quire*, and *Where*.
54 Geraldine Sherman qtd in Allemang 36.
55 Anna Porter qtd in Konotopetz.
56 Anna Porter qtd in Pitts 84.
57 Porter, "Discovering Words" R3.
58 King 303.
59 Jack McClelland to Anna Porter, 7 April 1977, M&S fonds, Mills Memorial Library, MU.
60 Marchand L4.
61 Porter, "Feedback" H12.
62 Porter, "Instead, We Became Cautious Friends."
63 Porter, "Instead, We Became Cautious Friends."
64 Porter, "The Master Storyteller" 317.
65 Porter, "Farley Mowat" 330.
66 Porter, "The Master Storyteller" 320.
67 See Goddard, "A Real Whopper" 46–50, 52, 54, 64.
68 Anna Porter qtd in Ross C1.
69 For a scholarly examination of the Goddard-Mowat affair, see Lee, "Goddard v. Mowat" 30–40.
70 Farley Mowat qtd in Baker 1.
71 Anna Porter qtd in Pitts 84.
72 Porter, "Discovering Words" R3.
73 Anna Porter qtd in Fotheringham 179.
74 Allan Fotheringham's other Key Porter titles include *Look Ma – No Hands: An Affectionate Look at Our Wonderful Tories* (1983), *Capitol Offences: Dr. Foth Meets Uncle Sam* (1986), *Birds of a Feather: The Press and the Politicians* (1989), *Last Page First* (1999), and *Fotheringham's Fictionary of Facts and Follies* (2001).
75 See Slopen, 'Monkeying around with Fraser's Book" L14.
76 See Porter's memoir, *The Storyteller: Memory, Secrets, Magic and Lies*.
77 MacDonald, "Literary Lights Out."
78 Founder Stan Bevington revived Coach House Press in 1997.
79 MacDonald, "Literary Lights Out."
80 Porter, "The Shaky State" A17.
81 Porter, "The Shaky State" A17.
82 A full account of Porter's leadership of Key Porter Books, which ceased operations in January 2011, is a large enough subject to warrant its own monograph and lies outside the scope of this study.
83 Porter, "The Shaky State" A17.

84 Porter, "The Shaky State" A17.
85 Sheppard.
86 Rae, Manji, and Porter, "A Call to Arms" A21.
87 Rae, Manji, and Porter, "A Call to Arms" A21.
88 Anna Porter qtd in de Mello, "TDR Interview."
89 Anna Porter qtd in Konotopetz.
90 See Porter, "Return of the Iron Fist."
91 PEN Canada stands for Poets, Playwrights, Editors, Essayists, Novelists Canada, which includes journalists and historians.
92 Stoffman A1.
93 Key Porter Books had published Jean Chrétien's memoir, *Straight from the Heart*, in 1994.
94 Anna Porter to Sarmite D. Bulte, 11 March 2003, Key Porter Books fonds, Mills Memorial Library, MU.
95 Anna Porter to Sarmite D. Bulte, 11 March 2003, Key Porter Books fonds, Mills Memorial Library, MU.
96 The other honorees were Patsy Aldana (Groundwood Books); Louise Dennys (Lester and Orpen Dennys); Diana Douglas (Self-Counsel Press); Valerie Hussey (Kids Can Press); Carol Martin (Peter Martin Associates); Anne Millyard (Annick Press); Libby Oughton (Ragweed Press); Ellen Seligman (McClelland and Stewart); Annabel Slaight (Owl); Ann Wall (House of Anansi Press); and Caroline Wood (on behalf of the Women's Press Collective). The President's Award is given annually in recognition of substantial long-term contributions to the Association of Canadian Publishers and the Canadian publishing industry. See www.publishers.ca.

7. The "Grande Dame" of Literary Agents: Bella Pomer

1 Bella Pomer, personal interview, 4 April 2012.
2 Turnbull B2.
3 Bella Pomer qtd in Turnbull B2.
4 Bella Pomer, personal interview, 4 April 2012. See Alice Kane, *Songs and Sayings of an Ulster Childhood* (ed. Edith Fowke, 1983) and *The Dreamer Awakes* (ed. Sean Kane, 1995).
5 M. Smith 5.
6 Parker, "The Struggle for Literary Publishing" 9.
7 Potter and Marsh.
8 Bella Pomer, personal interview, 4 April 2012.
9 Bella Pomer to Carol Shields, 17 May 2001, box 16, BP papers, Thomas Fisher Rare Book Library, UT.

10 Bella Pomer, personal interview, 4 April 2012.
11 Bella Pomer, personal interview, 4 April 2012.
12 Bella Pomer, personal interview, 4 April 2012.
13 Bella Pomer, personal interview, 4 April 2012. Harold Pomer did not live to see his wife succeed in her new venture; he died in 1980.
14 Fetherling 668.
15 Gillies 174, 35.
16 Gillies 26, 35.
17 York, *Margaret Atwood* 32.
18 Davey 112.
19 Lecker, "Canadian Authors and Their Literary Agents" 117–18. See also Litt, "The State and the Book" 34–44.
20 Joseph Regal qtd in Mayer 78.
21 York, *Margaret Atwood* 41.
22 York, *Margaret Atwood* 26.
23 York, *Margaret Atwood* 46.
24 Mayer 7, 11.
25 York, *Margaret Atwood* 56.
26 York, *Margaret Atwood* 59.
27 See Karr, *Authors and Audiences*; Dean, "Researching Sara Jeannette Duncan" 181–6; Morra, *Unarrested Archives*; McCaig, *Reading in Alice Munro's Archives*; and York, *Margaret Atwood*. For further work on Canadian authors and foreign agents, see Barbara Wales Meadowcroft, "Arthur Stringer as a Man of Letters"; and Gerson, "'Dragged at Anne's Chariot Wheels'" 143–59.
28 Gillies 61.
29 Gillies 61.
30 Gillies 61.
31 The Bella Pomer Literary Agency was established in 1978 and incorporated in 1983.
32 Bella Pomer qtd in Weiler 21.
33 Weiler 21.
34 Bella Pomer, personal interview, 4 April 2012.
35 Pomer charged the standard commission fee of 15 per cent.
36 Fitzgerald D8.
37 Bella Pomer qtd in Fitzgerald D8.
38 Fitzgerald D8.
39 Bella Pomer, email to author, 26 April 2015.
40 Bourdieu 291.

41 Bella Pomer to Nan Talese, 17 May 1990, box 2, file 23, BP papers, Thomas Fisher Rare Book Library, UT.
42 Bella Pomer to Nan Talese, 17 May 1990, box 2, file 23, BP papers, Thomas Fisher Rare Book Library, UT.
43 Bella Pomer to Penelope Hoare, 21 April 1997, box 2, file 25, BP papers, Thomas Fisher Rare Book Library, UT.
44 Bella Pomer to Matt Cohen, 8 March 1999, box 2, file 25, BP papers, Thomas Fisher Rare Book Library, UT.
45 Bella Pomer to Louise Dennys, 7 January 1998, box 4, file 2, BP papers, Thomas Fisher Rare Book Library, UT.
46 Kirchhoff C11.
47 Bella Pomer to Matt Cohen, 13 November 1995, box 2, file 26, BP papers, Thomas Fisher Rare Book Library, UT.
48 Bella Pomer to Matt Cohen, 13 November 1995, box 2, file 26, BP papers, Thomas Fisher Rare Book Library, UT.
49 Bella Pomer to Matt Cohen, 21 February 1996, box 2, file 25, BP papers, Thomas Fisher Rare Book Library, UT.
50 Bella Pomer, personal interview, 4 April 2012.
51 Bella Pomer to Matt Cohen, 9 May 1996, box 2, file 25, BP papers, Thomas Fisher Rare Book Library, UT.
52 Bella Pomer to Matt Cohen, 21 May 1996, box 2, file 25, BP papers, Thomas Fisher Rare Book Library, UT.
53 York, *Margaret Atwood* 49.
54 Bella Pomer to Matt Cohen, 10 April 1996, box 2, file 25, BP papers, Thomas Fisher Rare Book Library, UT.
55 Bella Pomer to Matt Cohen, 21 May 1996, box 2, file 25, BP papers, Thomas Fisher Rare Book Library, UT.
56 Bella Pomer to Matt Cohen, 7 July 1998, box 2, file 25, BP papers, Thomas Fisher Rare Book Library, UT.
57 Bella Pomer to Matt Cohen, 7 July 1998, box 2, file 25, BP papers, Thomas Fisher Rare Book Library, UT.
58 Bella Pomer to Matt Cohen, 7 July 1998, box 2, file 25, BP papers, Thomas Fisher Rare Book Library, UT.
59 Bella Pomer to Matt Cohen, 8 March 1999, box 2, file 25, BP papers, Thomas Fisher Rare Book Library, UT.
60 Bella Pomer to Matt Cohen, 8 March 1999, box 2, file 25, BP papers, Thomas Fisher Rare Book Library, UT.
61 Bella Pomer to Matt Cohen, 8 March 1999, box 2, file 25, BP papers, Thomas Fisher Rare Book Library, UT.

62 Bella Pomer to Matt Cohen, 8 March 1999, box 2, file 25, BP papers, Thomas Fisher Rare Book Library, UT.
63 Bella Pomer to Matt Cohen, 1 June 1999, box 2, file 25, BP papers, Thomas Fisher Rare Book Library, UT.
64 Bella Pomer, personal interview, 4 April 2012.
65 Wilson D3.
66 Bella Pomer to Jack Hodgins, 20 December 1999, box 3, file 22, BP papers, Thomas Fisher Rare Book Library, UT.
67 Bella Pomer to Jack Hodgins, 24 May 1989, box 4, BP papers, Thomas Fisher Rare Book Library, UT.
68 Bella Pomer to Jack Hodgins, 8 March 1994, box 3, file 29, BP papers, Thomas Fisher Rare Book Library, UT.
69 Bella Pomer to Jack Hodgins, 8 March 1994, box 3, file 29, BP papers, Thomas Fisher Rare Book Library, UT.
70 Bella Pomer to Jack Hodgins, 8 March 1994, box 3, file 29, BP papers, Thomas Fisher Rare Book Library, UT.
71 Jack Hodgins to Bella Pomer, 23 August 1997, box 3, BP papers, Thomas Fisher Rare Book Library, UT.
72 Bella Pomer to Jack Hodgins, 29 December 1997, box 6, file 6, BP papers, Thomas Fisher Rare Book Library, UT.
73 Bella Pomer to Jack Hodgins, 29 December 1997, box 6, file 6, BP papers, Thomas Fisher Rare Book Library, UT.
74 Bella Pomer to Douglas Gibson, 29 September 1992, box 6, file 1, BP papers, Thomas Fisher Rare Book Library, UT.
75 Jack Hodgins to Bella Pomer, 6 January 1994, box 3, file 30, BP papers, Thomas Fisher Rare Book Library, UT.
76 Bella Pomer to Douglas Gibson, 29 September 1992, box 6, file 1, BP papers, Thomas Fisher Rare Book Library, UT.
77 Bella Pomer to Douglas Gibson, 14 September 1993, box 6, file 1, BP papers, Thomas Fisher Rare Book Library, UT.
78 Bella Pomer to Douglas Gibson, 29 September 1992, box 6, file 1, BP papers, Thomas Fisher Rare Book Library, UT.
79 Bella Pomer to Douglas Gibson, 29 September 1992, box 6, file 1, BP papers, Thomas Fisher Rare Book Library, UT.
80 Bella Pomer to Jack Hodgins, 18 August 1997, box 3, BP papers, Thomas Fisher Rare Book Library, UT.
81 Bella Pomer to Douglas Gibson, 25 April 1995, box 6, file 3, BP papers, Thomas Fisher Rare Book Library, UT.
82 Bella Pomer to Jack Hodgins, 29 December 1997, box 6, file 6, BP papers, Thomas Fisher Rare Book Library, UT.

83 Bella Pomer to Jack Hodgins, 29 December 1997, box 6, file 6, BP papers, Thomas Fisher Rare Book Library, UT.
84 Bella Pomer to Jack Hodgins, 2 September 1997, box 3, BP papers, Thomas Fisher Rare Book Library, UT.
85 Bella Pomer to Douglas Gibson, 8 January 1998, box 6, file 7, BP papers, Thomas Fisher Rare Book Library, UT.
86 Bella Pomer to Jack Hodgins, 29 December 1997, box 6, file 6, BP papers, Thomas Fisher Rare Book Library, UT.
87 Jack Hodgins to Bella Pomer, 27 June 1994, box 3, file 28, BP papers, Thomas Fisher Rare Book Library, UT.
88 Bella Pomer to Jack Hodgins, 4 September 2000, box 5, file 23, BP papers, Thomas Fisher Rare Book Library, UT.
89 Bella Pomer to Jack Hodgins, 16 September 1996, box 3, file 26, BP papers, Thomas Fisher Rare Book Library, UT.
90 Bella Pomer to Jack Hodgins, 13 May 2001, box 5, file 24, BP papers, Thomas Fisher Rare Book Library, UT.
91 Joseph Regal qtd in Mayer 78.
92 Bella Pomer to Jack Hodgins, 3 January 1999, box 3, file 24, BP papers, Thomas Fisher Rare Book Library, UT.
93 Bella Pomer to Jack Hodgins, 12 March 1998, box 3, BP papers, Thomas Fisher Rare Book Library, UT.
94 Bella Pomer to Jack Hodgins, 18 August 1997, box 3, BP papers, Thomas Fisher Rare Book Library, UT.
95 Bella Pomer to Jack Hodgins, 2 September 1997, box 3, BP papers, Thomas Fisher Rare Book Library, UT.
96 Bella Pomer to Jack Hodgins, 18 August 1997, box 3, BP papers, Thomas Fisher Rare Book Library, UT.
97 Bella Pomer to Jack Hodgins, 5 September 1998, box 3, BP papers, Thomas Fisher Rare Book Library, UT.
98 Bella Pomer to Jack Hodgins, 15 August 1998, box 3, BP papers, Thomas Fisher Rare Book Library, UT.
99 Bella Pomer to Jack Hodgins, 26 August 2001, box 5, file 24, BP papers, Thomas Fisher Rare Book Library, UT.
100 Gibson 151.
101 Bella Pomer to Jack Hodgins, 15 November 2001, box 5, file 24, BP papers, Thomas Fisher Rare Book Library, UT.
102 Bella Pomer, email to author, 26 April 2015.
103 Bella Pomer, email to author, 25 April 2015.
104 Hobbs, "Voice and Re-vision" 35.
105 Bella Pomer, personal interview, 4 April 2012.

106 Bella Pomer, personal interview, 4 April 2012.
107 York, *Margaret Atwood* 49.
108 Bella Pomer to Carol Shields, 15 December 1983, box 6, BP papers, Thomas Fisher Rare Book Library, UT.
109 York, *Margaret Atwood* 49.
110 Bella Pomer to Carol Shields, 2 September 1982, box 6, BP papers, Thomas Fisher Rare Book Library, UT.
111 Bella Pomer to Carol Shields, 1 April 1983, box 16, BP papers, Thomas Fisher Rare Book Library, UT.
112 Bella Pomer to Carol Shields, 21 July 1998, box 16, BP papers, Thomas Fisher Rare Book Library, UT.
113 Bella Pomer to Carol Shields, 29 September 1997, box 16, BP papers, Thomas Fisher Rare Book Library, UT.
114 Bella Pomer to Carol Shields, 15 March 1999, box 16, BP papers, Thomas Fisher Rare Book Library, UT.
115 Bella Pomer to Carol Shields, 22 January 1985, box 6, BP papers, Thomas Fisher Rare Book Library, UT.
116 Bella Pomer to Carol Shields, 10 May 1988, box 6, BP papers, Thomas Fisher Rare Book Library, UT.
117 Bella Pomer to Carol Shields, 12 April 1984, box 6, BP papers, Thomas Fisher Rare Book Library, UT.
118 Bella Pomer to Carol Shields, 28 November 1994, box 6, BP papers, Thomas Fisher Rare Book Library, UT.
119 Bella Pomer to Carol Shields, 28 November 1994, box 6, BP papers, Thomas Fisher Rare Book Library, UT.
120 Shields's work was published in the following translations: Bulgarian, Catalan, Chinese, Croatian, Czech, Danish, Dutch, Estonian, Finnish, French, German, Greek, Hebrew, Hungarian, Icelandic, Italian, Japanese, Korean, Latvian, Norwegian, Polish, Portuguese, Romanian, Serbian, Spanish, Swedish, and Turkish.
121 Slopen, "Booker or Not" J18.
122 Carol Shields to Bella Pomer, 29 October 1993, box 6, BP papers, Thomas Fisher Rare Book Library, UT.
123 As a dual Canadian and American citizen – she was born and raised in Oak Park, Illinois – Shields was eligible for the Pulitzer Prize.
124 Slopen, "Persistent Pomer" K9.
125 Bella Pomer to Carol Shields, 5 September 1995, box 16, BP papers, Thomas Fisher Rare Book Library, UT.
126 Gillies 46.

127 Bella Pomer to Jocelyn Laurence, 3 January 1985, box 16, BP papers, Thomas Fisher Rare Book Library, UT.
128 Bella Pomer to Ted Mumford, 9 September 1993, box 17, BP papers, Thomas Fisher Rare Book Library, UT.
129 Bella Pomer to Douglas Pepper, [December 1993], box 17, BP papers, Thomas Fisher Rare Book Library, UT.
130 Bella Pomer to Bill Hanna, 7 June 1988, box 17, BP papers, Thomas Fisher Rare Book Library, UT.
131 Bella Pomer to Bill Hanna, 7 June 1988, box 17, BP papers, Thomas Fisher Rare Book Library, UT.
132 Bella Pomer to Bill Hanna, 7 June 1988, box 17, BP papers, Thomas Fisher Rare Book Library, UT.
133 Bella Pomer to Carol Shields, 17 July 1990, box 17, BP papers, Thomas Fisher Rare Book Library, UT.
134 Bella Pomer to Leona Trainer, 23 November 1993, box 16, BP papers, Thomas Fisher Rare Book Library, UT.
135 Bella Pomer to Jack Stoddart, 13 December 1994, box 16, BP papers, Thomas Fisher Rare Book Library, UT.
136 Bella Pomer to Jack Stoddart, 13 December 1994, box 16, BP papers, Thomas Fisher Rare Book Library, UT.
137 Bella Pomer to Bill Hanna, 7 February 1995, box 17, BP papers, Thomas Fisher Rare Book Library, UT.
138 Stoddart Publishing went bankrupt seven years later. For a full account of Stoddart's unfortunate and messy demise, see MacSkimming, *The Perilous Trade*.
139 Bella Pomer, personal interview, 4 April 2012.
140 Bella Pomer qtd in Stephen Smith 11.
141 Bella Pomer to Carol Shields, 22 February 1985, box 16, BP papers, Thomas Fisher Rare Book Library, UT.
142 Bella Pomer to Carol Shields, 21 May 1986, box 6, BP papers, Thomas Fisher Rare Book Library, UT.
143 Bella Pomer to Carol Shields, 11 July 1995, box 6, BP papers, Thomas Fisher Rare Book Library, UT.
144 Bella Pomer to Carol Shields, 31 May 1999, box 16, BP papers, Thomas Fisher Rare Book Library, UT.
145 Bella Pomer to Carol Shields, 17 May 2001, box 16, BP papers, Thomas Fisher Rare Book Library, UT.
146 Bella Pomer to Carol Shields, 17 May 2001, box 16, BP papers, Thomas Fisher Rare Book Library, UT.

147 "A Persistent Talent" C16.
148 *Unless* eventually was published in the following translations: Catalan, Czech, Dutch, Estonian, Finnish, French, German, Greek, Hebrew, Hungarian, Italian, Korean, Norwegian, Portuguese, Serbian, Spanish, and Swedish.
149 Bella Pomer to Carol Shields, 17 June 2002, box 16, BP papers, Thomas Fisher Rare Book Library, UT.
150 Bella Pomer to Carol Shields, 17 June 2002, box 16, BP papers, Thomas Fisher Rare Book Library, UT.
151 Bella Pomer to Carol Shields, 17 June 2002, box 16, BP papers, Thomas Fisher Rare Book Library, UT.
152 Bella Pomer to Carol Shields, 17 June 2002, box 16, BP papers, Thomas Fisher Rare Book Library, UT.
153 Bella Pomer to Carol Shields, 6 November 2002, box 16, BP papers, Thomas Fisher Rare Book Library, UT.
154 Bella Pomer, personal interview, 4 April 2012.
155 In addition to Cohen, Hodgins, and Shields, Pomer represented Joan Barfoot, Isabel Huggan, Ken Mitchell, Medora Sale, Diane Schoemperlen, Maggie Siggins, Merilyn Simonds, Eric Wright, and others. For a full client list, see the Bella Pomer papers, Ms Coll 00340, Ms Coll 00360, Thomas Fisher Rare Book Library, UT.
156 Bella Pomer qtd in Elash 12.
157 Elash 12.
158 Bella Pomer, personal interview, 4 April 2012.
159 Dennys 232.
160 Stephen Smith 11.
161 Davey 113.
162 Wilson D3.
163 Bella Pomer qtd in Stephen Smith 10–11.
164 Lecker, "Canadian Authors and Their Literary Agents" 118.
165 Lecker, "Canadian Authors and Their Literary Agents" 118.
166 Bella Pomer to Jack Hodgins, 11 July 1995, box 3, file 27, BP papers, Thomas Fisher Rare Book Library, UT.
167 George Fetherling wrote the entry. See Fetherling, "Literary Agents" 668.
168 Bella Pomer, personal interview, 4 April 2012.
169 Slopen, "Persistent Pomer" K9.
170 Honey, Posner, and Martin R2.
171 Bella Pomer, personal interview, 4 April 2012.
172 Bella Pomer, personal interview, 4 April 2012.
173 York, *Margaret Atwood* 88.

Conclusion

1 MacSkimming, *The Perilous Trade* 375.
2 Dewar 104.
3 MacSkimming, *The Perilous Trade* 377.
4 MacSkimming, *The Perilous Trade* 378, 379.
5 See MacSkimming, *The Perilous Trade* 383, 385.
6 MacSkimming, *The Perilous Trade* 387.
7 Dewar 241.
8 MacSkimming, *The Perilous Trade* 411.
9 Anna Porter qtd in MacSkimming, *The Perilous Trade* 412.
10 Anna Porter qtd in MacSkimming, *The Perilous Trade* 411. I have drawn on *The Perilous Trade* for details covering the years 2000 to 2005.
11 My focus on women whose careers spanned the twentieth century precludes a full discussion of the nature of present-day Canadian publishing.
12 Gerson, *Canadian Women in Print* 197.
13 McCleery 163. See Alistair McCleery, "The Return of the Publisher to Book History" 161–85. For a biography of Lane, see J. Lewis, *Penguin Special*.
14 McCleery 163.

Selected Bibliography

1. Archival Sources

British Columbia Archives

Emily Carr papers

David M. Rubenstein Rare Book and Manuscript Library, Duke University

Virginia Barber Literary Agency records

E.J. Pratt Library, Special Collections, Victoria University in the University of Toronto

Grace Irwin fonds
Mildred Claire Pratt fonds

Elizabeth Dafoe Library, Archives and Special Collections, University of Manitoba

Alice Cameron Brown fonds
Henry Kreisel fonds

John M. Kelly Library, Archival and Manuscript Collections, University of St Michael's College in the University of Toronto

Sheila Watson archives

Library and Archives Canada

Colbert Agency fonds

Mills Memorial Library, William Ready Division of Archives and Research Collections, McMaster University

Book Society of Canada fonds
Clarke, Irwin and Company Limited fonds
Key Porter Books fonds
McClelland and Stewart fonds

Thomas Fisher Rare Book Library, University of Toronto

Earle Birney papers
Robert Finch papers
Bella Pomer papers

University Library, University Archives and Special Collections, University of Saskatchewan

Ralph Gustafson literary papers

University of Toronto Archives

Francess Georgina Halpenny fonds
University of Toronto Press fonds

Western Libraries, Archives and Research Collections Centre, Western University

James Reaney fonds

2. Interviews

Clarke, William H. (Bill). Personal interview. 23 September 2010.
de Mello, Jessica. "TDR Interview: Anna Porter." *TDR: The Danforth Review* 6 November 2007. www.danforthreview.com/features/profiles/anna_porter.htm.
Gold, Jerome. "Dan Levant, Madrona Publishers." *Publishing Lives: Interviews with Independent Book Publishers in the Pacific Northwest and British Columbia*. By Gold. Seattle: Black Heron Press, 1995. 541–57.
Halpenny, Francess G. Personal interview. 21 May 2008.
Irwin, John W. Personal interview. 21 August 2013.
MacSkimming, Roy. "Francess Halpenny interview, 23 October 1998." Roy MacSkimming fonds. William Ready Division of Archives and Research Collections, Mills Memorial Library, MU. http://digitalcollections.mcmaster.ca/hpcanpub/media/francess-halpenny-interview-roy-macskimming-audio-interview-23-october-1998.

- Personal interview with William H. Clarke. 21 January 1999. Box 1, series 1, file 16, transcript. Roy MacSkimming fonds. William Ready Division of Archives and Research Collections, Mills Memorial Library, MU.
- "*The Perilous Trade* Conversations. Seven: Anna Porter." *Canadian Notes and Queries* 81 (Winter–Spring 2011): 74–82.

Pomer, Bella. Personal interview. 4 April 2012.
Porter, Anna. Personal interview. 25 October 2013.
Wallace, Susan. Personal interview. 17 February 2014.

3. Unpublished Sources

Brown, Lyle, and Jim Robertson. *Sunday Supplement*. CBC Radio, 5 March 1972. Transcript. CBC Archives.
Clarke, Irene Irwin. "Address by Irene Irwin Clarke in Convocation Hall, Saturday, May 10th, 1958." *The Diamond Jubilee of the Victoria College Alumnae Association, 1898–1958*. Ephemera Collection. Victoria University Archives, UT.
Clarke, W.H., to Eric Brown. 16 June 1941. National Gallery of Canada.
Halpenny, Francess G. "'Conference on Literary Biography.'" B2000-0023/006. FGH fonds, UTA.
- "Convocation Address, Carleton University, 1991." B2000-0023/005. FGH fonds, UTA.
- "Convocation Address, University of Toronto, 1994." B2000-0023/005. FGH fonds, UTA.
- "Teaching History with the DCB." B2000-0023/006. FGH fonds, UTA.

Harman, Eleanor. "Commission on Post-Secondary Education in Ontario." Memorandum, 25 January 1971. B1987-0051/065. FGH fonds, UTA.
Irwin, John W. Email to author. 2 December 2008.
Jordan, Tessa Elizabeth. "'Branching Out,' 1973–1980: Canadian Second-Wave Feminism, Periodical Publishing and Cultural Politics." Dissertation, University of Alberta, 2012.
Kim, Christine. "The Politics of Print: Feminist Publishing and Canadian Literary Production." Dissertation, York University, 2005.
Macleod, Laura. "Proper Care and Work Well Done: The University of Toronto Press, 1929–1960." 2000 research paper, Department of History, UT, January 1995.
Meadowcroft, Barbara Wales. "Arthur Stringer as a Man of Letters: A Selection of His Correspondence with a Critical Introduction." Dissertation, McGill University, 1993.

Niedzwiecki, Thaba. "Print Politics: Conflict and Community-Building at Toronto's Women's Press." MA thesis, University of Guelph, 1997.
Pomer, Bella. Email to author. 25 April 2015.
– Email to author. 26 April 2015.
Reaney, Susan. Email to author. 19 February 2014.
Van Remoortel, Marianne. "Agents of Change: Women Editors and Socio-Cultural Transformation in Europe (1710–1920)." European Research Council, Starting Grant 196793, Ghent University, 2015–20.

4. Published Sources

Adachi, Ken. "The Gofers Are Gaining Control: Women in Publishing." *Toronto Star* 21 March 1987: M3.
Allemang, John. "The Secret of Her Success: The Latest Chapter in Anna Porter's Drive for a Publishing Empire." *Globe and Mail* 31 July 1987: 36.
Association of Canadian Publishers. publishers.ca.
Audley, Paul. *Canada's Cultural Industries: Broadcasting, Publishing, Records and Film.* Toronto: James Lorimer, 1983.
Baker, Francis. "Friends and Fans Honor Farley Mowat." *Cobourg Daily Star* 22 April 2005: 1.
Baron, Naomi S. *Alphabet to Email: How Written English Evolved and Where It's Heading.* London/New York: Routledge, 2001.
Barrett, Renu. "Copp Clark Company." *Historical Perspectives on Canadian Publishing.* Mills Memorial Library, MU. http://digitalcollections.mcmaster.ca/hpcanpub/case-study/copp-clark-company.
Birney, Earle. *Spreading Time: Remarks on Canadian Writing and Writers. Book I: 1904–1949.* Montreal: Véhicule Press, 1980.
Bourdieu, Pierre. *Distinction: A Social Critique of the Judgement of Taste.* Trans. Richard Nice. Cambridge: Harvard UP, 1984.
Bowering, George. "Watson, Sheila Martin." *Encyclopedia of Literature in Canada.* Ed. William H. New. Toronto: U of Toronto P, 2002. 1199.
Brandeis, Robert C. "Claire Pratt: Art and Adversity." *DA: A Journal of the Printing Arts* 46 (Spring–Summer 2000): 3–28.
– "The Graphic Work of Claire Pratt." *DA: A Journal of the Printing Arts* 46 (Spring–Summer 2000): 29–33.
Brown, George Williams, Eleanor Harman, and Marsh Jeanneret. *The Story of Canada.* Toronto: Copp Clark Publishing, 1949.
Brydge, Kathryn. "Introduction: The Lost *Klee Wyck*." *Klee Wyck.* By Emily Carr. Vancouver: Douglas and McIntyre, 2003. 1–15.

Burr, Christina. "Defending 'The Art Preservative': Class and Gender Relations in the Printing Trade Unions, 1850–1914." *Labour/Le Travail* 31 (Spring 1993): 47–73.
– and Éric Leroux. "Working in the Printing Trades." *History of the Book in Canada, Volume 3, 1918–1980*. Ed. Carole Gerson and Jacques Michon. Toronto: U of Toronto P, 2007. 358–68.
Campbell, Sandra. *Both Hands: A Life of Lorne Pierce of Ryerson Press*. Montreal/Kingston: McGill-Queen's UP, 2013.
Canada's Early Women Writers. https://beta.cwrc.ca/project/canadas-early-women-writers.
Carey, Elaine. "'Tremendous Luck' and Energy Got Editor $50,000 Prize for Work." *Toronto Star* 13 November 1983: D5.
Carr, Emily. *An Address*. Toronto: Oxford UP, 1955.
– *Fresh Seeing: Two Addresses*. Toronto: Clarke, Irwin, 1972.
– *Growing Pains: The Autobiography of Emily Carr*. Toronto: Oxford UP, 1946.
– *The Heart of a Peacock*. Toronto: Oxford UP, 1953.
– *Hundreds and Thousands: The Journals of Emily Carr*. Toronto: Clarke, Irwin, 1966.
– *A Little Town and a Little Girl*. Toronto: Clarke, Irwin, 1951.
– *Pause: A Sketch Book*. Toronto: Clarke, Irwin, 1953.
Clark, Penney. "'A Grand Old House': Canadian Educational Publisher Copp Clark, 1841–2004." *Papers of the Bibliographical Society of Canada* 55.1 (Spring 2017): 51–90.
– "The Rise and Fall of Textbook Publishing in English Canada." *History of the Book in Canada, Volume 3, 1918–1980*. Ed. Carole Gerson and Jacques Michon. Toronto: U of Toronto P, 2007. 226–32.
"Clarke, Irwin." *Canadian Library Association Bulletin* 9 (May 1953): 151–4.
[Clarke, William Henry]. *William Henry Clarke, 1902–1955: A Memorial Volume*. Toronto: Clarke, Irwin, [1956].
Cooper, Afua. "'Out of a Cardboard Box beside Our Bed like a Baby': The Founders of Sister Vision Press." *Great Dames*. Ed. Elspeth Cameron and Janice Dickin. Toronto: U of Toronto P, 1997. 291–306.
Cullen, Darcy. "Introduction: The Social Dynamics of Scholarly Editing." *Editors, Scholars, and the Social Text*. Ed. Cullen. Studies in Book and Print Culture. Toronto: U of Toronto P, 2012. 3–32.
Daniells, Roy. *Deeper into the Forest*. Indian File Books. Toronto: McClelland and Stewart, 1948.
Danky, James P., and Wayne A. Wiegand, eds. *Women in Print: Essays on the Print Culture of American Women from the Nineteenth and Twentieth Centuries*. Madison: U of Wisconsin P, 2006.

Darnton, Robert. "What Is the History of Books?" *Daedalus* 111.3 (Summer 1982): 65–85.
Database of Canada's Early Women Writers. https://dhil.lib.sfu.ca/doceww.
Davey, Frank. "Economics and the Writer." *History of the Book in Canada, Volume 3, 1918–1980.* Ed. Carole Gerson and Jacques Michon. Toronto: U of Toronto P, 2007. 103–13.
Davies, Robertson. "The Revelation of Emily Carr." *Saturday Night* 8 November 1941: 18.
Davis, Laura K., and Linda M. Morra, eds. *Margaret Laurence and Jack McClelland, Letters.* Edmonton: U of Alberta P, 2018.
Deacon, William Arthur. "Critical Comments." *Globe and Mail* 3 June 1950: 10.
– "Far-Flung English Language Becoming a Jungle of Words." Review of *The Universal English Dictionary,* ed. H.C. Wyld; and *Webster's New World Dictionary of the American Language: College Edition. Globe and Mail* 20 February 1954: 25.
– "The Fly Leaf." *Globe and Mail* 5 December 1942: 8.
– "The Fly Leaf." *Globe and Mail* 23 February 1946: 8.
– "The Fly Leaf." *Globe and Mail* 10 December 1949: 14.
– "The Fly Leaf." *Globe and Mail* 1 November 1952: 13.
– "The Fly Leaf." *Globe and Mail* 24 January 1953: 22.
– "Introduces Younger Readers to Canada Past and Present." Review of *The Story of Canada,* by George Williams Brown, Eleanor Harman, and Marsh Jeanneret. *Globe and Mail* 15 October 1949: 12.
Dean, Misao. "'Researching Sara Jeannette Duncan in the Papers of A.P. Watt and Company." *Canadian Literature* 178 (Autumn 2003): 181–6.
Dennys, Louise. "Publishing and Women in Movement: Changing the Game." *Regenerations: Canadian Women's Writing.* Ed. Marie Carrière and Patricia Demers. Edmonton: U of Alberta P, 2014. 231–43.
Dewar, Elaine. *The Handover.* Windsor: Biblioasis, 2017.
"Diana Athill: Growing Old Disgracefully." Dir./Prod. Jill Nichols. *Imagine.* BBC Television One. 22 June 2010.
Dimson, C. Clare. "Emily Carr, Canadian Artist: She Made It as a Writer First." *Toronto Star* 19 February 1972: 67.
Dobbs, Kildare. *Running the Rapids: A Writer's Life.* Toronto: Dundurn Press, 2005.
Donaldson, Gordon. "Anna Porter." *Influence* October 1987: 24–7.
Donnelly, Judy. *The Archive of Clarke, Irwin & Company Limited.* Hamilton: MU Library P, 1992.
– "Clarke, Irwin and Company Limited." *Historical Perspectives on Canadian Publishing.* Mills Memorial Library, MU. http://digitalcollections.mcmaster.ca/hpcanpub/case-study/clarke-irwin-company-limited.

- "A History of Clarke, Irwin & Company Limited." *The Archive of Clarke, Irwin & Company Limited*, by Donnelly. Hamilton: MU Library P, 1992. iii–xi.
- "Jack McClelland and McClelland & Stewart." *Historical Perspectives on Canadian Publishing*. Mills Memorial Library, MU. http://digitalcollections.mcmaster.ca/hpcanpub/case-study/jack-mcclelland-and-mcclelland-stewart.

Elash, Anita. "The Rights Stuff." *Quill and Quire* July 1996: 12–13.

"Ernst and Ernst Report. Findings: A Summary." *Quill and Quire* 15 January 1971: 1.

Exceptional Women in Publishing. http://www.ewip.org.

Fetherling, George. "Literary Agents." *Encyclopedia of Literature in Canada*. Ed. William H. New. Toronto: U of Toronto P, 2002. 668.

Fitzgerald, Judith. "Bill Percy Turns His Back on the Sea." *Toronto Star* 21 June 1987: D8.

Fleming, Patricia Lockhart. "The Binding Trades." *History of the Book in Canada, Volume 2, 1840–1918*. Ed. Yvan Lamonde, Patricia Lockhart Fleming, and Fiona A. Black. Toronto: U of Toronto P, 2005. 101–6.

Fotheringham, Allan. *Boy from Nowhere: A Life in Ninety-One Countries*. Toronto: Dundurn Press, 2011.

"Francess Georgina Halpenny." *Globe and Mail* 6 January 2018: B19.

"Francess Halpenny Awarded Molson Prize." *University of Toronto Bulletin* 7 November 1983: n. pag.

Fredeman, William E. "Emily Faithfull and the Victoria Press: An Experiment in Sociological Bibliography." *The Library* 5th series 29.2 (June 1974): 139–64.

Friskney, Janet B. *New Canadian Library: The Ross-McClelland Years, 1952–1978*. Studies in Book and Print Culture. Toronto: U of Toronto P, 2007.

Fulford, Robert. "Notebook: Decline and Fall." *Saturday Night* August 1983: 5–7.

Galarneau, Claude, and Gilles Gallichan. "Working in the Trades." *History of the Book in Canada, Volume 1, Beginnings to 1840*. Ed. Patricia Lockhart Fleming, Gilles Gallichan, and Yvan Lamonde. Toronto: U of Toronto P, 2004. 80–6.

Gerson, Carole. *Canadian Women in Print 1750–1918*. Waterloo: Wilfrid Laurier UP, 2010.

- "'Dragged at Anne's Chariot Wheels:' L.M. Montgomery and the Sequels to *Anne of Green Gables*." *Papers of the Bibliographical Society of Canada* 35.2 (1997): 143–59.

- "Project Editing in Canada: Challenges and Compromises." *Editing as Cultural Practice in Canada*. Ed. Dean Irvine and Smaro Kamboureli. Waterloo: Wilfrid Laurier UP, 2016. 57–73.
- "Publishing by Women." *History of the Book in Canada, Volume 3, 1918–1980*. Ed. Carole Gerson and Jacques Michon. Toronto: U of Toronto P, 2007. 318–22.
- "Women and Print Culture." *History of the Book in Canada, Volume 1, Beginnings to 1840*. Ed. Patricia Lockhart Fleming, Gilles Gallichan, and Yvan Lamonde. Toronto: U of Toronto P, 2004. 354–60.

Gibson, Douglas. *Stories about Storytellers: Publishing Alice Munro, Robertson Davies, Alistair MacLeod, Pierre Trudeau, and Others*. Toronto: ECW Press, 2011.

Gillies, Mary Ann. *The Professional Literary Agent in Britain, 1880–1920*. Studies in Book and Print Culture. Toronto: U of Toronto P, 2007.

Goddard, John. "A Real Whopper." *Saturday Night* May 1996: 46–50, 52, 54, 64.

Gray, John Morgan. "Canadian Books: A Publisher's View." *Canadian Literature* 33 (Summer 1967): 25–36.

Gregor, Emily Walters. Review of *The Thesis and the Book: A Guide for First-time Academic Authors*, 2nd ed., ed. Eleanor Harman, Ian Montagnes, Siobhan McMenemy, and Chris Bucci. *Canadian Book Review Annual Online* (2009).

Gustafson, Ralph. *Rivers Among Rocks*. Design for Poetry. Toronto: McClelland and Stewart, 1960.

Halpenny, Francess G. "100 Books for 100 Years." *Papers of the Bibliographical Society of Canada* 40.2 (Fall 2002): 57–93.
- "A Canadian Publishing Programme." *Press Notes from the University of Toronto Press* 7.8–9 (August–September 1965): n. pag.
- "The Collection and the Book." *Press Notes from the University of Toronto Press* 9.1 (January 1967): n. pag.
- "The Editor on His Campus." *Scholarly Publishing: A Journal for Authors and Publishers* 2.4 (July 1971): 370–6.
- "An Editorial Career." *Press Notes from the University of Toronto Press* 7.4 (April 1965): n. pag.
- "The Editorial Function." *The University as Publisher*. Ed. Eleanor Harman. Toronto: U of Toronto P, 1961. 67–71.
- "Education and Training for Scholarly Publishing." *Scholarly Publishing: A Journal for Authors and Publishers* 4.2 (January 1973): 165–74.
- "The Ethics of Editing." *Press Notes from the University of Toronto Press* 5.4 (April 1963): n. pag.
- "Help the Humanities." *Globe and Mail* 29 March 1986: A6.

- "The Humanities in Canada: A Study in Structure." *Reinventing the Humanities: International Perspectives*. Ed. David Myers. Kew: Australian Scholarly Publishers, 1995. 155–65.
- "In Tribute: Russell Harper." *Quill and Quire* February 1984: 28.
- "Living a Project." *Journal of Scholarly Publishing* 32.4 (July 2001): 204–20.
- "Men in History." *Press Notes from the University of Toronto Press* 11.3 (March 1969): n. pag.
- "Research – Problems and Solutions: Problems and Solutions in the *Dictionary of Canadian Biography*, 1800–1900." *Re(dis)covering Our Foremothers: Nineteenth-Century Women Writers*. Ed. Lorraine McMullen. Reappraisals 15: Canadian Writers. Ottawa: U of Ottawa P, 1990. 37–48.
- "Responsibilities of Scholarly Publishers." *Scholarly Publishing: A Journal for Authors and Publishers* 24.4 (July 1993): 223–31.
- "The Scholarly Books of the University of Toronto Press." *The University as Publisher*. Ed. Eleanor Harman. Toronto: U of Toronto P, 1961. 59–62.
- "Shall We Join the Ladies?" *University of Toronto Graduate* (December 1968): 48–51, 102–4, 106.
- "[SIC]." *Press Notes from the University of Toronto Press* 10.5–6 (May–June 1968): n. pag.
- "Submitting a Manuscript." *Press Notes from the University of Toronto Press* 6.4 (April 1964): n. pag.
- "Teaching Publishing in a Master's Program in Library Science." *Book Research Quarterly* (Spring 1990): 74–82.
- "The Thesis and the Book." *The Thesis and the Book: A Guide for First-Time Academic Authors*. Ed. Eleanor Harman, Ian Montagnes, Siobhan McMenemy, and Chris Bucci. 2nd ed. Toronto: U of Toronto P, 2003. 3–10.
- "Twenty Years of Canadian Biography." *Transactions of the Royal Society of Canada* 5.1 (1986): 193–201.
- "University Presses." *Canadian Forum* August 1967: 110–14.
- *A World of Words*. Francess G. Halpenny, 2017.
- and J.C.J. "House Style." *Press Notes from the University of Toronto Press* 8.5 (May 1966): n. pag.
- ed. *Editing Canadian Texts*. Toronto: A.M. Hakkert, 1975.
- ed. *Editing Twentieth-Century Texts*. Toronto: U of Toronto P, 1972.

Hammill, Faye. *Literary Culture and Female Authorship in Canada 1760–2000*. Cross/Cultures 63. Amsterdam: Rodopi, 2003.

Hampton, Edna. "Francess Halpenny Will Edit Dictionary." *Globe and Mail* 30 May 1969: 10.

Harman, Eleanor. "AAUP Meets in Toronto." *Press Notes from the University of Toronto Press* 9.7–8 (July–August 1967): n. pag.
- "The Art of Book Designing." *Press Notes from the University of Toronto Press* 16.3 (April 1974): n. pag.
- "Buchmesse." *Press Notes from the University of Toronto Press* 9.11 (November 1967): n. pag.
- "Copy Editing: Can We Afford It?" *IEEE Transactions on Professional Communication* 18.3 (September 1975): 133–4.
- "Five Persons from Alberta: Emily Murphy 1868–1933, Nellie McClung 1874–1951, Louise McKinney 1868–1933, Irene Parlby 1878–1965, Henrietta Edwards 1849–1933." *The Clear Spirit: Twenty Canadian Women and Their Times*. Ed. Mary Quayle Innis. Toronto: U of Toronto P, 1966. 158–78.
- "Founding a University Press." *The University as Publisher*. Ed. Harman. Toronto: U of Toronto P, 1961. 19–58.
- "Ghost Writing Learned Books." *Globe and Mail* 8 February 1947: 10.
- "Hints on Proofreading." *Press Notes from the University of Toronto Press* 5.12 (December 1963): n. pag.
- "Is 'Hopefully' Viable?" *Press Notes from the University of Toronto Press* 15.1 (October 1973): n. pag.
- "A Reconsideration of Manuscript Editing." *Scholarly Publishing: A Journal for Authors and Publishers* 7.2 (January 1976): 146–56.
- Review of *The Building of the House: Houghton Mifflin's Formative Years*, by Ellen B. Ballou. *Scholarly Publishing: A Journal for Authors and Publishers* 2.1 (October 1970): 96–9.
- "Royal Commission on Publications." *Press Notes from the University of Toronto Press* 3.1 (January 1961): n. pag.
- "University Press Association." *Press Notes from the University of Toronto Press* 2.5 (May 1960): n. pag.
- and Ian Montagnes. Preface to the First Edition. *The Thesis and the Book: A Guide for First-Time Academic Authors*. 2nd ed. Ed. Eleanor Harman, Ian Montagnes, Siobhan McMenemy, and Chris Bucci. Toronto: U of Toronto P, 2003. ix–x.

Haycock, Ken. "Impression." *Expression* 1.2 (1977): 26–8, 60–1.

Hobbs, Catherine. "Personal Ethics: Being an Archivist of Writers." *Basements and Attics, Closets and Cyberspace: Explorations in Canadian Women's Archives*. Life Writing. Ed. Linda M. Morra and Jessica Schagerl. Waterloo: Wilfrid Laurier UP, 2012. 181–92.
- "Voice and Re-vision: The Carol Shields Archival Fonds." *Carol Shields and the Extra-Ordinary*. Ed. Marta Dvořák and Manina Jones. Montreal/Kingston: McGill-Queen's UP, 2007. 33–58.

Honey, Kim, Michael Posner, and Sandra Martin. "Publishing's Big Players." *Globe and Mail* 27 November 2000: R2.
Howsam, Leslie. "In My View: Women and Book History." *SHARP News* 7.4 (Autumn 1998): [1]–2.
– "Thinking Through the History of the Book." *Mémoires du livres* 7.2 (Spring 2016).
– "Women in Publishing and the Book Trades in Britain, 1830–1914." *Anschrift der Redaktion: Leipziger Jahrbuch zur Buchgeschichte* 6 (31 March 1996): 67–79.
Hurtig, Mel. *A Twilight in the Country: Memoirs of A Canadian Nationalist*. Don Mills, ON: Stoddart Publishing, 1996.
Hutchinson, Sybil. "Kettleful of Sunshine." *First Statement* 1.8 [1942]: 2–8.
– "Second Sight." *Canadian Accent: A Collection of Stories and Poems by Contemporary Writers from Canada*. Ed. Ralph Gustafson. Middlesex: Penguin Books, 1944. 77–83.
Igartua, José E. "What Nation, Which People? Representations of National Identity in English-Canadian History Textbooks from 1945 to 1970." *History in Global Perspective: Proceedings of the 20th International Congress of Historical Sciences, Sydney, 2005*. Ed. Martyn Lyons. Sydney: University of New South Wales, 2006. CD-ROM.
Inkster, Tim. "Chapter One: The French Connection." *Porcupine's Quill* 26 August 2010. http://porcupinesquill.ca/blog/?p=179.
"Irene Irwin Clarke: Publisher Fostered Canadian Authors." *Globe and Mail* 27 March 1986: D9.
"Irene Irwin Clarke, 83, Founded Publishing House with Husband." *Toronto Star* 27 March 1986: A28.
Irvine, Dean. *Editing Modernity: Women and Little-Magazine Cultures in Canada, 1916–1956*. Studies in Book and Print Culture. Toronto: U of Toronto P, 2008.
Isay, Jane. "Editing Scholars in Three Modes for Three Audiences." *Editors on Editing*. Ed. Gerald Gross. 3rd ed. New York: Grove Press, 1993. 252–9.
Jaillant, Lise. "Reading Ian McEwan's Correspondence." *Times Literary Supplement Online* 21 November 2017.
Jeanneret, Marsh. "Editorial: Universities as Publishers." *Scholarly Publishing: A Journal for Authors and Publishers* 1.1 (October 1969): 3–4.
– *God and Mammon: Universities as Publishers*. Toronto: Macmillan Company of Canada, 1989.
Jordan, John O., and Robert L. Patten. Introduction. *Literature in the Marketplace: Nineteenth-Century British Publishing and Reading Practices*. Ed. Jordan and Patten. Cambridge: Cambridge UP, 1995. 1–18.

Kachergis, Joyce, ed. *One Book/Five Ways: The Publishing Procedures of Five University Presses*. 2nd ed. Chicago: U of Chicago P, 1994.

Kane, Alice. *The Dreamer Awakes*. Ed. Sean Kane. Peterborough, ON: Broadview Press, 1995.

– *Songs and Sayings of an Ulster Childhood*. Ed. Edith Fowke. Toronto: McClelland and Stewart, 1983.

Karr, Clarence. *Authors and Audiences: Popular Canadian Fiction in the Early Twentieth Century*. Montreal/Kingston: McGill-Queen's UP, 2000.

Kelly, Cathal. "U of T's Leonard Cohen Collection Digs Up Diamonds in the Mine." *Globe and Mail* 28 December 2017.

King, James. *Jack: A Life with Writers. The Story of Jack McClelland*. Toronto: Knopf Canada, 1999.

Kirchhoff, H.J. "Kidlit Stars Celebrate 10 Years of Success." *Globe and Mail* 5 November 1988: C11.

Kome, Penney. "Reading between the Lines." *Quest* March 1983: 38a–f.

Konotopetz, Gyle. "Literary Dynamo Kindles Lifelong Passion." *Business Edge News Magazine* 22 December 2005.

Kreisel, Henry. "Reflections on Being 'Archived.'" *Canadian Literature* 127 (Winter 1990): 62–72.

Lagacé, Patricia. "The Art of Editing." *Press Notes from the University of Toronto Press* 16.2 (February 1974): n. pag.

Langan, Fred. "Francess Halpenny, 98, Was an Undisputed Star of the Editing World." *Globe and Mail* 14 January 2018.

Layton, Irving. *The Swinging Flesh*. Toronto: McClelland and Stewart, 1961.

Lecker, Robert. "Canadian Authors and Their Literary Agents, 1890–1977." *Papers of the Bibliographical Society of Canada* 54.1–2 (Spring–Fall 2016): 93–120.

– *Dr. Delicious: Memoirs of a Life in CanLit*. Montreal: Véhicule Press, 2006.

Lee, Katja. "Goddard v. Mowat: F***ing the Facts Fifteen Years Later." *Canadian Literature* 206 (Autumn 2010): 30–40.

Lennox, John, and Ruth Panofsky, eds. *Selected Letters of Margaret Laurence and Adele Wiseman*. Toronto: U of Toronto P, 1997.

Leroux, Éric. "Printers: From Shop to Industry." *History of the Book in Canada, Volume 2, 1840–1918*. Ed. Yvan Lamonde, Patricia Lockhart Fleming, and Fiona A. Black. Toronto: U of Toronto P, 2005. 75–87.

Levy, Michelle. "Do Women Have a Book History?" *Studies in Romanticism* 53.3 (Fall 2014): 297–317.

Lewis, Jeremy. *Penguin Special: The Life and Times of Allen Lane*. London: Penguin Books, 2005.

Lewis, Laurie. *Love, and All That Jazz*. Erin, ON: Porcupine's Quill, 2013.

Litt, Paul. "The State and the Book." *History of the Book in Canada, Volume 3, 1918–1980*. Ed. Carole Gerson and Jacques Michon. Toronto: U of Toronto P, 2007. 34–44.
Long, Elizabeth. Foreword. *Women in Print: Essays on the Print Culture of American Women from the Nineteenth and Twentieth Centuries*. Ed. James P. Danky and Wayne A. Wiegand. Madison: U of Wisconsin P, 2006. xv–xxi.
Lopez, Ken. "Literary Archives: How They Have Changed and How They Are Changing." *Forging the Future of Special Collections*. Ed. Melissa A. Hubbard, Robert H. Jackson, and Arnold Hirshorn. Chicago: American Library Association, 2016. 95–100.
Lorimer, Roland. *Ultra Libris: Policy, Technology, and the Creative Economy of Book Publishing in Canada*. Toronto: ECW Press, 2012.
Lowman, Ron. "Books Study Says Canada Must Block Foreign Takeovers." *Toronto Star* 22 February 1973: 1, 4.
Lownsbrough, John. "High-Powered Women in Canadian Book Publishing." *Chatelaine* August 1985: 50–1, 64–6, 68.
MacDonald, Marci. "Literary Lights Out." *Maclean's* 29 July 1996.
MacDonald, Mary Lu. "*The Montreal Museum*, 1832–1834: The Presence and Absence of Literary Women." *Women and the Literary Institution/ L'écriture au feminine et l'institution littéraire*. Ed. Claudine Potvin and Janice Williamson. Edmonton: University of Alberta Research Institute for Comparative Literature, 1992. 139–50.
MacLaren, Eli. "Canadian Book History." *The Oxford Handbook of Canadian Literature*. Ed. Cynthia Sugars. New York: Oxford UP, 2016. 799–812.
– "'Significant Little Offerings': The Origin of the Ryerson Poetry Chap-Books, 1925–26." *Canadian Poetry: Studies/Documents/Reviews* 72 (Spring–Summer 2013): 9–49.
MacSkimming, Roy. *The Perilous Trade: Book Publishing in Canada 1946–2006*. Updated ed. Toronto: McClelland and Stewart, 2007.
Marchand, Philip. "Birney Loved Life Too Much to Court Only Muse." *Toronto Star* 9 September 1995: L4.
Maude, Mary McDougall. "Francess Georgina Halpenny." *The Canadian Encyclopedia*. http://www.thecanadianencyclopedia.com/en/article/Francess-georgina-halpenny/.
Mayer, Debbie. *Literary Agents: The Essential Guide for Writers*. New York: Penguin Books, 1998.
McCaig, JoAnn. *Reading in Alice Munro's Archives*. Waterloo: Wilfrid Laurier UP, 2002.
McCleery, Alistair. "The Return of the Publisher to Book History: The Case of John Allen." *Book History* 5 (2002): 161–85.

Metcalf, John. *An Aesthetic Underground: A Literary Memoir*. Toronto: Thomas Allen Publishers, 2003.
Modernist Archives Publishing Project. http://www.modernistarchives.com.
Montagnes, Ian. "In Tribute: Eleanor Harman." *Quill and Quire* November 1988: 8–9.
– "University of Toronto Press." *The Oxford Companion to Canadian Literature*. 2nd ed. Ed. Eugene Benson and William Toye. Toronto: Oxford UP, 1997. 1148–9.
Moore, Christopher. "Portraits of a Nation." Review of *Dictionary of Canadian Biography, Volume VI: 1821–35*, ed. Francess G. Halpenny. *Books in Canada* October 1987: 34–5.
Morra, Linda M. *Unarrested Archives: Case Studies in Twentieth-Century Canadian Women's Authorship*. Toronto: U of Toronto P, 2014.
– ed. *Corresponding Influence: Selected Letters of Emily Carr and Ira Dilworth*. Toronto: U of Toronto P, 2006.
Mount, Nick. *Arrival: The Story of CanLit*. Toronto: House of Anansi Press, 2017.
"Mrs. Clarke Opens Emily Carr Show." *Quill and Quire* March 1972: 6.
Murray, Simone. *Mixed Media: Feminist Presses and Publishing Politics*. London: Pluto Press, 2004.
Nash, Andrew. "Reading the Nation." Review of *Print in Motion: The Expansion of Publishing and Reading in the United States, 1880–1940*, ed. Carl F. Kaestle and Janice A. Radway. *Papers of the Bibliographical Society of America* 104.3 (September 2010): 365–75.
Neale, Gladys. "In Tribute: Irene Irwin Clarke." *Quill and Quire* July 1986: 38.
Nelson, Adie. *Gender in Canada*. 4th ed. Toronto: Pearson Canada, 2010.
New Canadian Library Collecting: A Blog by the Ignorant Intellectual. nclcollecting.ca.
Newfeld, Frank. *Drawing on Type*. Erin, ON: Porcupine's Quill, 2008.
Newman, Christina McCall. "Adventure: How John Diefenbaker Confounded His Collaborators, Terrorized His Publisher, and Finessed a Big Best-Seller." *Saturday Night* November 1976: 33–4, 36–8.
Panofsky, Ruth. *The Literary Legacy of the Macmillan Company of Canada: Making Books and Mapping Culture*. Studies in Book and Print Culture. Toronto: U of Toronto P, 2012.
– "'A Press with Such Traditions': Oxford University Press of Canada." *Papers of the Bibliographical Society of Canada* 42.1 (Spring 2004): 7–29.
Parker, George L. "The Sale of Ryerson Press: The End of the Old Agency System and Conflicts over Domestic and Foreign Ownership in the Canadian Publishing Industry, 1970–1986." *Papers of the Bibliographical Society of Canada* 40.2 (Fall 2002): 7–55.

- "The Struggle for Literary Publishing: Three Toronto Publishers Negotiate Separate Contracts for Canadian Authors 1920–1940." *Papers of the Bibliographical Society of Canada* 55.1 (Spring 2017): 5–50.
Pascoe, Allan H. "Basic Advice for Novice Authors." *Journal of Scholarly Publishing* 33.2 (January 2002): 75–89.
- "A Persistent Talent." *Ottawa Citizen* 9 September 2001: C16.
Pike, Lois. "A Selective History of Feminist Presses and Periodicals in English Canada." *In the Feminine: Women and Words/Les Femmes et les mots*. Ed. Ann Dybikowski. Edmonton: Longspoon Press, 1983. 209–18.
Pitts, Gordon. "On the Shelf." *Report on Business Magazine* [*Globe and Mail*] June 2005: 84.
Poole, Carmen. ""Not of the Nation': Canadian History Textbooks and the Impossibility of an African-Canadian Identity." *Southern Journal of Canadian Studies* 5.1–2 (December 2010): 81–102.
Porter, Anna. *The Appraisal*. Toronto: ECW Press, 2017.
- *The Bookfair Murders*. Toronto: Little, Brown and Company Canada, 1997.
- *Buying a Better World: George Soros and Billionaire Philanthropy*. Toronto: Dundurn Press, 2015.
- "A Canadian Education." *Passages: Welcome Home to Canada*. Ed. Michael Ignatieff. Toronto: Doubleday Canada, 2002. 93–117.
- "Discovering Words to Live By." *Globe and Mail* 1 October 2001: R1, R3.
- "Farley Mowat 1921–2014." *Queen's Quarterly* 121.3 (Fall 2014): 326–33.
- "Feedback." *Toronto Star* 30 September 1995: H12.
- *The Ghosts of Europe: Journeys through Central Europe's Troubled Past and Uncertain Future*. Vancouver: Douglas and McIntyre, 2010.
- *Hidden Agenda*. Toronto: Irwin Publishing, 1985.
- "I'm All Right, Jack." *Toronto Life* March 1990: 49.
- *In Other Words: How I Fell in Love with Canada One Book at a Time*. Toronto: Simon and Schuster Canada, 2018.
- "Instead, We Became Cautious Friends." *Hazlitt* 14 May 2014. https://hazlitt.net/blog/remembering-farley-mowat.
- *Kasztner's Train: The True Story of Rezso Kasztner, Unknown Hero of the Holocaust*. Vancouver: Douglas and McIntyre, 2007.
- "The Master Storyteller." *Writing Life: Celebrated Canadian and International Authors on Writing and Life*. Ed. Constance Rooke. Toronto: McClelland and Stewart, 2006. 315–20.
- *Mortal Sins*. Toronto: Irwin Publishing, 1987.
- "Return of the Iron Fist." *Maclean's* 25 January 2011.
- "The Shaky State of Canadian Book Publishing." *Globe and Mail* 15 March 2011: A17.

- *The Storyteller: Memory, Secrets, Magic and Lies*. Toronto: Doubleday Canada, 2000.
- ed. *Jack McClelland: The Publisher of Canadian Literature*. Guadalajara: University of Guadalajara, 1996.
- and Marjorie Harris, eds. *Farewell to the 70s: A Canadian Salute to a Confusing Decade*. A Discovery Book. Don Mills, ON: Thomas Nelson, 1979.

Potter, Jessica, and James H. Marsh. "English-Language Book Publishing." *The Canadian Encyclopedia*. 16 December 2013. www.thecanadianencyclopedia.ca.

Pratt, Mildred Claire, ed. *Viola Whitney Pratt: Papers and Speeches*. Toronto: Lugus Productions 1990.

- *Viola Whitney Pratt: A Testament of Love*. Toronto: Lugus Productions, 1990.

"Professor Jack Morpurgo." *Telegraph* 16 October 2000. http://www.telegraph.co.uk/culture/books/1370520/Professor-Jack-Morpurgo.html.

Publishing Lives. Narr. Robert McCrum. Prod. Melissa FitzGerald. BBC Radio Four. 30 September–4 October 2013; 10–14 March 2014.

Rae, Arlene Perly, Irshad Manji, and Anna Porter. "A Call to Arms on Anti-Semitism." *Toronto Star* 15 October 2004: A21.

Rimstead, Roxanne. Review of *Canadian Women in Print 1750–1918*, by Carole Gerson. *Tulsa Studies in Women's Literature* 30.1 (Spring 2011): 175–6.

Rohmann, Paul. "Recommends *The Thesis and the Book*." *The Exchange* [Education and Training Committee, Association of American University Presses] 11 (June 1976): n. pag.

Ross, Val. "Did *Saturday Night* Cry Wolf?" *Globe and Mail* 11 May 1996: C1.

Rutherford, Paul. Review of *Dictionary of Canadian Biography, Volume X: 1871–1880*, ed. Marc La Terreur. *Canadian Historical Review* 55 (September 1974): 197–9.

Serra, Fabrizio, ed. *Bibliologia: An International Journal of Bibliography, Library Science, History of Typography and the Book* 9 (2014).

Sheppard, Robert. "Anna's Journey." *Maclean's* 10 February 2000.

Shipton, Rosemary. "An Academic Rock Star's Advice for Editors." *Editor's Weekly: Official Blog of Canada's National Editorial Association*, 17 April 2018. http://blog.editors.ca/?p=4732.

Slopen, Beverley. "Booker or Not, Shields Is Hot." *Toronto Star* 13 November 1993: J18.

- "Monkeying around with Fraser's Book." *Toronto Star* 11 June 1994: L14.
- "Persistent Pomer." *Toronto Star* 6 January 1996: K9.

Smith, Michael. "Publishing Should Be a Subject in Colleges, Book Inquiry Is Told." *Globe and Mail* 17 April 1971: 5.

Smith, Stephen. "Rights Rites: Agents Have Arrived – And So Has the Superagency." *Quill and Quire* April 1994: 1, 10–11.

Solecki, Sam, ed. *Imagining Canadian Literature: The Selected Letters of Jack McClelland*. Toronto: Key Porter Books, 1998.
Speller, Randall. "Frank Newfeld and McClelland & Stewart's Design for Poetry Series." *DA: A Journal of the Printing Arts* 56 (Spring–Summer 2005): 3–36.
St Onge, Anna. *The Sheila Watson Archives*. Toronto: John M. Kelly Library, University of St Michael's College, UT, 2009.
Stoffman, Judy. "Info Highway Must Stay Canadian, Group Says." *Toronto Star* 2 October 1995: A1.
Stone, James S. "More Light on Emily Faithfull and the Victoria Press." *The Library* 5th series 33.1 (March 1978): 63–7.
Stursberg, Richard. "Royal Commission on Publications." *Canadian Encyclopedia*. 16 December 2013. www.thecanadianencyclopedia.ca.
Surridge, Jennifer, and Ramsay Derry, eds. *A Celtic Temperament: Robertson Davies as Diarist*. Toronto: McClelland and Stewart, 2015.
Szigethy, Anna, and Anne Graves. *Vampires: From Vlad Drakul to the Vampire Lestat*. Toronto: Key Porter Books, 2002.
Tarver, Julidta. Review of *Revising Your Dissertation: Advice from Leading Editors*, ed. Beth Luey. *Environmental History* 10.3 (July 2005): 562–3.
"Three Heads Are Better than One: The Story behind 'The Story of Canada.'" *Quill and Quire* November 1949: 18–20.
Tippett, Maria. *Emily Carr: A Biography*. Toronto: Oxford UP, 1979.
Toller, Carol. "A Fine Balance: Can Women Juggling Work and Family Make It to the Top?" *Quill and Quire* April 1999: 1, 12–13.
– "The Pink Ghetto." *Quill and Quire* April 1999: 14.
Toner, Patrick. *If I Could Turn and Meet Myself: The Life of Alden Nowlan*. Fredericton: Goose Lane Editions, 2000.
Travis, Trysh. "The Women in Print Movement: History and Implications." *Book History* 11 (2008): 275–300.
Turnbull, Barbara. "Storyteller Still Spins Wonder Tales: Alice Kane Has Enthralled Thousands of All Ages." *Toronto Star* 18 August 1992: B2.
"UBC Medal Honours Editor and Biography Series." *University of British Columbia News Bulletin* 4 June 1986: n. pag.
Webb, Thompson, Jr. Review of *The University as Publisher*, ed. Eleanor Harman. *Library Quarterly: Information, Community, Policy* 32.2 (April 1962): 166–7.
Weiler, Derek. "Talk like an Egyptian." *Quill and Quire* April 1999: 21.
Werner, Sarah. "Weaving a Feminist Book History." *Wynken de Worde* 17 March 2018. sarahwerner.net/blog/.
Wilson, Peter. "Writers Agree – They Couldn't Make It without Their Agents." *Vancouver Sun* 29 August 1987: D3.

Women in Book History Bibliography. http://www.womensbookhistory.org.
Women in Publishing. http://www.womeninpublishing.org.uk.
"Women in Publishing." Narr. Kate Mossen. Prod. Lucinda Montefiore. Ed. Alice Feinstein. *Woman's Hour*. BBC Radio Four. 19 August 2013.
Wood, Gaby. "A Touch of Frost: The Story of Penguin's Secret Editor." *Telegraph* 5 August 2010.
Wright, Donald. *The Professionalization of History in English Canada*. Toronto: U of Toronto P, 2005.
York, Lorraine. *Literary Celebrity in Canada*. Toronto: U of Toronto P, 2007.
– *Margaret Atwood and the Labour of Literary Celebrity*. Toronto: U of Toronto P, 2013.

Index

Page numbers in italics refer to photographs

"100 Books for 100 Years"
(Halpenny), 77, 209n13

Acis in Oxford (Finch), 105
Adachi, Ken, 18–19
Adamson, Anthony: *Hallowed Walls*, 38
Address, An (Carr), 204n54
AFG Agency, 95
"Agents of Change" (Van Remoortel), 20
Alcuin Society Award for Excellence in Book Design in Canada, 106
Aldana, Patsy, 6, 223n96
Alfred A. Knopf, 11, 21, 174, 200n33
Allen, Ralph, 36
Almighty Voice (Peterson), 101
Alumnae Theatre Company. *See* University Alumnae Dramatic Club
Amazon, 191
Amen House, 31, *32*
American Bookseller Association, 146, 186
Ancestral Roof, The (MacRae), 38
Anderson, Doris, 141

Anderson, Patrick: *The Colour as Naked*, 92
André Deutsch, 20, 141
Annick Press, 6, 223n96
Anthology (radio program), 99
anti-Semitism, 148
Antoinette de Mirecourt (Leprohon), 216n17
Appraisal, The (Porter), 219n1
Armstrong, Jeannette, 6
Arrival (Mount), 126
"Arrivals" (Birney), 143
Arthur, Eric, 92
Arthur, Paul, 92, 95
Arthur Ellis Award, 179
"Arthur Stringer as a Man of Letters" (Meadowcraft), 224n27
As For Me and My House (Ross), 95, 118
Association of American University Presses, 56, 60–1, 67, 79
Association of Canadian Publishers, 151, 223n96
Athill, Diana, 20
Atwood, Margaret, 12, 158, 189
Authors and Audiences (Karr), 158
A.Y.'s Canada (Groves), 38

Backwoods of Canada, The (Traill), 216n17
Bailey, Alfred Goldsworth: *Border River*, 92
Baker, Tom, 60
Baldwin House, 49
Balland, 159
Balls for a One-Armed Juggler (Layton), 127
Ballstadt, Carl, 216n17
Bantam Books, 131, 140–1
Barber, Virginia, 21, 158, 175–6
Barfoot, Joan, 230n155
Barzun, Jacques, 56
Bathurst Street Theatre, 112
Bawden, H.N., 108–9
BBC Radio Four, 21
BBC Television One, 20
"Beauty of Miss Beatty, The" (Reaney), 107
Becker, Maximilian, 95
Beginnings (Wylie), 137
Bella Pomer Literary Agency, 152, 159–61, 224n31
Bennett, Avie, 144, 189, 191–2
Benson, D.C., 103
Bentley, George, 200n33
Bentley, Richard, 200n33
Bentley Publishers, 11
Beresford-Howe, Constance, 159
Bergsma, Peter, 164
Bertelsmann and Pearson, 189, 193
Berton, Pierre, 36, 96, 133
Betrayal, The (Kreisel), 97, 122
Between Tears and Laughter (Le Pan), 39
Beverley Slopen Literary Agency, 24
Bevington, Stan, 222n78
Bible (King James), 90
Biblioasis, 200n34

Bibliologia, 20
Bilodeau, Charles: *Notre Histoire*, 48–9
Bird, Will R.: *Ghosts Have Warm Hands*, 39
Bird in the House, A (Laurence), 218n44
Birds of a Feather (Fotheringham), 222n74
Birney, Earle, 9, 16, 89–92, 131–3, 142–3; "Arrivals," 143; *Ice Cod Bell or Stone*, 119; "Maritime Faces," 143; *Selected Poems 1940–1966*, 143; *Turvey*, 89
Blackwood, William, 200n33
Blackwood Publishing, 11
Blaise, Clark: *A North American Education*, 136
Blake, Carole, 178
Blake Friedmann Agency, 178
Bloomsbury Press, 19
Bohne, Harald, 53, 60
book awards: Alcuin Society Award for Excellence in Book Design in Canada, 106; Arthur Ellis Award, 179; Booker Prize, 178; British Columbia National Award for Canadian Non-Fiction, 150; Commonwealth Literature Prize, 168; Ethel Wilson Fiction Prize, 171, 197; Giller Prize, 150, 185; Governor General's Literary Award, 38–40, 49, 77, 90, 93, 99, 109, 125, 160, 163, 167, 178–80, 197; Leipzig Award, 38; National Book Critics Circle Award, 183; National Business Book Award, 150; Orange Prize, 182; Prix de Lire, 182; Pulitzer Prize, 178; Seal Books First Novel Award, 141; Search-for-

a-New-Novelist competition, 159; Stephen Leacock Memorial Medal for Humour, 39; Women's Prize for Fiction, 182
Book of Small, The (Carr), 41–2, 47, 90
Book of Strange, The (Fraser), 146
Book Publishers' Professional Association, 159
Book Publishing Industry Development Plan, 11
Book Society of Canada, 18, 88, 97, 101–6; Searchlight series, 102
Booker Prize, 178
BookExpo. *See* American Bookseller Association
Bookfair Murders, The (Porter), 219n1
Book-of-the-Month Club, 154
Bookseller, The (Cohen), 164–5
booksellers, 190–1
Border River (Bailey), 92
Both Hands (Campbell), 208n89
Bourdieu, Pierre, 13; *Distinction*, 160
Bousille and the Just (Gélinas), 39
Box Garden, The (Shields), 175
Boy with an R in His Hand, The (Reaney), 106
Boys and Girls House, 153
Bradley, W.A. *See* W.A. Bradley
Bread, Wine and Salt (Nowlan), 39
Brébeuf and His Brethren (Pratt), 217n23
British Columbia National Award for Canadian Non-Fiction, 150
"Brocksden" (screenplay) (Reaney), 111
Broken Ground (Hodgins), 169–71, 173
Brooke, Frances, 12; *The History of Emily Montague*, 117, 216n17

Brown, Alice Cameron: "Ghosts," 105; "November Garden," 105
Brown, E.K., 16, 70; *Rhythm in the Novel*, 71
Brown, George Williams, 16, 50, 56, 67, 80; *Canada in North America 1800–1901*, 49; *Canada in North America to 1800*, 49; *Notre Histoire*, 48–9; *The Story of Canada*, 48–9, 206n29
Bruce, Phyllis, 140
Bubblegum Delicious (Lee), 220n20
Buchmesse. *See* Frankfurt Book Fair
Bukowski, Denise, 130
Burr, Christina: *History of the Book in Canada*, 12
Bushell, Elizabeth, 4
Bushell, John, 3–4
Buying a Better World (Porter), 219n1

Calder, Liz, 19–20
Callaghan, Morley, 133
"Call to Arms on Anti-Semitism, A" (Manji, Perly, and Porter), 148
Callil, Carmen, 20–1
Callwood, June, 141
Camp, Dalton, 44
Campbell, Sandra: *Both Hands*, 208n89
Campbell Thompson Limited, 104
Canada Book Fund, 11
Canada Council for the Arts, 9–10, 80, 90, 130, 149, 156, 191, 210n57
Canada (Fulford), 220n7
Canada in North America 1800–1901 (Brown, Harman, Jeanneret), 49
Canada in North America since 1800 (Harman and Jeanneret), 49
Canada in North America to 1800 (Brown, Harman, Jeanneret), 49

Canada's Early Women Writers, 12
Canadian Accent, 89
"Canadian Authors and Their Literary Agents" (Lecker), 36, 103, 156, 187, 214n60
Canadian Authors Association, 96
"Canadian Book History" (MacLaren), 9
Canadian Book Publishing Development Program, 10
Canadian Brothers, The (Richardson), 216n17
Canadian Business, 222n53
Canadian Centenary series, 121
Canadian Conference of the Arts, 127
Canadian Crusoes (Traill), 216n17
Canadian Forum, 153
Canadian Geographic, 222n53
Canadian Historical Review, 49, 73
Canadian Journal of Economics and Political Science, 73
Canadian Journal of Mathematics, 57
Canadian Literature, 97
Canadian Mathematical Bulletin, 57
Canadian Organization for Development through Education (CODE), 150
Canadian Peoples, The (Sandwell), 90
Canadian Publishers and Canadian Publishing, 44
"Canadian Publishing Programme, A" (Halpenny), 209n20
Canadian Short Stories (radio program), 99
Canadian Speakers' and Writers' Service, 24, 103–4
Canadian Woman Studies, 6
Canadian Women's Educational Press, 6
Canadian Writers' Guild, 96, 153
Canadian Writers' Service, 88, 103
Canadian Writing Research Collaboratory, 12
Cape, Jonathan, 36
Capitol Offences (Fotheringham), 222n74
Carleton University, 118
Carr, Emily, 30, 35, 40–3, 102, 194; *An Address*, 204n54; *The Book of Small*, 41–2, 47, 90; *Emily Carr: Her Paintings and Sketches*, 90; *Fresh Seeing*, 204n54; *Growing Pains*, 204n54; *The Heart of a Peacock*, 204n54; *The House of All Sorts*, 41, 90; *Hundreds and Thousands*, 41–2; *Klee Wyck*, 40, 43, 47, 90–1; *Klee Wyck* (abridged version), 204n54; *A Little Town and a Little Girl*, 204n54; *Pause*, 204n54; *A Sketch Book*, 204n54
Carson, Ed, 179–80
Carver, Brent, 39
Case, Nora: *Ten Little Nigger Boys*, 34
Cassell & Co, 132, 139
Caswell, Edward, 214n60
Cat and the Wizard, The (Lee), 220n20
CBC Wednesday Night (radio program), 99
Centennial Commission, 55, 82, 210n57
Centre for Editing Early Canadian Texts, 118, 216n17
Chalmers, Floyd, 54
Chapters, 190
Chapters/Indigo, 190
Chatto and Windus, 21, 36
Chequered Shade, The (Daniells), 119

chien d'or, Le (Kirby), 216n17
Child of the Morning (Gedge), 159–60
Chrétien, Jean, 150; *Straight from the Heart*, 223n93
Churchill, Winston, 54
Claire Pratt Book Service, 113
Clara Thomas Archives and Special Collections (York University), 24
Clark, Henry J., 47
Clark, Penney: "'A Grand Old House' ...", 7; "The Rise and Fall of Textbook Publishing in English Canada," 47
Clarke, Garrick, 35
Clarke, Irene, 5, 8, 11–18, 22–5, 30–45, 193–4
   character: feminism, 30, 33; hypocrisy and prejudices, 31, 34; public image and the media, 43
   editorial contributions: "care and nurture of authors," 39; mentorship of Harman, Hutchinson, and Neale, 46, 194
   personal life: appreciation for theatre, 38; public persona, 34; role model for Anna Porter, 196
   work with Emily Carr: "114 letters from" her, 204n56; interest in and affection for her, 41–3, 194; oversees her publications, 194, 204n54
Clarke, Irwin & Company, 5–10, 18–19, 22, 25, 30–44, 45–7, 90, 154, 193–4, 196, 200n34; acquires copyright for all of Emily Carr works, 41; Amen House, 31, *32*; awards received, 38–40; Canadian Paperback series, 39, 203n37; ceases operations, 44; children's books, 44; Clarwin House, 36; commitment to fostering French and English dialogue, 39; fiftieth anniversary, 43; loss of educational sales, 37–8; loss of Robertson Davies contract, 37; publishing houses represented by, 36; quality of editing and book design, 38; receives government assistance, 44; trade books published by, 38–9
Clarke, William H. (Bill) Jr., 33, 35, 37, 44, 91
Clarke, William H. (Bill) Sr., 3, 11, 16, 18, 25, 31, 35, 40–3, 46–7, 90–1, 200n34
Clarwin House, 36
Clockmaker, The (Haliburton), 117, 216n17
Close, Ann, 21, 174
Coach House Press, 6, 147, 222n78
Cohen, Leonard, 133; *The Spice-Box of Earth*, 119
Cohen, Matt, 9, 27, 160–7, 175, 185, 230n155; *The Bookseller*, 164–5; *Elizabeth and After*, 163; *Emotional Arithmetic*, 162–3; *Emotional Arithmetic* (film version), 167; *Getting Lucky*, 163; *Last Seen*, 163
Coker, Cait, 21
Colbert, Nancy, 152
Collected Works of John Stuart Mill, 55, 207n59
Collier Macmillan, 132, 139
Colour as Naked, The (Anderson), 92
Colours in the Dark (Reaney), 109–10

Commonwealth Literature Prize, 168
Copp, William Walter, 47
Copp Clark, 5, 7, 18, 45, 47–9
Copyright Act of Canada (1921), 9
Cosgrave, Basil H., 60
Cossée, Eva, 164
Coteau Books, 191
Coward, McCann and Geoghegan, 139
Critical Years, The (Morton, ed.), 121–2
Critically Speaking (radio program), 99
Cronk, Douglas, 216n17
Crown Publishing, 139
Cullen, Darcy, 75
Cutler, May, 6

Dalton, Sophia Simms, 4
Daniells, Roy: *The Chequered Shade*, 119; *Deeper into the Forest*, 92
Danky, James P.: *Women in Print*, 21
Darnton, Robert, 13
Data Protection Act (UK 2018), 18
Database of Canada's Early Women Writers, 12
Davey, Frank: "Economics and the Writer," 156
Davey, Linda, 6
Davies, Gwendolyn, 216n17
Davies, Robertson, 36, 39–40; *The Diary of Samuel Marchbanks*, 38; *Leaven of Malice*, 39; *A Mixture of Frailties*, 37, 203n35; *Renown at Stratford*, 38; *Samuel Marchbanks' Almanack*, 203n35; *Shakespeare for Young Players*, 38; *The Table Talk of Samuel Marchbanks*, 38; *Tempest-Tost*, 39; *Thrice the Brinded Cat Hath Mew'd*, 38; *Twice Have the Trumpets Sounded*, 38
Davis, Bill, 37
Dawson, Robert MacGregor, 69; *The Government of Canada*, 53, 77; *William Lyon Mackenzie King*, 54, 77
Dawson, Sarah, 77
D.C. Benson, 103
De Mille, James: *A Strange Manuscript Found in a Copper Cylinder*, 116, 216n17
de Pencier, Michael, 142
Deacon, William Arthur, 48–9
Dean, Misao: "Researching Sara Jeannette Duncan," 158
"December 25" (Finch), 106
Deep Hollow Creek (Watson), 98–9
Deeper into the Forest (Daniells), 92
Deficit Made Flesh, The (Glassco), 92
Dennys, Louise, 19, 151, 162, 223n96; "Publishing and Women in Movement," 185
Department of Canadian Heritage, 11, 190–1
Design for Poetry series, 113, 119
Desperate People, The (Mowat), 145
Dever, Maryanne, 24
Dewar, Elaine, 190; *The Handover*, 200n25
Diary of Samuel Marchbanks, The (Davies), 38
Dictionary of American Biography, 80
Dictionary of Canadian Biography/ Dictionnaire biographique du Canada (DCB/DBC), 55–6, 69, 72, 79–85, 195, 210n57, 211n76
Dictionary of National Biography, 80
Diefenbaker, John, 120

Dilworth, Ira, 40
Distican, 191
Distinction (Bourdieu), 160
Diviners, The (Laurence), 218n44
"Do Women Have a Book History" (Levy), 201n47
Dobbs, Kildare, 11, 200n34
Dominion Drama Festival, 108
Donnelly, James, 108
Donnelly, Judy: "A History of Clarke, Irwin & Company Limited," 36–7, 202n3; "Clarke, Irwin and Company Limited," 44; "Jack McClelland and McClelland & Stewart," 8, 10
Double Hook, 190
Double Tuning (Finch), 106
Doubleday, 8, 21, 139, 162
Doubleday Canada, 130, 136, 172
Douglas, Diana, 223n96
Douglas and McIntyre, 172
Douglas Gibson Books, 130, 168, 170
Doyle, Roddy: *Paddy Clarke Ha Ha Ha*, 178
"Dragged at Anne's Chariot Wheels" (Gerson), 224n27
Drummond, W.H.: *Habitant Poems*, 117
Duncan, Sara Jeannette, 158
Duval, Paul: *Four Decades*, 38; *Ken Danby*, 38

Each Man's Son (MacLennan), 118
Eayrs, Carl, 214n60
Eayrs, Hugh, 47
e-books, 193
"Economics and the Writer" (Davey), 156
ECW Press, 200n34

Editing Canadian Texts (Halpenny, ed.), 79
Editing Modernity (Irvine), 12
Editing Twentieth-Century Texts (Halpenny, ed.), 79
"Editor on His Campus, The" (Halpenny), 209n20
Edwards, Henrietta Muir, 206n28
Edwards, Mary Jane, 216n17
Elizabeth and After (Cohen), 163
Elizabeth II, Queen, 54
Elliott, Ellen, 23
email, 26–8
Emily Carr: A Biography (Tippett), 41
Emily Carr: Her Paintings and Sketches (Carr), 90
"Emily Faithfull and the Victoria Press" (Fredeman), 201n63
Emotional Arithmetic (Cohen), 162–3
Emotional Arithmetic (film version) (Cohen), 167
Encyclopedia of Literature in Canada (New, ed.), 187
Endicott, Norman J., 93
Engel, Howard: *Murder on Location*, 39; *The Ransom Game*, 39; *The Suicide Murders*, 39
"English-Language Book Publishing" (Potter and Marsh), 154
En'owkin Centre, 6
Enschedé, Royal Joh. (printers), 54
Enseignement primaire, 49
Ernst and Ernst, 65
Ethel Wilson Fiction Prize, 171, 197
European Research Council, 20
Even Your Right Eye (Webb), 92
Ewart, Alison, 71–2
Exceptional Women in Publishing, 21

Fable of the Goats and Other Poems, The (Pratt), 217n23
Falcon and Grey Walls Press, 99
"Famous Five," 206n28
Farewell to the 70s (Porter and Harris, eds.), 219n1
Farrar, Straus and Giroux, 162
Farrar and Rinehart, 40
Farrell, Patrick, 109
feminism, 15, 17, 30, 193; feminist periodicals, 6, 14, 20; second-wave, 6
Fenn, H.B., 192
Fetherling, George, 230n167; "Literary Agents," 155
Finch, Robert, 104; *Acis in Oxford*, 105; *For the Back of a Likeness*, 106; "December 25," 106; *Double Tuning*, 106; *The Grand Duke of Moscow's Favourite Solo*, 105; *Has and Is*, 105; *Poems*, 105; *Sail-boat and Lake*, 106; *The Strength of the Hills*, 92, 105; *Twelve for Christmas*, 105; *Variations and Theme*, 105–6
Findley, Timothy: *The Wars*, 39
Finova, 190
Firebrand (Kilbourn), 38
Fire-Dwellers, The (Laurence), 218n44
First Statement, 89
Fisher Rare Book Library (University of Toronto), 24
Fleming, Patricia Lockhart: *History of the Book in Canada*, 12
"Flitting Behaviour" (Shields), 179, 181
"Flying a Red Kite" (Hood), 102
For the Back of a Likeness (Finch), 106
Ford Foundation, 53, 210n57

Forsey, Eugene: *The Royal Power of Dissolution of Parliament ...*, 90
Fotheringham, Allan, 143; *Birds of a Feather*, 222n74; *Capitol Offences*, 222n74; *Fotheringham's Fictionary of Facts and Follies*, 222n74; *Last Page First*, 222n74; *Look Ma – No Hands*, 222n74; *Malice in Blunderland*, 145
Fotheringham's Fictionary of Facts and Follies (Fotheringham), 222n74
Foundation to Underwrite New Drama for Pay Television, 182
"Founding a University Press" (Harman), 63, 209n13
Four Decades (Duval), 38
Fourth Estate, 184
"Frank Newfeld and McClelland & Stewart's Design for Poetry Series" (Speller), 92
Frankfurt Book Fair, 134, 173, 185, 187
Fraser, Sylvia, 137, 143; *The Book of Strange*, 146; *The Quest for the Fourth Monkey*, 146
Fredeman, William E.: "Emily Faithfull and the Victoria Press," 201n63
French, David, 91
French, Donald, 214n60
Fresh Seeing (Carr), 204n54
Fricker, Brenda, 182
Friskney, Janet: *New Canadian Library*, 116, 118
Frost, Eunice, 21
Frost, Robert, 54
Frye, Northrop, 117
Fulford, Robert, 134; *Canada*, 220n7; "Notebook," 35

Gage, W.J., 10, 65, 79
Gainsburg, Joseph C.: *Introduction to Better Reading*, 102
Galarneau, Claude: *History of the Book in Canada*, 12
Gallant, Mavis, 177
Gallichan, Gilles: *History of the Book in Canada*, 12
Garbage Delight (Lee), 220n20
Gay, Elizabeth, 4
Gayfield Press, 20
Gazette du commerce et littéraire, pour la ville et district de Montréal, La, 4
Gedge, Pauline: *Child of the Morning*, 159–60
Gélinas, Gratien: *Bousille and the Just*, 39; *Tit-coq*, 39; *Yesterday the Children Were Dancing*, 39
General Distribution Services, 190–2
General Publishing, 190
George G. Harrap, 36
Gerson, Carole, 19, 197; "Dragged at Anne's Chariot Wheels," 224n27; *History of the Book in Canada*, 3, 12, 14; "Publishing by Women," 5; "Women and Print Culture," 199n5
Getting Lucky (Cohen), 163
"Ghost Writing Learned Books" (Harman), 57
"Ghosts" (Brown), 105
Ghosts Have Warm Hands (Bird), 39
Ghosts of Europe, The (Porter), 148, 219n1
Gibson, Douglas, 11, 130, 167–74, 179, 186, 191, 197, 200n34
Gibson, Shirley, 6
Gill, Keith, 107
Giller Prize, 150, 185

Gillies, Mary Ann: *The Professional Literary Agent in Britain, 1880–1920*, 156, 159
Gilmour, George, 155
Glassco, John: *The Deficit Made Flesh*, 92
Globe and Mail, 20, 26, 36, 48, 57, 164, 179
God and Mammon (Jeanneret), 209n13
Goddard, John, 144–5, 222n69
Godfrey, Dave, 111, 136
Godfrey, Ellen, 111
Good, Cynthia, 151
Goodchild, Frederick G., 91
Goodings, Lennie, 21
Gordon, Lillian G.: *Introduction to Better Reading*, 102
Gosselin, Mary Graddon, 12
Gotlieb, Phyllis: *Within the Zodiac*, 119
Government of Canada, The (Dawson), 53, 77
Governor General's Literary Award, 38–40, 49, 77, 90, 93, 99, 109, 125, 160, 163, 167, 178–80, 197, 217n23
Graham, Martha, 54
Grand Duke of Moscow's Favourite Solo, The (Finch), 105
"'Grand Old House, A' ..." (Clark), 7
Graves, Anne: *Vampires*, 219n1
Gray, John Morgan, 11, 101, 200n34
Groundwood Books, 6, 223n96
Grove, Frederick Philip, 133
Groves, Naomi Jackson: *A.Y.'s Canada*, 38
"Growing Old Disgracefully" (television documentary), 20
Growing Pains (Carr), 204n54

Gustafson, Ralph, 89; *Rivers Among Rocks*, 119
Gutenberg Galaxy, The (McLuhan), 55
Guthrie, Tyrone: *Renown at Stratford*, 38; *Twice Have the Trumpets Sounded*, 38
Gwyn, Richard, 39; *The Shape of Scandal*, 38

Habitant Poems (Drummond), 117
"Hagar." See *Stone Angel, The* (Laurence)
Haliburton, Thomas Chandler: *The Clockmaker*, 117, 216n17
Halifax Gazette, 4
Hallowed Walls (MacRae and Adamson), 38
Halpenny, Francess, 11–12, 15–18, 22–4, 45, 50–3, 56, 64, 69–87, 83, 194
  articles: "100 Books for 100 Years," 77, 87, 209n13; "A Canadian Publishing Programme," 209n20; "In Tribute: Russell Harper," 78; "Living a Project," 209n20; "Men in History," 81; "Research – Problems and Solutions," 81; "Responsibilities of Scholarly Publishers," 209n20; "The Editor on His Campus," 209n20; "The Humanities in Canada," 86; "The Scholarly Books of the University of Toronto Press," 209n20; "The Thesis and the Book," 65; "University Presses," 209n20
  editorial contributions: analysis of the editorial function, 61; attention to the needs of scholarly writers, 77; belief in formal preparation for editorial skills, 73, 195; capacity for leadership, 82; career advancement strategy, 72; champion for humanities, 85; collaboration with authors, 77–8; editor of *Editing Canadian Texts*, 79; editor of *Editing Twentieth-Century Texts*, 79; general editor of DCB/DBC, 72, 79–85, 195; mentorship and training for scholarly editors, 78–9; reverence for scholarship, 74, 195; scholarly editing – practice, 77–9; scholarly editing – theory, 74–6; "The Business of Editing" (presentation), 79; thoughtful diligence, 71; understanding of books as artefacts, 73
  honours: Molson Prize and UBC Medal, 84; Order of Canada, 85
  legacy, 84–7
  personal and professional life outside of publishing: dean of Faculty of Library Science, 85; interest in theatre, 70; RCAF meteorologist during Second World War, 72
Hamilton, Lyn, 164
Hammill, Faye: *Literature Culture and Female Authorship in Canada 1769–2000*, 12
Handcuffs (Reaney), 108
Handover, The (Dewar), 200n25
Harman, Eleanor, 12, 15–18, 22–4, 31, 45–68, *61*, 90, 153, 194

articles: "Five Persons
    from Alberta," 206n28;
    "Founding a University
    Press," 63, 209n13; "Ghost
    Writing Learned Books,"
    57; "A Reconsideration of
    Manuscript Editing," 64, 102
  books (co-authored): *Canada in
    North America 1800–1901*, 49;
    *Canada in North America since
    1800*, 49; *Canada in North
    America to 1800*, 49; *The Story of
    Canada*, 48–9, 206n29; *A Story
    Workbook in Canadian History*, 48;
    The University as Publisher, 63
  character: biases, 51; ingenuity,
    54; interest in historic women,
    206n28; pursuit of lifelong
    learning, 56
  editorial contributions: analysis
    of the editorial function, 61;
    attention to detail, 53; career
    advancement strategy, 52, 72;
    "common sense" approach
    to editing, 57–8; consultant to
    universities, 66–7; editor of
    and contributor to *Press Notes*,
    59–65, 194; editor of *Scholarly
    Publishing*, 64–5; editor of
    The Thesis and the Book, 64–5;
    knowledge of business, 55;
    large projects, 55; meetings
    with colleagues from the
    United States and Europe,
    61; mentorship of Francess
    Halpenny, 56; negotiating
    skills, 53; preference for
    serious literature, 46; quality
    of publications, 58; scholarly
    publishing, 50

  honours: Queen Elizabeth II
    Silver Jubilee Medal, 67
  personal life: bequeaths estate to
    Scholarly Publishing, 65
Harold Greenberg Fund. *See*
  Foundation to Underwrite
  New Drama for Pay
  Television
Harper, J. Russell, 69; *Kreighoff*, 78;
  Painting in Canada, 78; *Paul
  Kane's Frontier*, 78; *A People's
  Art*, 78
HarperCollins Canada, 172, 180
Harrap, George G., 36
Harris, Mike, 10
Hart, Julia Catherine Beckwith:
  St Ursula's Convent, 216n17
Hart-Davis, Rupert, 36
Harvard University Press, 114
Has and Is (Finch), 105
Havel, Václav, 148
Hayne, David, 79, 81
H.B. Fenn, 192
Heart of a Peacock, The (Carr), 204n54
Hedges, Doris, 104
Hedges, Southam and de Merian,
  103–4, 214n60
Hellmer, Kurt, 158
Hemingway, Ernest, 54
Hémon, Louis: *Marie Chapdelaine*, 41
Henderson, Gavin, 135
Henry Holt, 36
Hepburn, Audrey, 54
Hewitt, Alison. *See* Ewart, Alison
Hidden Agenda (Porter), 219n1
Hiebert, Paul: *Sarah Binks*, 118
Hinitt, Robert N., 108
"History of Clarke, Irwin &
  Company Limited, A"
  (Donnelly), 36

History of Emily Montague, The (Brooke), 117, 216n17
History of the Book in Canada/Histoire du livre et de l'imprimé au Canada (Gerson), 3, 12–14, 156
Hoare, Penelope, 163
Hobbs, Catherine, 24; "Voice and Re-vision," 175
Hodgins, Jack, 9, 27, 160, 167–75, 179, 185, 230n155; *Broken Ground*, 169–71, 173–4; *The Honorary Patron*, 168; *The Invention of the World*, 168; *Left Behind in Squabble Bay*, 168; "Letter to Venice," 169; *The Macken Charm*, 169–72; *Over 40 in Broken Hill*, 170; *A Passion for Narrative*, 170; *Spit Delaney's Island*, 168
Hogarth Press, 20, 36
Holt, Henry, 36
Honorary Patron, The (Hodgins), 168
Hood, Hugh: "Flying a Red Kite," 102
House of All Sorts, The (Carr), 41, 90
House of Anansi Press, 6, 136, 223n96
Houston, Jean, 78
Howsam, Leslie, 13–14; "In My View," 30; "Thinking through the History of the Book," 3
Huggan, Isabel, 230n155
Hugh Scobie Publisher, 5
Hundreds and Thousands (Carr), 41–2
Hurtig, M.G., 39
Hurtig, Mel, 11, 200n34
Hurtig Publishers, 200n34
Hussey, Valerie, 223n96
Hutchinson, Sybil, 12, 15–18, 22, 24–5, 31, 88–112, 98, 122, 152, 155–6
  character: assertiveness, 106; capacity for sustained effort, 91, 109; frankness, 100; incompatibility with Jack McClelland, 100, 195; lapses in professional etiquette, 103; low tolerance for unprofessional conduct, 110–11; nationalist orientation, 96, 102; natural intelligence, 91; openness and curiosity, 98; optimism, 101; reserve, 99
  editorial contributions: acquisitions, 101; encouragement and mentorship of authors, 93–9, 195; esteem for writers, 102–3; as series editor, 102, 195; trade and educational books, 88, 102
  literary agent, 88, 103–12; for Alice Cameron Brown, 105; for James Reaney, 106–12, 196–7; for Robert Finch, 105–6, 196–7
  skills and attributes as literary agent: calmness and precision, 107; encouragement and mentorship of authors, 105; as negotiator and promoter, 106; as publicist, 102
  personal life: bequest of personal library, 112; homes, 104
  short stories: "Kettleful of Sunshine," 89; "Second Sight," 89; writing skills, 90, 102, 112

Ian McEwan Papers, 26
Ice Cod Bell or Stone (Birney), 119
Ideas (radio program), 107
Idiot Joy, An (Mandel), 39

Igartua, José E.: "What Nation, Which People," 206n29
Imagining Canadian Literature (McClelland), 147
In Other Words (Porter), 11, 219n1
"In Praise of Eros" (Layton), 128–9
In Search of Greatness (Karsh), 54–5
"In Tribute: Russell Harper" (Halpenny), 78
Independent Literary Agents Association, 159
Indian File series, 92, 105–6, 195
Indigenous peoples, 40, 145; Keewatin Caribou Inuit, 145; motifs used in book designs, 92; publishing houses, 6; writers, 102
Indigo, 190
Information Highway Advisory Council, 150
Inkster, Tim, 105–6
Intersect (Shields), 175
Introduction to Better Reading (Gainsburg and Gordon), 102
Invention of the World, The (Hodgins), 168
Irvine, Dean: *Editing Modernity*, 12
Irving, John, 117
Irwin, John C.W., 16, 18, 31, 91, 101–4
Irwin, John W., 25, 103, 214n58
Isay, Jane, 76

"Jack McClelland and McClelland & Stewart" (Donnelly), 8, 10
Jack McClelland (Porter, ed.), 219n1
Jackson, A.Y., 39; *A Painter's Country*, 38
Jaillant, Lise: "Reading Ian McEwan's Correspondence," 26–8

Jam, Teddy, 163–6 (Matt Cohen pseud.)
Jamieson, Jean, 78
Jeanneret, François Charles Archile, 50
Jeanneret, Marsh, 11, 44–8, 51–5, 59–60, 64–7, 71–2, 80, 84, 194, 200n34, 207n59; *Canada in North America 1800–1901*, 49; *Canada in North America since 1800*, 49; *Canada in North America to 1800*, 49; *God and Mammon*, 209n13; *Notre Histoire*, 48–9; *The Story of Canada*, 48–9, 206n29; *A Story Workbook in Canadian History*, 48; "The University as Publisher," 63
Jest of God, A (Laurence), 218n44
Johnson, Kenneth, 39
Jonathan Cape, 36
Jordan, John O.: *Literature in the Marketplace*, 22
Jordan, Tessa Elizabeth, 12
Judith Hearne (Moore), 118
Jung, Carl, 54

Kachergis, Joyce: *One Book/Five Ways*, 209n13
Kane, Alice, 153–4
Kane, Hugh, 16, 91, 154
Karr, Clarence: *Authors and Audiences*, 158
Karsh, Yousuf: *Portraits of Greatness*, 54; *In Search of Greatness*, 54–5
Kasztner, Rezsö (Rudolf Kastner), 149
Kasztner's Train (Porter), 149, 219n1
Keewatin Caribou Inuit, 145
Kelly, Cathal, 26
Ken Danby (Duval), 38
Kennedy, Jacqueline, 126–7

Kennedy, John F., 127–8
"Kettleful of Sunshine" (Hutchinson), 89
Key Porter Books, 19, 140–7, 151, 162, 192, 196, 220n7, 220n11, 220n20, 222nn74, 82, 223n93
Key Publishers, 142, 222n53
Kids Can Press, 223n96
Kilbourn, William, 39; *The Firebrand*, 38
Killdeer and Other Plays, The (Reaney), 109
Kim, Christine, 12
Kirby, William: *Le chien d'or*, 216n17
Kirchhoff, H.J., 164
Klee Wyck (abridged version) (Carr), 204n54
Klee Wyck (Carr), 40, 43, 47, 90–1
Klein, A.M.: *The Second Scroll*, 118
Klinck, Carl, 117
Knopf, Alfred A., 11, 21, 174, 200n33
Knopf Canada, 162–4
Knowles, Stanley: *The New Party*, 119–20
Konrád, György (George Konrad), 148
Kraulis, J.A.: *The National Parks of Canada*, 220n11
Kreighoff (Harper), 78
Kreisel, Henry, 9, 88, 100, 104, 195; *The Betrayal*, 97, 122; "Reflections on Being 'Archived,'" 97; *The Rich Man*, 93–7
Kroetsch, Robert, 36
Kruschchev, Nikita, 128

La Terreur, Marc, 55
Lagacé, Patricia, 61
Lane, Allen, 197, 231n13
Larmore, Phoebe, 158

Larry's Party (Shields), 182–3
Last Page First (Fotheringham), 222n74
Last Seen (Cohen), 163
Laughing Rooster, The (Layton), 127–9
Laurence, Jocelyn, 179
Laurence, Margaret, 9, 26, 36, 113, 133, 143–5, 196; *A Bird in the House*, 218n44; *The Diviners*, 218n44; *The Fire-Dwellers*, 218n44; *A Jest of God*, 218n44; Manawaka series, 218n44; *The Stone Angel*, 123–4, 218n44; *This Side Jordan*, 122–3; *The Tomorrow-Tamer*, 123
Layton, Irving, 9, 113, 124–9, 133, 196; *Balls for a One-Armed Juggler*, 127; Governor General's Literary Award for poetry, 125; "In Praise of Eros," 128–9; *The Laughing Rooster*, 127–9; *A Red Carpet for the Sun*, 124–5, 127; *The Swinging Flesh*, 125–7, 129; "Why I Don't Make Love to the First Lady," 126–7, 129
Le Pan, Douglas: *The Mysterious Naked Man*, 39; *The Net and the Sword*, 39; *Between Tears and Laughter*, 39
Leacock, Stephen, 133
Leaven of Malice (Davies), 39
Lebel, Maurice, 49
Lecker, Robert, 11, 200n34; "Canadian Authors and Their Literary Agents," 36, 103, 156, 187, 214n60
Lee, Dennis: *Bubblegum Delicious*, 220n20; *The Cat and the Wizard*, 220n20; *Garbage Delight*, 220n20; *Savage Fields*,

136; *Silverly/Good Night, Good Night*, 220n20; *So Cool*, 220n20
Lee, Jennie: *This Great Journey*, 33
Lee, Katja: "Goddard v. Mowat," 222n69
Left Behind in Squabble Bay (Hodgins), 168
Left Wing and a Prayer (Mellor and Michel), 134
Leipzig Award, 38
Leprohon, Rosanna: *Antoinette de Mirecourt*, 216n17
Leroux, Éric: *History of the Book in Canada*, 12; "Printers: From Shop to Industry," 4, 199n7
Lester and Orpen Dennys, 19, 151, 160–2, 223n96
"Letter to Venice" (Hodgins), 169
"Letters in Canada," 70
Letters of Mephibosheth Stepsure (McCulloch), 117. See also *Mephibosheth Stepsure Letters, The* (McCulloch)
Levine, Norman, 133
Levy, Michelle: "Do Women Have a Book History?" 201n47
Lewis, David, 135
Lewis, Jeremy: *Penguin Special*, 231n13
Lewis, Laurie, 11
Library, The, 20
Library and Archives Canada, 9
Lingner, Antje, 51
Listen to the Wind (Reaney), 108
literary agencies, 8, 18, 22–5, 36, 95, 103–4, 155–9; foreign, 158, 224n27
"Literary Agents" (Fetherling), 155
"Literary Archives" (Lopez), 28
Literary Legacy of the Macmillan Company of Canada, The (Panofsky), 23

Literature Culture and Female Authorship in Canada 1769–2000 (Hammill), 12
Literature in the Marketplace (Jordan and Patten, eds.), 22
Litt, Paul: "The State and the Book," 156
Little, Brown, 21, 93, 141
Little Town and a Little Girl, A (Carr), 204n54
"Living a Project" (Halpenny), 209n20
Lochhead, Douglas G., 117, 216n17
London Book Fair, 186–7
Lonely Passion of Judith Hearne, The. See *Judith Hearne* (Moore)
Long, Elizabeth: Foreword. *Women in Print*, 29
Longman Canada, 55
Look Ma – No Hands (Fotheringham), 222n74
Lopez, Ken: "Literary Archives," 28
Lovell, Anne, 4
Lownsbrough, John, 18
Lunn, Janet, 44
Lynn, Marion, 6

MacDonald, Mary Lu, 12
Macfarlane, John, 191
Macfarlane, Walter and Ross, 191–2
Macken Charm, The (Hodgins), 169–72
Mackenzie, Ursula, 21
Mackenzie, William Lyon, 106
MacLaren, Eli: "Canadian Book History," 9
Maclean Hunter, 54, 155
MacLennan, Hugh: *Each Man's Son*, 118
Macleod, Laura: "Proper Care and Work Well Done," 209n13

Macmillan, Alexander, 200n33
Macmillan, Daniel, 200n33
Macmillan Company of Canada, 5, 10, 16, 18, 23, 32, 37, 40, 47, 101, 106, 114, 130, 152–5, 159, 167–8, 194, 200n34; Governor General's Literary Award title, 109–10
Macmillan Publishers (UK), 11
MacRae, Marion: *The Ancestral Roof*, 38; *Hallowed Walls*, 38
MacSkimming, Roy: *The Perilous Trade*, 33, 50, 56, 64, 141, 190, 229n138, 231n10
Malice in Blunderland (Fotheringham), 145
Manawaka series (Laurence), 218n44
Mandel, Eli: *An Idiot Joy*, 39
Manji, Irshad: "A Call to Arms on Anti-Semitism," 148
Mann, Thomas, 54
Mann Booker Prize. *See* Booker Prize
Mansfield, Katherine, 89
Marchand, Philip, 144
Margaret Atwood and the Labour of Literary Celebrity (York), 107, 156–8, 165
Marie Chapdelaine (Hémon), 41
"Maritime Faces" (Birney), 143
Marsh, James H.: "English-Language Book Publishing," 154
Marshall, Joyce, 96
Martin, Carol, 223n96
Martin, Stephanie, 6
Massey, Vincent, 9
Massey Commission, 9, 156
McCaig, JoAnn: *Reading in Alice Munro's Archive*, 158

McCleery, Alistair: "The Return of the Publisher to Book History," 197
McClelland, Jack, 7–11, 16, 91, 99–100, 112–20, 127–8, 133, 139–40, 195, 200nn33, 34; conflict with Earle Birney, 143; *Imagining Canadian Literature*, 147; mentorship of and admiration for Anna Porter, 136–8, 142; nationalism, 9, 118, 135, 142–3, 189, 196; offers to sell company to Porter, 141; personal characteristics, 137; retires from publishing, 144; sells Seal to Key Porter, 162
McClelland, John, 91, 200n33
McClelland and Goodchild, 5
McClelland and Stewart, 5–10, 18, 25, 88–9, 90–101, 113–41, 154, 168, 172–4, 186, 191–6, 200n34, 223n96; Canadian Centenary series, 121; "caste system for its authors," 170; Design for Poetry series, 113, 119; Governor General's Literary Awards titles, 93, 125; Hollinger House location, 116, 134; Indian File series, 92, 105; New Canadian Library (NCL), 113, 116–19, 133–4, 136; sale of 25 per cent to Random House, 189–90; Seal Books, 140; sold to Avie Bennett, 144; "The Canadian Publishers," 133; transfer to Random House, 200n25
McClelland Publishers, 11
McCulloch, Thomas: *Letters of Mephibosheth Stepsure*, 117;

The Mephibosheth Stepsure Letters, 216n17
McDermid, Anne, 20, 166
McDougall, Robert, 117
McEwan, Ian (papers), 26
McGill-Queen's University Press, 67
McGraw-Hill, 10
McInnis, Edgar: *The War*, 91
McKeon, Clare, 140
McKnight, Linda, 130, 140
McLuhan, Marshall, 104; *The Gutenberg Galaxy*, 55
McMullen, Lorraine: *Re(dis)covering Our Foremothers*, 81
McNamee, Kevin: *The National Parks of Canada*, 220n11
Meade, Edward: *Remember Me*, 118
Meadowcraft, Barbara Wales: "Arthur Stringer as a Man of Letters," 224n27
Mellor, Bob: *Left Wing and a Prayer*, 134
"Men and Women in the Book Trade" (conference), 20
"Men in History" (Halpenny), 81
Mephibosheth Stepsure Letters, The (McCulloch), 216n17. See also *Letters of Mephibosheth Stepsure* (McCulloch)
Mesplet, Fleury, 4
Metal and the Flower, The (Page), 92–3
Metcalf, John, 11, 200n34
Methodist Book and Publishing House, 5, 10
M.G. Hurtig, 39
Michel, Doug: *Left Wing and a Prayer*, 134
Michnik, Adam, 148
Mill, John Stuart, 55, 207n59

Miller, Lily Poritz, 130, 140
Millyard, Anne, 6, 223n96
Mirabeau, Marie, 4
Mitchell, Ken, 159, 230n155
Mitchell, W.O., 36
Mixed Media (Murray), 14
Mixture of Frailties, A (Davies), 37, 203n35
Modernist Archives Publishing Project, 20
Molinaro, Matie, 24, 88, 103–4, 156
Montagnes, Ian: *The Thesis and the Book*, 64–5; "University of Toronto Press," 209n13
Montgomery, Lucy Maude (L.M.), 12, 133
Montreal Gazette/La Gazette de Montréal, 4
Montreal Museum, or Journal of Literature and Arts, 12
Montreal Women's Printing Office, 206n28
Moodie, Susanna, 12; *Roughing It in the Bush*, 117, 216n17
Moore, Brian, 36, 133; *Judith Hearne*, 118
Moore, Christopher, 84
Moore, Mavor, 39, 70
"More Light on Emily Faithfull and the Victoria Press" (Stone), 201n63
Morpugo, John Eric, 99
Morra, Linda M., 24; *Unarrested Archives*, 158
Mortal Sins (Porter), 219n1
Morton, W.L.: Canadian Centenary series, 121; *The Critical Years*, 121–2
Motor Car in Britain, The (radio program), 107

Mott, Ann, 4
Mount, Nick: *Arrival*, 126
Mowat, Claire, 144
Mowat, Farley, 9, 115, 131–3, 142; conflict with John Goddard, 144–5, 222n69; *The Desperate People*, 145; *Never Cry Wolf*, 145; *People of the Deer*, 145; *Sibir*, 144
Muir, Amelia, 206n28
Mul, Klaasje, 165
Munro, Alice, 158, 175–7
Murder on Location (Engel), 39
Murray, Simone: *Mixed Media*, 14–15
Mysterious Naked Man, The (Le Pan), 39

Nash, Andrew, 13
National and Provincial Parks Association of Canada, 135
National Book Critics Circle Award, 183
National Book Festival, 145
National Business Book Award, 150
National Library of Canada, 9
National Parks of Canada, The (McNamee and Kraulis), 220n11
National Post, 20
Neale, Gladys, 23, 31–3
Ne'er-Do-Well Thespians (NDWT), 112
Nelson, James Gordon, 135
Net and the Sword, The (Le Pan), 39
Never Cry Wolf (Mowat), 145
New, William H.: *Encyclopedia of Literature in Canada*, 187
New Canadian Library Collecting (blog), 203n37
New Canadian Library (Friskney), 116–18

New Canadian Library (NCL), 9, 113, 116–19, 133–6, 195
New Democratic Party, 119
New Party, The (Knowles), 119–20
New York Times Book Review, 183
New Yorker, 177
Newfeld, Frank, 11, 119, 127–9, 133
Newman, Peter C., 113, 134, 196; *Renegade in Power*, 120–1
"Next Best Kiss, The" (Shields), 177
Nicholson, James, 79–80, 210n57
Niedzwiecki, Thaba, 12
Nielsen-Ferns Limited, 111
Noble and Noble, 36
North American Education, A (Blaise), 136
"Not of the Nation" (Poole), 206n29
"Notebook" (Fulford), 35
Notre Histoire (Brown, Harman, Marsh, Bilodeau), 48–9
"November Garden" (Brown), 105
Nowlan, Alden, 33; *Bread, Wine and Salt*, 39

Of Time and the Lover (Watson), 92–3
O'Keefe, Georgia, 54
Old Woman at Play (Wiseman), 39
O'Leary, Gratton, 60
Ondaatje, Michael, 189
One Book/Five Ways (Kachergis, ed.), 209n13
Ontario Arts Council, 10
Ontario Development Corporation, 10
Ontario Media Development Corporation Book Fund, 11
Ontario Royal Commission on Book Publishing, 10, 44, 65–7, 153
"Orange Fish, The" (Shields), 177

Orange Fish, The (short story collection) (Shields), 180
Orange Prize, 182
Order of Canada, 151
Order of Ontario, 151
Others (Shields), 175
Oughton, Libby, 223n96
Over 40 in Broken Hill (Hodgins), 170
Owen, Ursula, 20
Owl, 223n96
Oxford Companion to Canadian History and Literature, The (Story and Toye, eds.), 130
Oxford Dictionary of National Biography. See *Dictionary of National Biography*
Oxford University Press, 50, 59
Oxford University Press Canada, 5, 18, 23–4, 31–3, 41–7, 67, 88, 130, 192, 200n34; Governor General's Literary Awards titles, 90–1; King James Bible, 90–1
Ozment, Kate, 21

Paddy Clarke Ha Ha Ha (Doyle), 178
Page, P.K.: *The Metal and the Flower*, 92–3
Painted Ladies (Percy), 160
Painter's Country, A (Jackson), 38
Painting in Canada (Harper), 78
Pandora Press, 14
Panofsky, Ruth: *The Literary Legacy of the Macmillan Company of Canada*, 23
Papers of the Bibliographical Society of Canada, 77
Parker, George L., 216n17; "The Struggle for Literary Publishing," 8
Parker, Morten: *The Red Kite* (film), 102

Parks, Malcolm, 216n17
Passion for Narrative, A (Hodgins), 170
Paterson, Barbara, 206n28
Patriot, 4
Patten, Robert L.: *Literature in the Marketplace*, 22
Paul Kane's Frontier (Harper), 78
Pause (Carr), 204n54
Pearce, John, 172
PEN Canada, 149, 223n91
Penguin Books, 21, 99, 197
Penguin Books Canada, 151
Penguin Random House Canada, 9, 148, 151, 189. See also Random House of Canada
Penguin Special (Lewis), 231n13
People of the Deer (Mowat), 145
People's Art, A (Harper), 78
Pepper, Douglas, 179
Percy, H.R.: *Painted Ladies*, 160
Perilous Trade, The (MacSkimming), 33, 56, 64, 141, 190, 229n138, 231n10
Perly, Arlene: "A Call to Arms on Anti-Semitism," 148
Peter Martin Associates, 223n96
Peterman, Michael A., 216n17
Peterson, Len, 101–2; *Almighty Voice*, 102
Phelps, Arthur J., 117
Pierce, Lorne, 11, 200n34, 208n89
Pike, Lois, 12
Pius XII, Pope, 54
Plewman, Barbara, 51
Plummer, Christopher, 167
Poems (Finch), 105
Pomer, Bella, 12, 15–18, 22–5, 152–88, *161*
 character: aversion to rejection, 162; mischievousness, 166; persistence, 163 email

correspondence, 26–8; entrepreneurship: Bella Pomer Literary Agency, 155
literary agent, 155; for Carol Shields, 175–85, 189, 193, 197; client list, 230n155; commission fees, 183, 224n31; first international success, 159–60; "*grande dame* of the Canadian scene," 187; "'hot' author representative[s]," 187; for Jack Hodgins, 167–75, 197; for Matt Cohen, 161–7, 197
personal life: childhood love of books and reading, 153; friendships, 187; née Lieberman, 153
skills and attributes as literary agent: ally of and attentive listener to authors, 179; awareness of cultural trends, 173; boldness, 171; businesslike composure and tact, 165, 181; conciliatory approach, 165; dedication to authors, 169; editorial review, 165, 168–70, 176–7; emotional support for authors, 172–3; expertise in mystery genre, 164; integrity and commitment, 169; knowledge of the publishing business, 152; practical realism, 176; professionalism, 185; promotion at book fairs, 185–6; shrewdness as negotiator, 186; straightforwardness, 152; vision and tenacity, 175
spheres of influence: Canadian literary agents, 187; Canadian writers in Canada and abroad, 152, 186; literary culture of Canada, 152; publishing contracts in Canada and abroad, 186

Pomer, Harold, 16, 153–5

Poole, Carmen: "Not of the Nation," 206n29

Porcupine's Quill, 105–6, 200n34

Porte, William, 108–9

Porter, Anna, 6, 12, 15–19, 22, 25, 131–51, *132*, 162
articles: "A Call to Arms on Anti-Semitism," 148; "The Shaky State of Canadian Book Publishing," 147
awards and honours, 131, 219n1; Association of Canadian Publishers President's Award, 151; Order of Canada, 151; Order of Ontario, 151
books: *The Appraisal*, 219n1; *The Bookfair Murders*, 219n1; *Buying a Better World*, 219n1; *Farewell to the 70s* (co-edited with Marjorie Harris), 219n1; *The Ghosts of Europe*, 148, 219n1; *Hidden Agenda*, 219n1; *Jack McClelland*, 219n1; *Kasztner's Train*, 149, 219n1; *Mortal Sins*, 219n1; *In Other Words*, 11, 219n1; *The Storyteller*, 219n1; *Vampires* (under the name Anna Szigethy; co-authored with Anne Graves), 219n1
character: enthusiasm, talent, and drive, 133; tenacity, 137
editorial contributions: advocacy, 142–6; discernment

and intuition, 135; incisive intelligence, 135; initiative, 135; knowledge of publishing, 137; nationalist ideology, 135, 143, 196; organizational and interpersonal skills, 137, 143; role model, 139
entrepreneurship: *see* Key Porter Books
personal life: activism against injustice, 148; birth of children, 139; close friendships, 141; demands of family and career, 140–1; early life; 132, 143, 148; environmentalism, 135; heritage, 132, 146, 149; outspokenness on freedom of speech, 148; retirement from publishing, 192; spouse Julian Porter, 135, 139, 145
spheres of influence: government groups, 150; literary culture in Canada, 131, 137, 149–50; publishing in Canada, 146–51, 151; women in publishing, 151
Porter, Julian, 135, 145
Portraits of Greatness (Karsh), 54
Potter, Jessica: "English-Language Book Publishing," 154
Prashker, Betty, 139
Pratt, Claire, 12, 15–18, 22, 113–30, *114*, 131, 134
book: *The Silent Ancestors*, 130
character: calmness, 120; compassion, 122; diplomacy, 121; intelligence, resolve, and good humour, 130; "perceptivity and honesty," 127; vivaciousness, 124
editorial contributions: affinity for Canadian literature, 116; attentiveness to authors, 118, 125, 196; attention to detail, policy, and procedure, 117; "best book editor in the country," 130; effectiveness as a communicator, 127; executive ability, 127; expertise and dedication, 115, 119; with fiction writers, 122–3; for freelance work, 130; guiding and conciliatory, 129; as indexer, 120; insight into writerly personality, 120, 124–6; as Irving Layton's editor, 124–9, 196; as Margaret Laurence's editor, 122–4, 196; as Peter C. Newman's editor, 120–1, 196; relationships with authors, 120–2; "ruthless" approach, 120; as series editor, 113, 116–19, 195; for trade books, 119–24, 195
entrepreneurship: Claire Pratt Book Service, 113
personal life: childhood polio and resulting illnesses, 115, 129, 215n2; daughter of poet E.J. Pratt, 120; woodcut artist, 119; writer of genealogical study, 130
spheres of influence: literary culture in Canada, 113; professionalization of editors, 113, 130; publishing in Canada, 113, 130
Pratt, Edwin John (E.J.), 120, 130; *Brébeuf and His Brethren*, 217n23; *The Fable of the Goats*

and Other Poems, 217n23;
Governor General's Literary
Awards, 217n23; *Towards the
Last Spike*, 217n23
Pratt, Viola Whitney, 120, 217n23
Press Gang Publishers, 6
*Press Notes from the University of
Toronto Press*, 45, 56–65, 81,
194
Press Porcépic, 110, 130
Les Presses de l'Université Laval, 80
"Printers: From Shop to Industry"
(Leroux), 4
Prix de Lire, 182
Procunier, Edwin, 101–2
*Professional Literary Agent in Britain,
1880–1920, The* (Gillies), 156,
159
"Proper Care and Work Well Done"
(Macleod), 209n13
publishers in Canada: agents
for American and British
publishers, 8–9, 36; agents
in the United States, 36, 93;
of Canadian history, 48; of
Canadian works, 9, 92, 113,
133, 216n17; of children's
books, 6, 44, 220n20; of
children's magazines, 217n23;
digital archives of, 28; of
educational textbooks, 7,
30–1, 37, 47, 101, 154, 194;
encouragement of women
in the trade, 16; expansion
into US market, 146; family
businesses, 30–1; of feminist
periodicals and books, 6, 20;
financial assistance to, 44;
first full-time staff designer,
51; first paperback reprint
series, 116; first to receive
Ford Foundation grant, 53;
first woman publisher of
English-language books, 30;
funding available to, 10–11;
histories of, 20, 36–7, 63,
201n63, 202n3; Indigenous-
owned, 6; of magazines,
222n53; male domination of,
11; marketing problems in the
US, 36; of medical textbooks,
47; memoirs of, 11; of non-
fiction, 191; opportunities for
immigrant writers, 96; papers
of, 13; of poetry series, 119;
present-day, 192–3; Royal
Commission on Status of, 65;
sales to American companies,
10, 65; of scholarly books,
18, 25, 50, 67, 121, 194; of
scientific books and journals,
57; simultaneous publication
in the US, 93; subsidiary
rights for, 18; takeovers and
collapses of, 189–93; of trade
books, 18, 30–1, 38, 91, 194; of
works by Black women and
women of colour, 6
Publishers Weekly, 19, 154, 183
"Publishing and Women in
Movement" (Dennys), 185
"Publishing by Women" (Gerson), 5
Publishing Lives (radio series), 21
Puffin Books, 21
Pulitzer Prize, 178, 228n123

Quest for the Fourth Monkey, The
(Fraser), 146
Quill and Quire, 10, 20, 48, 78, 179,
222n53

racial discrimination, 34
Rácz, Vili, 146, 149
Raddall, Thomas H., 133
Ragweed Press, 223n96
Randolph Theatre. *See* Bathurst Street Theatre
Random House, 93, 189–92
Random House of Canada, 179–81, 184, 189, 200n25. *See also* Penguin Random House Canada
Ransom Game, The (Engel), 39
Reader's Digest, 155
"Reading Ian McEwan's Correspondence" (Jaillant), 26
Reading in Alice Munro's Archive (McCaig), 158
Reaney, James, 9, 25, 88, 104–12, 152, 195; literary executors, 215n72; website, 215n72
works: *The Boy with an R in His Hand*, 106; "Brocksden" (screenplay), 111; *Colours in the Dark*, 109–10; Donnelly family trilogy, 108, 111; *Handcuffs*, 108; *The Killdeer and Other Plays*, 109; *Listen to the Wind*, 108; *The Red Heart*, 92–3, 106; *Selected Longer Poems*, 110; *Selected Shorter Poems*, 110; *The St Nicholas Hotel*, 108; *Sticks and Stones*, 108; "The Beauty of Miss Beatty," 107; "Traffic," 107
Reaney, James Stewart, 215n72
Reaney, Susan, 112
"Reconsideration of Manuscript Editing, A" (Harman), 64
Red Carpet for the Sun, A (Layton), 124–5, 127

Red Heart, The (Reaney), 92–3, 106
Red Kite, The (film) (Parker), 102
Re(dis)covering Our Foremothers (McMullen, ed.), 81
"Reflections on Being 'Archived'" (Kreisel), 97
Regal, Joseph, 157, 173
Remember Me (Meade), 118
Renegade in Power (Newman), 120
Renouf, Susan, 140
Renown at Stratford (Guthrie and Davies), 38
Republic of Love, The (Shields), 182
"Research – Problems and Solutions" (Halpenny), 81
"Researching Sara Jeannette Duncan" (Dean), 158
"Responsibilities of Scholarly Publishers" (Halpenny), 209n20
"Return of the Publisher to Book History, The" (McCleery), 197
Reynal and Hitchcock, 95
Reynolds, Paul, 158
Rhythm in the Novel (Brown), 71
Ricciutelli, Luciana, 6
Rich Man, The (Kreisel), 93–7
Richardson, John: *The Canadian Brothers*, 216n17; *Wacousta*, 216n17
Richardson, Miranda, 182
"Rights Rites" (Smith), 186
Rimstead, Roxanne, 14
Rinehart, 36
"Rise and Fall of Textbook Publishing in English Canada, The" (Clark), 47
Rivers Among Rocks (Gustafson), 119
Robarts, John, 65
Robinson, David, 110

Rockefeller Foundation, 60
Rohmer, Richard, 44
Rolph, Ernest, 31
Rooke, Leon, 135–6
Roosevelt, Eleanor, 54
Roper, Don, 134
Ross, Gary, 191
Ross, Malcolm, 116–17, 134
Ross, Sinclair, 36; *As For Me and My House*, 95, 118
Roughing It in the Bush (Moodie), 117, 216n17
Roy, Gabrielle, 133
Royal Commission on National Development in the Arts, Letters and Sciences, 9
Royal Commission on Publications, 60–1
Royal Commission on the Status of Women in Canada, 6, 15
Royal Joh. Enschedé (printers), 54
Royal Power of Dissolution of Parliament ..., The, 90
Rule, Jane, 36, 158
Rupert Hart-Davis, 36
Rutherford, Paul, 84
Ryerson Press, 5, 10, 40, 65, 90, 114, 200n34; Ryerson Poetry Chapbooks series, 92
Ryerson University, 78

Sail-boat and Lake (Finch), 106
Sale, Medora, 164, 230n155
Salkeld, Blanaid, 20
Salter, Fred, 91
Samuel Marchbanks' Almanack (Davies), 203n35
Sandwell, B.K.: *The Canadian Peoples*, 90
Sarah Binks (Hiebert), 118

Sarandon, Susan, 167
Saturday Night, 40, 105, 144–5
Savage Fields (Lee), 136
"Scarf, The" (Shields), 177
Schieder, Rupert, 216n17
Schoemperlen, Diane, 230n155
"Scholarly Books of the University of Toronto Press" (Halpenny), 209n20
Scholarly Publishing, 45, 58–9, 64–7, 194
Schuster, M. Lincoln ("Max"), 200n33
Scobie, Hugh, 5, 47
Scotiabank Giller Prize. *See* Giller Prize
Scott, Jack, 95
Scott Foresman, 10
Seal Books, 25, 131, 139–42, 162, 196
Seal Books First Novel Award, 141
Search-for-a-New-Novelist competition, 159
Searchlight series, 102
Second Scroll, The (Klein), 118
"Second Sight" (Hutchinson), 89
Selected Longer Poems (Reaney), 110
Selected Poems 1940–1966 (Birney), 143
Selected Shorter Poems (Reaney), 110
Self-Counsel Press, 223n96
Seligman, Ellen, 99, 130, 140, 223n96
Serra, Fabrizio, 20
Shakespeare Association of America, 21
Shakespeare for Young Players (Davies), 38
"Shaky State of Canadian Book Publishing, The" (Porter), 147
Shape of Scandal, The (Gwyn), 38
Shaw, George Bernard, 54

Sheard, Sarah, 6
Sheba Feminist Publishers, 14
Sheila Watson Archives, The (St Onge), 99
Sherman, Geraldine, 142
Shields, Carol, 12, 22, 27, 152, 160, 175–85, 230n155; association with Bella Pomer, 181–4, 189, 193; dual Canadian and American citizen, 228n23
  works: *The Box Garden*, 175; "Flitting Behaviour," 179, 181; *Intersect*, 175; *Larry's Party*, 182–3; "The Next Best Kiss," 177; "The Orange Fish," 177; *The Orange Fish* (short story collection), 180; *Others*, 175; *The Republic of Love*, 182; "The Scarf," 177; *Small Ceremonies*, 175; *The Stone Diaries*, 175, 177–80, 184; *Swann*, 179–81; *Swann* (film), 182; translations of, 228n120, 230n148; *Unless*, 183–5, 230n148; *Various Miracles*, 179–81; "Weather," 177
Shields, Donald, 176
Shipton, Rosemary, 78
Sibir (Mowat), 144
Siggins, Maggie, 230n155
Silent Ancestors (C. Pratt), 130
Silvera, Makeda, 6
Silverly/Good Night, Good Night (Lee), 220n20
Simon, Richard L., 200n33
Simon and Schuster, 11, 139, 191
Simonds, Merilyn, 230n155
Sinclair, Lister, 95–6, 101
Sinclair-Stevenson, 163
Sister Vision Press, 6

Skelton, Robin, 42
Sketch Book, A (Carr), 204n54
Slaight, Annabel, 223n96
Slopen, Beverley, 24, 146, 152, 187
Small Ceremonies (Shields), 175
Smallwood, Norah, 21
Smith, J. Merle, 48
Smith, Olive, 113
Smith, Russell E., 204n56
Smith, Stephen: "Rights Rites," 186
So Cool (Lee), 220n20
Solecki, Sam, 147
Soliman, Patricia, 139
Speller, Randall: "Frank Newfeld and McClelland & Stewart's Design for Poetry Series," 92
Spice-Box of Earth, The (Cohen), 119
Spit Delaney's Island (Hodgins), 168
Sproatt, Henry, 31
St Martin's Press, 163
St Nicholas Hotel, The (Reaney), 108
St Onge, Anna: *The Sheila Watson Archives*, 99
St Ursula's Convent (Hart), 216n17
"State and the Book, The" (Litt), 156
Steinbeck, John, 54
Stephen Leacock Memorial Medal for Humour, 39
Stephens, Donald, 216n17
Stepsure Letters, The. See *Letters of Mephibosheth Stepsure* (McCulloch)
Sticks and Stones (Reaney), 108
Stockdale, John C., 216n17
Stoddart, Jack Jr., 180, 190–1
Stoddart Publishing, 179–81, 190, 229n138
Stone, James S.: "More Light on Emily Faithfull and the Victoria Press," 201n63

Stone Angel, The (Laurence), 123–4, 218n44
Stone Diaries, The (Shields), 175, 177–80, 184
Stories with John Drainie (radio program), 99
Story, Norah: *The Oxford Companion to Canadian History and Literature*, 130
Story of Canada, The (Brown, Harman, Marsh), 48–9, 206n29
Story Workbook in Canadian History, A (Harman and Jeanneret), 48
Storyteller, The (Porter), 219n1
Straight from the Heart (Chrétien), 223n93
Strange Manuscript Found in a Copper Cylinder, A (De Mille), 116, 216n17
Strength of the Hills, The (Finch), 92, 105
Stringer, Arthur, 158
"Struggle for Literary Publishing, The" (Parker), 8
Suicide Murders, The (Engel), 39
Sullivan, Alan: *Three Came to Ville Marie*, 91
Sutherland, Donald, 110
Sutherland, John, 89
Swann (film) (Shields), 182
Swann (Shields), 179–81
Swinging Flesh, The (Layton), 125–9
Szigethy, Anna. *See* Porter, Anna

Table Talk of Samuel Marchbanks, The (Davies), 38
Talese, Nan, 21, 162–3
Talonbooks, 109–10
Task Force on Women Entrepreneurs, 150

Taylor, James, 60
Taylor, Peter, 134
Taylor, Ruth, 128
Telegraph, 21
Tempest-Tost (Davies), 39
Temptations of Big Bear, The (Wiebe), 136
Ten Little Nigger Boys (Case), 34
"Thesis and the Book, The" (Halpenny), 65
Thesis and the Book (Harman and Montagnes, eds.), 64–5
Theytus Books, 6
Thibaudeau, Colleen, 92, 107
"Thinking Through the History of the Book" (Howsam), 3
This Great Journey (Lee), 33
This Side Jordan (Laurence), 122–3
Thomas Archives and Special Collections (York University), 24
Thomas Fisher Rare Book Library (University of Toronto), 24
Three Came to Ville Marie (Sullivan), 91
Thrice the Brinded Cat Hath Mew'd (Davies), 38
Times Literary Supplement, 26
Tippett, Maria: *Emily Carr: A Biography*, 41
Tison, Marie-Anne, 4
Tit-coq (Gélinas), 39
Toller, Carol, 20
Tomorrow-Tamer, The (Laurence), 123
Toronto International Film Festival, 167
Toronto Life, 179, 222n53
Toronto Public Library, 153, 186
Toronto Public Library Foundation, 150
Toronto Star, 18, 144, 187

"Touch of Frost, A" (Wood), 202n66
Towards the Last Spike (Pratt), 217n23
Toye, William, 11, 200n34; *The Oxford Companion to Canadian History and Literature*, 130
"Traffic" (Reaney), 107
Traill, Catharine Parr: *The Backwoods of Canada*, 216n17; *Canadian Crusoes*, 216n17
Travis, Trysh, 14
Trudel, Marcel, 80
Tundra Books, 6
Turnbull, Keith, 112
Turvey (Birney), 89
Twelve for Christmas (Finch), 105
Twice Have the Trumpets Sounded (Guthrie and Davies), 38

Uhtoff, Ina, 41
Unarrested Archives (Morra), 158
Universal Copyright Convention, 9
Université de Montréal, 66
Universities of Ontario Press, 66
University Alumnae Dramatic Club, 70–1
University as Publisher, The (Harman), 63
"University as Publisher, The" (Jeanneret), 63
University of Alberta, 67
University of British Columbia, 67
University of British Columbia Press, 75
University of California Press, 67
University of Manitoba Press, 61
University of Ottawa Press, 67
University of Toronto, 189; Faculty of Library Science (now Faculty of Information), 79
University of Toronto Law Journal, 73

University of Toronto Press, 5, 11, 16–18, 25, 45, 50–3, 69–87, 114, 186, 192–5, 200n34, 209n13; 70 Bond Street shipping and warehouse location, 60; 21 King's College Circle location, 52–3; awards for DCB/DBC, 55, 84; Baldwin House location, 49, 71–3, 77; brief to Royal Commission, 66–7; Collected Works of John Stuart Mill, 55, 207n59; distinctive publishing aesthetic, 69; first full-time staff designer in Canada, 51; Ford Foundation grant, 53; foundation for editorial practice in Canada, 61; Governor General's Literary Award for *The Government of Canada* (Dawson), 77; history of, 63, 68, 87; house organ *Press Notes*, 45, 56–65, 81, 194; Huron Street textbook store, 60; international scholarly contributions, 207n59; journal *Scholarly Publishing*, 45, 58–9, 64–5
"University of Toronto Press" (Montagnes), 209n13
University of Toronto Quarterly, 70, 73
"University Presses" (Halpenny), 209n20
Unless (Shields), 183–5

Vampires (Porter and Graves), 219n1
Van Remoortel, Marianne: "Agents of Change," 20
Vardey, Lucinda, 152
Variations and Theme (Finch), 105–6

Various Miracles (Shields), 179–81
Véhicule Press, 191
Verrall, Arthur, 60
Victoria Daily Times, 42
Viking Penguin, 177
Viking Press, 21
Virago Press, 14, 21
"Voice and Re-vision" (Hobbs), 175
Voyer, Marie Josephte, 4

W.A. Bradley, 104
Wacousta (Richardson), 216n17
Wall, Ann, 6, 223n96
Wallace, Susan, 107, 215n72
Walter, Jan, 191
War, The (McInnis), 91
Wars, The (Findley), 39
Watson, James Wreford: *Of Time and the Lover*, 92–3
Watson, Sheila, 9, 88, 100, 104, 195; *Deep Hollow Creek*, 98–9
Watt, A.P., 159
A.P. Watt and Company, 158
"Weather" (Shields), 177
Weaver, Robert, 99, 105
Webb, Kaye, 21
Webb, Phyllis: *Even Your Right Eye*, 92
Werner, Mindy, 21, 178
"What Nation, Which People" (Igartua), 206n29
Where, 222n53
"Why I Don't Make Love to the First Lady" (Layton), 126–9
Whyte, Kenneth, 145
Wicks, Ben, 104
Wiebe, Rudy, 175; *The Temptations of Big Bear*, 136
Wiegand, Wayne A.: *Women in Print*, 21
Wilder, Thornton, 54
Wilfrid Laurier University, 67

Wilkinson, Shelagh, 6
William Lyon Mackenzie King (Dawson), 54, 77
Williams, Rex, 202n66
Williams, Tennessee, 54
Wing, Willis Kingsley, 36, 158
Wiseman, Adele, 26, 36; *Old Woman at Play*, 39
Within the Zodiac (Gotlieb), 119
W.J. Gage, 10, 65, 79
Woman's Hour (radio program), 21
Woman's Missionary Society of the United Church of Canada, 217n23
Woman's Work in Canada (newspaper), 206n28
women: dearth of documentation for biographies, 81; discrimination against, 34, 150; educational and occupational restrictions, 69–71, 84; eligibility to sit in the Canadian Senate, 206n28; entrepreneurs, 150; the "Famous Five," 206n28; first female member of University of Toronto board of governors, 34; gender biases against, 69, 150; missionary societies, 217n23; prize for fiction by women, 182; rights of, 30–1; university and other organizations for, 34; youngest woman elected to British House of Commons, 33
"Women, Gender, and Book History" (seminar), 21
Women in Book History Bibliography, 21
Women in Print, Foreword (Long), 29
women in print and publishing trades: as agents of change,

Index 279

18–19; archival collections of, 11, 23–6; balance of career and motherhood for, 17, 131, 139–40; bibliographies about, 21; Black and of colour, 6; career professionals in trade publishing, 6; class bias against, 12, 16, 31, 34, 72; digital projects about, 12, 21; discrimination against in workforce, 4–5, 155; domination of the trades, 20, 78; early involvement in print production, 3–4; education and support for, 21; email archives of, 26–8; feminist orientation, 193; feminist press movement, 14; first career literary agents, 155; first elected vice-president of Association of American University Presses, 67; first female editor-in-chief, 88, 91; first female editors in trade and scholarly publishing, 6; first female publisher of English-language books in Canada, 5, 30; first full-time staff designer, 51; first periodical for female readers, 12; first successful commercial literary agency founded by women, 24–5, 88, 103, 156; gender bias against, 12–20, 31, 46, 50–2, 71–2, 79, 139, 181, 201n47; as "generators of meaning," 13; historical context for, 22; important figures in Canadian publishing, 140; influence of, 16; international scholarly interest in, 20–1; interviews with, 24; lack of formal recognition for, 19–20; literary agents, 152, 155–9; mentorship of authors, 97; Montreal Women's Printing Office, 206n28; paths crossed, 18; present-day, 231n11; professional methods of, 17; progress and accomplishments of, 22–3; promotion of, 20–1; public curiosity about, 21; radio documentaries about, 21; role models and mentors for other women, 15–16, 46, 56, 139, 194, 196; role of marital status for, 17, 72; scholarship on, 12; support from men for, 16, 71; television documentaries about, 20; Women's Press Collective, 223n96

Women in Print (Danky and Wiegand, eds.), 21
Women in Print Movement, 14
Women in Publishing, 20
"Women in Publishing" (radio documentary), 21
Women's Press, 6, 14
Women's Press Collective, 223n96
Women's Prize for Fiction. *See* Orange Prize
Wood, Caroline, 223n96
Wood, Gaby, 21; "A Touch of Frost," 202n66
Woodcock, George, 179
Woodhouse, A.S.P., 16, 70–1
Word on the Street, 150
World Friends, 217n23
Wright, Eric, 164, 230n155
Writers' Guild of Alberta, 175, 186

Writers' Union of Canada, 153
Wylie, Betty Jane: *Beginnings*, 137

Yale University Press, 76
Yesterday the Children Were Dancing (Gélinas), 39

York, Lorraine, 12; *Margaret Atwood and the Labour of Literary Celebrity*, 107, 156–8, 165, 176, 187
Young, Helen Granger, 206n28
Young, Scott, 36

STUDIES IN BOOK AND PRINT CULTURE

General Editor: Leslie Howsam

Hazel Bell, *Indexers and Indexes in Fact and Fiction*
Heather Murray, *Come, bright Improvement! The Literary Societies of Nineteenth-Century Ontario*
Joseph A. Dane, *The Myth of Print Culture: Essays on Evidence, Textuality, and Bibliographical Method*
Christopher J. Knight, *Uncommon Readers: Denis Donoghue, Frank Kermode, George Steiner, and the Tradition of the Common Reader*
Eva Hemmungs Wirtén, *No Trespassing: Authorship, Intellectual Property Rights, and the Boundaries of Globalization*
William A. Johnson, *Bookrolls and Scribes in Oxyrhynchus*
Siân Echard and Stephen Partridge, eds., *The Book Unbound: Editing and Reading Medieval Manuscripts and Texts*
Bronwen Wilson, *The World in Venice: Print, the City, and Early Modern Identity*
Peter Stoicheff and Andrew Taylor, eds., *The Future of the Page*
Janet Badia and Jennifer Phegley, eds., *Reading Women: Literary Figures and Cultural Icons from the Victorian Age to the Present*
Elizabeth Sauer, *"Paper-contestations" and Textual Communities in England, 1640–1675*
Nick Mount, *When Canadian Literature Moved to New York*
Jonathan Earl Carlyon, *Andrés González de Barcia and the Creation of the Colonial Spanish American Library*
Leslie Howsam, *Old Books and New Histories: An Orientation to Studies in Book and Print Culture*
Deborah McGrady, *Controlling Readers: Guillaume de Machaut and His Late Medieval Audience*
David Finkelstein, ed., *Print Culture and the Blackwood Tradition*
Bart Beaty, *Unpopular Culture: Transforming the European Comic Book in the 1990s*
Elizabeth Driver, *Culinary Landmarks: A Bibliography of Canadian Cookbooks, 1825–1949*
Benjamin C. Withers, *The Illustrated Old English Hexateuch, Cotton Ms. Claudius B.iv: The Frontier of Seeing and Reading in Anglo-Saxon England*
Mary Ann Gillies, *The Professional Literary Agent in Britain, 1880–1920*
Willa Z. Silverman, *The New Bibliopolis: French Book-Collectors and the Culture of Print, 1880–1914*
Lisa Surwillo, *The Stages of Property: Copyrighting Theatre in Spain*

Dean Irvine, *Editing Modernity: Women and Little-Magazine Cultures in Canada, 1916–1956*
Janet B. Friskney, *New Canadian Library: The Ross-McClelland Years, 1952–1978*
Janice Cavell, *Tracing the Connected Narrative: Arctic Exploration in British Print Culture, 1818–1860*
Elspeth Jajdelska, *Silent Reading and the Birth of the Narrator*
Martyn Lyons, *Reading Culture and Writing Practices in Nineteenth-Century France*
Robert A. Davidson, *Jazz Age Barcelona*
Gail Edwards and Judith Saltman, *Picturing Canada: A History of Canadian Children's Illustrated Books and Publishing*
Miranda Remnek, ed., *The Space of the Book: Print Culture in the Russian Social Imagination*
Adam Reed, *Literature and Agency in English Fiction Reading: A Study of the Henry Williamson Society*
Bonnie Mak, *How the Page Matters*
Eli MacLaren, *Dominion and Agency: Copyright and the Structuring of the Canadian Book Trade, 1867–1918*
Ruth Panofsky, *The Literary Legacy of the Macmillan Company of Canada: Making Books and Mapping Culture*
Archie L. Dick, *The Hidden History of South Africa's Book and Reading Cultures*
Darcy Cullen, ed., *Editors, Scholars, and the Social Text*
James J. Connolly, Patrick Collier, Frank Felsenstein, Kenneth R. Hall, and Robert G. Hall, eds., *Print Culture Histories Beyond the Metropolis*
Kristine Kowalchuk, *Preserving on Paper: Seventeenth-Century Englishwomen's Receipt Books*
Ian Hesketh, *Victorian Jesus: J.R. Seeley, Religion, and the Cultural Significance of Anonymity*
Kirsten MacLeod, *American Little Magazines of the Fin de Siècle: Art, Protest, and Cultural Transformation*
Emily C. Francomano, *The Prison of Love: Romance, Translation, and the Book in the Sixteenth Century*
Kirk Melnikoff, *Elizabethan Publishing and the Makings of Literary Culture*
Amy Bliss Marshall, *Magazines and the Making of Mass Culture in Japan*
Scott McLaren, *Pulpit, Press, and Politics: Methodists and the Market for Books in Upper Canada*
Ruth Panofsky, *Toronto Trailblazers: Women in Canadian Publishing*

www.ingramcontent.com/pod-product-compliance
Lightning Source LLC
Chambersburg PA
CBHW052014070526
44584CB00016B/1751